What if?

Character Sketches from the Bible

Junior Devotional

Bradley Booth

Pacific Press®
Publishing Association

Nampa, Idaho | Oshawa, Ontario, Canada
www.pacificpress.com

Cover design by Gerald Lee Monks
Cover design resources from iStockphoto.com / Halfpoint
Inside design by Kristin Hansen-Mellish

The author assumes full responsibility for the accuracy of all facts and quotations as cited in this book.

You can obtain additional copies of this book by calling toll-free 1-800-765-6955 or by visiting http://www.adventistbookcenter.com.

Library of Congress Cataloging-in-Publication Data
Names: Booth, Bradley, 1957- author.
Title: What if? / Bradley Booth.
Description: Nampa : Pacific Press Publishing Association, 2017.
Identifiers: LCCN 2017021971 | ISBN 9780816362981 (pbk. : alk. paper)
Subjects: LCSH: History—Religious aspects—Christianity. | Choice
  (Psychology)—Religious aspects—Christianity. | Bible—Biography.
Classification: LCC BR115.H5 B58 2017 | DDC 242/.2—dc23 LC record available at https://lccn.loc.gov/2017021971

July 2017

Dedication

This book is dedicated to young people everywhere who have faced decisions like the thousands of Bible characters who lived before them. May Jesus help us make the choices that will let us prosper spiritually and live long in the land that the Lord our God has given us.

Abel

The tongue is a fire, a world of iniquity. James 3:6

Have you ever been beaten up by a bully? Maybe at school, or in your neighborhood? Has your older brother or sister ever made fun of you? Not much fun, is it? And if you have ever suffered and been mistreated because you were standing up for what's right, you might know how Abel felt being picked on by his big brother. And it didn't end up a pretty picture. We don't know exactly what happened that fateful day, but it's likely Cain began by calling his brother names. "Momma's boy!" or "Chicken!"

"If being right with God makes you want to make fun of me, then I'll take it," Abel might well have replied. And, of course, for Cain it was probably hard not to get angry with someone who always seemed to say the right thing at the right time for the right reason.

You know the rest of the story. Cain killed Abel, and we've been paying the price ever since. Anger leads to fists, and fists bring fights. Fights lead to war, and war ends in murder and death. In American history alone, we've sure had our fair share of wars: the Indian wars, the Revolutionary War, the War of 1812, the war with Mexico, the Civil War, the Spanish-American War, World War I, World War II, the Korean War, Vietnam, the Cold War with the Soviet Union, the first and second wars in Iraq, the war in Afghanistan, and most recently the worldwide war on terror. Millions have died, and hundreds of millions have suffered.

But let's go back to how this story began. I mean, what if Cain hadn't gotten angry with Abel? What if he had listened to Abel's advice? What if Cain hadn't lost his temper and killed Abel? Would the antediluvian world have become so wicked that God would have to destroy it with a flood of waters? We'll never know the answers to those questions this side of heaven, but one thing is sure: Control your tongue, or it will control you. Abel could tell you all about that.

Abraham

By faith Abraham obeyed when he was called to go out to the place
which he would receive as an inheritance. And he went out,
not knowing where he was going. Hebrews 11:8

Abraham was quite a guy! Called by God to leave his pagan hometown of Ur, he obeyed, not even knowing where he was headed. When we realize what kind of a city Ur was, we might understand how difficult it must have been to leave. In those days, Ur was a port city of great wealth on the Persian Gulf. It had schools, libraries, and a sophisticated system of laws and courts. Homes were comfortable, many of them with second-story balconies and skylights, plumbing, indoor pools, and lush gardens.

And what did Abraham trade all this for? The life of a nomad camping out 24/7. Now he and his family had to cook over a campfire instead of a courtyard grill. Instead of farming crops in one place, he and his guys had to move around constantly to herd his sheep, goats, and cattle. They had to fight against lions, bears, and Amorite giants. Why? Because God asked him to do it. That's a pretty good reason. But there was an upside to all this too. Ur was the center of a corrupt form of worship in which people worshiped the moon and offered human sacrifices. It was not a good place to raise kids. Then, too, the city was later completely destroyed, another excellent reason for Abraham to get out of town. Answering God's call, Abraham journeyed to Canaan and started a new clan that worshiped the Creator God of heaven and earth, not the things He created.

So, what if Abraham hadn't obeyed God and left Ur? What if he had refused to go camping nonstop? What if he had not obeyed God in everything asked of him? Quite clearly the Jewish nation would have never existed. The promise of a Savior would have had to be fulfilled in some other way. We would not have Abraham's example of what it means to obey God, no matter how hard that might seem.

Adam

"Believe on the LORD Jesus, and you will be saved." Acts 16:31

How many push-ups can you do? How many push-ups can you do with one hand tied behind your back? What's your official time in the forty-yard dash? Can you do a 360-degree windmill dunk? Can you do a double rodeo 1080 on a half-pipe?

Adam could do all this and more. He could swim with the fastest of dolphins. He could outclimb mountain goats on the face of a rocky cliff. He could outrun zebras, outsiwng monkeys, and outsmart tigers! And given time, he would have eventually learned how to fly with the eagles. He was at least twelve feet tall, weighed as much as 1,300 pounds, boasted abs that would put today's best body-builders to shame, and likely had an IQ of eight hundred.

That's cool. Don't you sometimes wish you had those advantages? Putting it plainly, Adam was like Superman in more ways than not. Most important, he was made in God's image, and that means he had the capacity to love like God. He was kind and compassionate like Jesus and willing to share like the Holy Spirit.

But in the end Adam was not smart. Quite simply, he blew it! He was not wise enough to trust in the Creator who gave him life. When Eve came home carrying an armload of fruit from Eden's forbidden tree, Adam fell for the oldest game in history. He chose Eve and the temptation she offered him to be wise like the gods. What a shame! Obeying the God of the universe from the start would have saved Adam a world of sadness.

What if you could go back to Eden and help Adam make that choice all over again? Would you do it? Today we have a chance to make those same kinds of choices, to get it right this time, to make the decisions Adam did not. Today we can say courageously, "Get behind me, Satan. I choose Jesus and His words of life."

JANUARY 4

Cain

"Am I my brother's keeper?" Genesis 4:9, NIV

Anyone who has younger brothers or sisters knows how annoying they can be at times. They get into your personal things. They get in the way when your friends are around. They just don't understand simple language like "No!" Psychologists tell us that sibling rivalry is one of the most powerful emotions on earth. It makes us compete for our parents' attention. It causes us to fight over possessions and food. It can even cost us a boyfriend or girlfriend.

However, brothers and sisters can be pretty wonderful too. Think about it. The longer you live, the more you will probably appreciate your siblings, especially in the case of sisters. Who sticks with you through the tough times of life? Who shows up for all those important events like baptisms, graduations, weddings, and the first babies that come along? And there's something else you may not have thought about. Our brothers and sisters will be around for longer than any of our other earthly relationships. Our parents are gone before we are, and our children outlive us by at least a generation. But brothers and sisters? They may spend as much as eighty or ninety years together.

Now, Cain and his brother Abel were destined to spend a lot of time together. According to Genesis most of the antediluvians at that time lived eight or nine hundred years. Wow! That's a long time if you have a hard time getting along. And that was the problem. Cain and Abel didn't agree on many things, and their worship of God was one of the biggest differences. To put it simply, Cain was an angry young man. He resented everybody, it seemed, and it all went back to how he felt about God.

But what if he hadn't let his anger get the best of him? Well, he wouldn't have murdered his brother, for starters, and he wouldn't have had to leave his family and home for the rest of his life. Wow! That's a serious price to pay for a temper tantrum! So, what's the message here? Don't let anger and resentment control you. It's not worth it.

Eliezer

The LORD has heard my supplication; The LORD will receive my prayer. Psalm 6:9

How would you like being sent across the desert on a scavenger hunt to find a wife for your CEO's son? That's what happened to Eliezer. Abraham asked his chief servant, Eliezer, to find a wife for his son, a common custom of that era. People bartered for such things in those days, hoping that the match made by the family would be a happy one. There was no other way to do it, but that didn't make it any easier for Eliezer. This is how the story turned out. Eliezer grabbed ten of Abraham's fastest camels and raced pell-mell across the desert to Haran. When he finally got to his destination, the camels were on empty. How do we know? Because of the water they had to draw for the camels at the watering trough when he arrived.

Eliezer was very worried about his assignment. How was he going to know which girl was the right one to bring home to Isaac? Should he put an ad in Haran's local newspaper? Could he post Isaac's profile on Facebook, Twitter, or a dating Web site? Should he make an announcement on the radio or local TV stations? They didn't have such things in those days, so Eliezer did the only sensible thing. He prayed. Would God show him the right girl to take home for Isaac? He asked that the one who offered to water his camels would be the girl of choice. Really! What an awesome prayer of faith. Eliezer must have truly been in touch with God to make such a request!

And, of course, God heard his cry for help. But what if Eliezer hadn't prayed such a prayer? Well, Isaac would not have married Rebekah, the new bride-to-be. Jacob would not have been born. Joseph would not have been born, and millions would have died in Egypt's coming famine. And the list goes on. That's the difference prayer can make. So what's the catch? God expects us to pray specific prayers, that much is sure. If we are more like Eliezer, maybe we will have more success.

Enoch

Enoch walked with God; then he was no more, because God took him away.
Genesis 5:24, NIV

noch is one of the most famous characters in history, maybe not so much for what he did but for what he didn't do. To put it simply, he never died. Excuse me, someone might say. How does that sort of thing happen in this world? Well, it doesn't. Not very often, anyway. As far as we know, it happened only one other time in world history.

Clearly Enoch was out of place in a world gone crazy with wickedness. He was a man after God's own heart, of unusual character because he was in constant communion with heaven. Inspiration tells us he preached against the world's growing wickedness, pleading with folks to turn back to God. He even predicted the end of the world, first by a flood of waters, and second by fire on the judgment day. So, you see, it's not surprising that a good man like Enoch couldn't be kept in a world as bad as ours. He walked and talked so much with angels that God finally took him to his new home in the sky.

Imagine what it must have been like to see such an event! Enoch didn't disappear mysteriously, leaving everyone to wonder where he had gone. In fact, many were present to see the amazing phenomenon. As he spoke one last time to the scoffing crowds, Enoch's face probably shone like an angel's. And then, as with Elijah, we can imagine a flash of light streaking down to the narrow city street. In an instant it caught up the prophet in its glorious grasp before curving heavenward and out of sight somewhere among the clouds.

What a moment in time! Imagine now, what if Enoch hadn't spent so much time with God? Well, then, he would have stayed in this world longer and then died like everyone else. For a man as godly as him, that would have been such a waste! Don't you wish you could experience such a thing? You can. Jesus has promised us that very same ride one day soon when Jesus comes.

Gabriel

"I am Gabriel. I stand in the presence of God, and I have been sent
to speak to you and to tell you this good news." Luke 1:19, NIV

Other than Lucifer, the angel name mentioned most often in the war between good and evil is Gabriel. When Lucifer abandoned his position beside God's throne to stage a rebellion in heaven, someone had to take his place, and that someone was Gabriel. What an awesome privilege that would have been for him! Lucifer decided he would no longer take orders from the Sovereign of the universe, and Gabriel was asked to fill his shoes. Can you imagine that? Wouldn't you feel excited and honored at being given such a job?

One of Gabriel's major roles down through history has been to stand in the presence of God and serve as a special messenger to humans on earth. On one occasion he was sent to Babylon to explain a vision to Daniel. Then there's the story of his visit to the temple to tell Zacharias he would have a son named John, who turned out to be the one who announced the Messiah. And, of course, Gabriel appeared to Mary, a young maiden in Nazareth, to tell her that she would give birth to the Son of God.

But the greatest moment in the years of Gabriel's service must have been when he was sent by the Father to call Jesus from the grave. As he sped through the far reaches of space, he split the darkness of night with his supersonic speed. Then he rolled that massive stone from its place as though it were a pebble and commanded, "Jesus, Your Father calls You! Come forth!"

Can you imagine Gabriel following in Lucifer's footsteps and refusing to obey the commands of the Father? I can't, but what if he had? Certainly we would be calling him the second-biggest fool the universe has ever seen. When God gives us a job to do, as He did for Gabriel, we should do it. It's an honor to serve our Creator, and who knows what exciting missions He will send us on?

JANUARY 8

Esau

When Esau was forty years old, he married Judith daughter of Beeri the Hittite, and also Basemath daughter of Elon the Hittite. They were a source of grief to Isaac and Rebekah. Genesis 26:34, 35, NIV

Esau was a man's man! He was a rough character with lots of wild hair, and he felt most at home when he was hunting and fishing and doing all kinds of extreme sports. Unfortunately, he cared little for spiritual things. He didn't want to live by God's laws, and that's where all the trouble started. Exhibit A: When he turned forty he trashed all the rules by marrying pagan women, and that really broke his mother and father's heart. His parents were the head of a clan that worshiped the God of heaven, so marrying pagans created a big family scandal, as you can imagine. But it gets worse.

As the oldest son, Esau was in line for the family birthright, but he couldn't have cared less, at least for the spiritual end of it. Exhibit B: One afternoon he came home exhausted after a wild and woolly hunt. On Jacob's campfire was a pot of bubbling stew, and Esau had smelled it for miles downwind. He was ravenous, and within minutes he bartered away his birthright for a bowl of the campfire stew. "What good is a birthright to a dead man?" he growled.

And yet, we see as the story develops further, Esau had a fit when Jacob stole the birthright, which, by the way, Esau had already traded away for a bowl of stew. That's how Esau did things. But what if he had taken his responsibilities in the family more seriously? What if he had wished to honor God and live by heaven's rules? He would have saved Jacob a lot of trouble, and future generations of their descendants wouldn't have fought against each other constantly. As it turned out, Esau's descendants, the Edomites and Amalekites, made life miserable for the Israelites. Over and over again in the generations that followed, they were constantly at war with Israel. And to think that it all started over a bowl of stew.

Isaac

And Abraham said, "My son, God will provide for Himself the lamb
for a burnt offering." Genesis 22:8

Isaac was one of the most wanted babies in history. For twenty-five years, God had been promising Abraham that Sarah would have a son. God always has His reasons for making His people wait, but to Abraham and Sarah it must have seemed like it would never happen. And we would have to agree. By the time Isaac finally came along, Abraham was a hundred years old and Sarah was ninety. Isaac was truly a miracle baby!

He was a good boy as he grew, obedient to his parents, and, like his father, had a strong faith in God. Everyone in his father's village loved him as the promised son. But it was the famous sacrifice he and his father made on Mount Moriah that made history. That Abraham would consider sacrificing Isaac seems barbaric to us today, and yet the story is classic. Isaac was about twenty years old by then, and he could have told his father, "Take a hike," but he didn't. Inspiration tells us he supported his father because he understood why God was asking them to do such a thing.

And, of course, the story has a good ending. As Isaac watched his father raise a knife to the sky, he heard an angel's voice from heaven telling them it was enough. Abraham and Isaac had helped God make His point. God would one day send His only Son to die. And then a ram in a nearby thorny ticket was found to take Isaac's place, thus bringing the test of faith to an end. But what if Isaac had not agreed to go through with the sacrifice? What if he had said, "I'm out of here," and walked down off that mountain? Then, quite frankly, God's classic illustration for the universe about the coming sacrifice of Jesus would have never happened. No one would have blamed Isaac for refusing to take part. But, fortunately, he made it happen. Because of his part in the saga, he has a place in one of the greatest stories of all time.

Jacob

Lying lips are an abomination to the Lord, but those who deal truthfully
are His delight. Proverbs 12:22

How would you like your nickname to be "cheater," or "swindler," or "sneak thief"? Take your pick, because that's exactly what people called Jacob. In one afternoon he told his father three fateful lies that would haunt him for the rest of his life. In the years to come, how often he would wish he could go back to relive those moments. This is how it happened.

His mother knew he should get the family birthright instead of Esau. A birthright represented an inheritance of both money and spiritual leadership in the family, and Esau wasn't fit to have either. God had told her this prophetically, but Isaac wouldn't listen and finally decided one fateful day to give the birthright blessing to Esau anyway. Both Rebekah and Jacob knew the prize should be his, and to get it they were willing to go through quite a charade, but it was the lies that proved to be the clincher. When Isaac asked, "Who are you?" Jacob said, "I am Esau your firstborn." When Isaac asked how Jacob had managed to catch the wild deer and prepare the meal so quickly, the smooth talker replied, "The Lord God brought it to me." When Isaac pressed for further proof that he was indeed Esau, Jacob outright lied: "I am!" That's how it is with lies. One lie calls for another to cover up the deceptions we weave.

But what if Jacob had refused to play the part of a lying cheat? Well, for one thing, he wouldn't have had to leave home abruptly, and God would have honored him with the birthright in his own time. Secondly, Jacob wouldn't have had to work fourteen long years to marry four angry women, who gave him twelve sons whose violent rivalries would make his life miserable over and over again. And finally, he never saw his mother again, the one who arranged the little scheme in the first place. Quite a price to pay for a pack of lies, don't you think?

Laban

"Your father has deceived me and changed my wages ten times,
but God did not allow him to hurt me." Genesis 31:7

What would it have been like to be a member of Laban's family? Who was this man, and why did he have such a bad rep? We don't know much about his younger days before Jacob showed up, except that he was the son of Bethuel, who was the son of Nahor, who was the brother of Abraham—making him the grand-nephew of Abraham. But he was nothing like Uncle Abraham.

Laban was known to be a sneaky, conniving snake of a man. He jumped at the chance to have Jacob work seven years for the right to marry his daughter Rachel, only to deceive him by giving him Leah instead. And then Laban forced him to work another seven years for Rachel. How he managed to pull that off, we'll probably never know. Leah wore a veil to the wedding, but that probably wouldn't have been enough. Likely Laban got Jacob good and drunk at the feast so he would be clueless until the "I dos" were in his rearview mirror.

In addition, Laban was a nasty boss; he changed Jacob's wages ten times because his son-in-law was getting richer every day. His plan was to get back some of that wealth, but it didn't work out that way. Even worse, when Jacob tried to leave town with his wives and kids, Laban claimed they all belonged to him. What a nut! Not the relative you want to see at a family reunion.

What if he hadn't been such a jerk? What if Laban had been kind to his daughters and Jacob? For one thing he would have had a happier life. Then, too, Jacob might have stuck around much longer and made Laban a very rich man. But that's the way it is with greed. It makes us mean and spiteful, and it poisons our lives. Unfortunately, Laban knew all about that.

JANUARY 12

Eve

"You may be sure that your sin will find you out." Numbers 32:23, NIV

This one is for the young ladies. Imagine for a moment that you are the most beautiful woman in the history of the world. No one can compare with you. Your skin tone is perfect, your hair the color of honey, your pearly whites the envy of all women in every age to come!

Imagine you have been given a home in paradise with cascading waterfalls spilling into pools of crystal-clear water ringed with lily pads. Your house is a forest glen scented with roses and jasmine, its roof a canopy of fruit-laden vines. You sleep on soft mosses in a moonlit glade and wake to the sweet songs of exotic birds.

Imagine that God has introduced you to the man of your dreams—tall, dark, and handsome. He is noble and funny and swifter than the eagles when he races through the open fields with zebras and cheetahs and every creature that was ever made to run with the wind. And he adores you. This man brings you flowers that will never fade. He climbs the highest trees to reach the most delightful of fruits for your noonday meal together. He smiles at your little antics, laughs at your silliest jokes, and worships the Creator with you every day as the gorgeous sun sets in the painted western sky.

Imagine your heavenly Father has given you all these gifts and more, and that He requires only one simple test of faith to demonstrate your gratefulness for these gifts—obedience to His Word. What will you do with this challenge?

Now, what if, like Eve, you should cast all these blessings aside for a few careless minutes of shopping at a forbidden tree? Imagine the price you must pay for freedom and independence from your Father in heaven. Let's rethink that choice and make the right ones today.

Job

In all this Job did not sin nor charge God with wrong. Job 1:22

What's the worst thing that's ever happened to you? You had to get braces? You didn't make the basketball team? Your best friend stole your boyfriend or girlfriend? OK, those things can seem pretty bad sometimes, but what would it be like to have your whole world come crashing down in one day? You lose your Lamborghini, your house, your family business, any money you had in your Swiss bank accounts, and all your kids! In one day! That's ridiculous, you say!

Well, maybe, but that's exactly what happened to Job from the land of Uz, minus the car and Swiss bank accounts, of course. And if that weren't enough, he got really, really sick. His friends came by to share his grief, but they did more to discourage him than help.

Now, while all this was happening, Satan was doing his own brand of trash talking. He told God that Job wasn't worth saving, that he was only being faithful because God made him rich. But Job proved Satan wrong when he declared, "Though He slay me, yet will I trust in Him," and, "I know that my Redeemer lives, and that He will raise me up in the resurrection." Wow! Now that's a testimony!

But what if Job hadn't held true to his beliefs? What if he hadn't trusted God? What if he had cursed Him instead? Then Satan would have celebrated, and God would have been left holding the bag, so to speak. But praise God, Job did hang on! He knew God never asks us to endure more than we are able, and that good always wins in the end. And God blessed Job and gave him back everything he had lost, twice over.

JANUARY 14

Jabal, Jubal, and Tubal-Cain

Although they knew God, they did not glorify Him as God,
nor were thankful, but became futile in their thoughts,
and their foolish hearts were darkened. Romans 1:21

Jabal, Jubal, and Tubal-Cain. Who were these characters? The three stooges? A band of brothers? Maybe. All were descendants of Cain, six generations removed from their evil great-great-great-great-grandfather. All of them chased the things of this world, and all became famous for being firsts in their generation.

Jabal was the first man to get rich breeding livestock for a living. In those days wealth was measured by how many animals you had. Cattle, sheep, goats, donkeys, and horses. And who knows? Maybe even elephants!

Jubal became a legend as a musician. We read in Genesis that he invented the harp and organ especially, and played them as well. His harp was a stringed instrument, probably very much like the one David played more than two thousand years later. The organ he made was maybe more like a flute, or perhaps several fastened together, like bagpipes.

And then there was Tubal-Cain. He was the first metal worker of the antediluvian world, the first to successfully use copper, bronze, and iron. This meant he knew how to shape metals into tools and weapons.

That's all we really know about the three brothers individually. We do know that they lived during the time of Enoch and Methuselah, and they may have even watched Noah build his ark and preach about a coming flood.

We have no word that they ever accepted Noah's message, but what if they had? What if they hadn't gotten caught up in making money and becoming famous? What if they had decided the wisdom of their Creator was more important than the foolishness of their own minds? Sad, isn't it. They gained much in this world, but lost their own souls in the process.

Judah

"Now therefore, please let your servant remain instead of the lad as a slave to my
lord, and let the lad go up with his brothers. For how shall I go up to my father if the
lad is not with me, lest perhaps I see the evil that would come upon my father?"
Genesis 44:33, 34

Early on, Judah was not a very nice guy. In fact, he was quite the bully, like his
brothers Simeon and Levi. When they ripped Joseph's coat of many colors off
his back, it was Judah who suggested they sell him into slavery. They all thought
they hated Joseph enough to commit such a crime, but they had no idea how much
grief it was going to cause their father. From that moment forward, every day for
Jacob was like a funeral. And just as big a shock to Judah was the realization that
because of their shameful deed, he and his brothers would never again get a good
night's sleep. How could they when Joseph's cries for mercy kept ringing in their
ears?

Twenty years passed, but by now Judah was living in another world. No longer
was he the cruel villain who had sold his brother to Ishmaelite traders for twenty
pieces of silver. When famine hit the Mediterranean lands, the brothers traveled
down to Egypt to buy grain. And, of course, this is where Joseph's magical dreams
came true, when the brothers all bowed before him. Joseph was now prime minister of Egypt, and through the weeks that followed he tested his brothers to the
max, finding they had changed remarkably. No longer were they the angry, harsh
men of his younger years, and Judah was a prince, the most noble of them all. He
had changed so much, in fact, that he now offered to suffer Benjamin's fate when
the boy was accused of stealing the prime minister's silver divining cup.

What if Judah had not repented of his crimes and given his heart to the God of
his fathers? Likely he would not have gone down in history as the father of Israel's
greatest tribe, the clan from which King David and Jesus Himself would one day
be born. Good choice, Judah. You passed the test with flying colors, and you didn't
need a coat of many colors to do it. You set a first-class example for all of us.

JANUARY 16

Lamech

"He who is faithful in what is least is faithful also in much; and he who is unjust in what is least is unjust also in much." Luke 16:10

Lamech was the father of Noah, the famous builder who took everyone safely through the worldwide flood. Good job, father Lamech. You must have been a pretty good dad.

Interestingly enough, Lamech didn't live to see that day. He didn't live to see the ark finished, or the animals go into the ark, or the rain come down for forty days and forty nights.

Well, you might be thinking, *He was probably pretty old. What can we expect? No one lives forever.* So how old did he live to be? Only 777 years. Wait a minute, you might be saying, that's pretty old, isn't it? It would be by today's standards, for sure.

Yes, but did you know his son Noah lived to be 950 years old? And his father lived for almost a thousand years! Actually, 969 years to be specific. Wow! That's really old! By now you may have guessed who his father was. If you said Methuselah, you would be right.

One of the most interesting bits of trivia about Lamech is that he died only five years before the flood. Five years? Why did God allow that? Why not let Lamech live to help his son Noah finish the ark and then stand with him during the greatest trial of his life?

We don't know. Maybe he would have been too depressed seeing the world destroyed by a flood. The Bible doesn't say much about Lamech except that Noah was his oldest son, and that he had big plans for his firstborn (Genesis 5:29). Evidently he didn't like doing hard farm work like plowing the soil and weeding. Maybe he was hoping Noah would help save the world from the curse God put on the earth after Adam and Eve sinned (Genesis 3:17, 18). Maybe. But it also sounds as though he was hoping his son would be the long-hoped-for Savior of the world. Well, Noah didn't save the world from its sins, but he did help save the world by building an ark.

Leah

And he [Jacob] said to Laban, "What is this you have done to me? Was it not for Rachel that I served you? Why then have you deceived me?" Genesis 29:25

Weddings are supposed to be wonderful—the happiest day of your life—but that's not how it turned out for Leah. Her tale and the part she played in it is one of the most famous, and yet saddest, wedding stories in all the Bible. Jacob had fallen in love with Leah's beautiful *younger* sister Rachel, and Leah probably watched the whole thing with a breaking heart. Would no one ever seek her hand in marriage? The Bible suggests she was as plain as Rachel was pretty.

So who was responsible for the wedding that became a fiasco? Laban knew if he married off his younger daughter first, he might never get a suitor for Leah. Something about the customs of the day. And so the wedding became a sham. The girl that Jacob thought he was getting turned out to be Leah. Of course, Jacob was furious at his father-in-law Laban when he realized he had been hoodwinked, but in those days, in that culture, he had few choices. What a sick joke, especially for Leah and Rachel, who were pawns of their father, Laban.

But one question remains. Was Leah a party to the cruel, underhanded, nasty plan designed by her father? Was she in on the wedding heist? Maybe, but if she was in on the deal she may have done so thinking this was her only chance at happiness. Wow! Nothing could have been further from the truth. Deceiving your husband- or wife-to-be is not the way to begin a life of happiness together.

So what would have happened if she had refused to go through with the deception? Culture or no culture, customs or not, what if she had told her father she would rather be an old maid the rest of her life than live a life full of desperate heartache and miserable rejection? We'll never know, but if she had, she would have saved a lot of people a lot of tears.

Simeon and Levi

"Simeon and Levi are brothers—their swords are weapons of violence. . . .
Cursed be their anger, so fierce, and their fury, so cruel!" Genesis 49:5, 7, NIV

What a pair! Coming number two and three in the birth order of Jacob's family, Simeon and Levi were quite a handful, and among his twelve sons they were the most trouble. Like their grandfather, Laban, they were conniving, cruel, and always angry, it seems. Not surprisingly, they kept doing the most horrendous things that shamed their father Jacob and threatened the safety of his clan.

The first deed to rear its ugly head came after the marriage of their sister Dinah to a young prince, a man named Shechem, from the town near their campsite. Shechem had humiliated their sister by having relations with her, but other than force the young man to marry her, Jacob took no further action. Simeon and Levi were furious at this atrocity and decided to take things into their own hands. After dark one night, the two of them invaded the citadel with vengeance and killed every man in the city. Jacob was horrified and fled, afraid that Shechem's relatives would come to avenge their murders, but God protected his family, and no harm came to the clan. A few years later, Simeon and Levi hatched another evil plan, this one for their younger brother Joseph, because they felt he was a spoiled brat. The coat Jacob gave him was proof enough to them. With a heart of stone, Simeon influenced Levi and his other brothers to rip the coat off and throw Joseph in a pit.

That's the tale of two brothers driven by hate to become cruel monsters, and at what a price! But what if they had listened to the Holy Spirit? What if they hadn't allowed their feelings of anger to control their lives? Their wicked characters forced Jacob to skip over both Simeon and Levi and give the family birthright to his fourth son, Judah. Both boys missed the chance to join the family line through which Jesus would come. And just as tragic, Simeon eventually lost his tribal inheritance in the land of Canaan, causing his clan to disappear from history altogether.

Lot

Then Lot chose for himself all the plain of Jordan, and . . . dwelt in the cities of the plain and pitched his tent even as far as Sodom. Genesis 13:11, 12

Life is all about choices, isn't it? If Lot were here today, we could ask him about that. Unfortunately, he didn't do so well in the choices department. For starters, he allowed trouble to develop between his family and Abraham's. He was a guest in Abraham's village, so that should have been a red flag for him. And then choice number two. When Abraham called for peace negotiations between the two families and suggested they separate, Lot agreed. He knew God had made a covenant of protection with his uncle Abraham, but still he chose to leave.

Then Abraham did the unthinkable. He let Lot choose where he preferred to live, and once again Lot forgot about everyone but himself. "I'll take the river valley," we can hear him saying a bit smugly. Choice number three. Once again, bad idea. What looked good on the surface turned out to be selfish and toxic for him and his family. Choice number four. He pitched his tent toward Sodom, that great city of wickedness. Eventually he moved his family right into the city—choice number five. And when enemy armies swept into Sodom, taking him and his family captive, God spared him miraculously by sending Abraham to his rescue. The captives were brought home unhurt, but still Lot remained in the city. Choice number six.

And that brings us to choice number seven. When the angels brought Lot a warning from heaven that the city was about to be destroyed by fire, he lingered, and because of his hesitancy, his wife was lost. Seven poor choices, each one progressively more damaging than the one before it. But what if Lot had used better judgement in making these choices? What if he had asked Abraham for advice? What if he had listened to the Holy Spirit? The history of his family would have been quite different.

Lot's Wife

"Remember Lot's wife." Luke 17:32

Why does Jesus tell us to remember Lot's wife in the Gospel of Luke? Quite simply, she made bad choices like her husband, Lot. Sadly, we don't even know her name. So focused was she on the sumptuous luxuries of her home in Sodom that today she has almost no identity at all except as "Lot's wife." Why? Because of the fateful, fatal choice she made during the early morning of Sodom's destruction. Though she was a worshiper of the one true God, her connection with Him was not a good one, and when crisis came to her life she crashed and burned. Literally.

"Don't look back!" the angel told her. "Flee the city!" but she had so much wealth in Sodom, she could think of nothing else. Not even the hand of the angel who was trying to lead her out of Sodom. History tells us the rift valley floor under Sodom was unstable, a seam in the earth's crust where the earth's tectonic plates come together. At the time of Sodom's destruction these plates were probably still settling from the effects of the Flood five hundred years before. When the plates shifted dramatically that fateful morning, liquid "fire and brimstone" came shooting out of giant fissures in the valley floor. Not surprisingly, this destroyed Sodom and four other cities in the valley. Unfortunately, Lot's wife lingered, and as she turned to look back she died. Volcanic ash and salt that can still be found in the area must have covered her, turning her into what the Bible calls a "pillar of salt." What a tragic end to something that didn't have to happen!

But what if she had willingly escaped with Lot and her anxious girls? What if she had obeyed the angel and headed for the mountains? There is no doubt she would be remembered today as one of only four people who escaped the destruction of that fabled city. She would be a legend out of time, representing those who are fleeing this world to inherit a city whose Builder and Maker is God.

Lucifer

Be alert and of sober mind. Your enemy the devil prowls around
like a roaring lion looking for someone to devour. 1 Peter 5:8, NIV

When was the last time you saw a lion up close? Close enough to see his bare teeth and the look in his eye that told you he'd like to hunt you for his next meal. Lions are among the most dangerous creatures on earth. They weigh as much as five hundred pounds, have two-inch claws to hook their prey, and are outfitted with four-inch fangs for biting through skulls.

Interestingly enough, the Bible compares Satan to a lion, but whatever for? The fact is, in the beginning, before the cancer of sin took root in the universe, Satan looked like anything but a lion. He was a majestic angel, handsome and magnificent beyond description! Lucifer, the morning star, was created to take first place as covering cherub beside the Father's crystal throne. His robe of iridescent light radiated a kaleidoscope of brilliance, and on his head was a crown of brightest white. His smile was warm, his eyes kind, his intelligence beyond anything yet created. In humbleness and gratitude he lived to serve, always ready to praise his almighty Creator.

So what went wrong? How did Lucifer become Satan? Proud of his good looks and influence near God's throne, Lucifer foolishly desired Jesus' place in the Father's presence. The Father begged him to reconsider, but Lucifer would not turn back. He then led a revolt to take God's throne, and there was war in heaven. This was the beginning of great sadness in the universe, because Lucifer and his evil angels were cast out of heaven.

Think of it. If Lucifer had repented of his evil plans when God offered him a pardon, we would be telling a far different tale today. Instead, we must now share the story of the great controversy between the lion and the Lamb, and all those who have been players in that story.

Melchizedek

And having been perfected, He became the author of eternal salvation to all who
obey Him, called by God as High Priest "according to the order of Melchizedek."
Hebrews 5:9, 10

W ho was Melchizedek? Well, for starters, he was the king of Salem and a priest
of the Most High God. Except for the story where he appears in the script to
receive tithes from Abraham, we know almost nothing about him. No one knew
who his father or mother was, or any of his ancestors for that matter. No one had
any record of his family genealogy. So who was he? Some say he could have been
Shem, the son of Noah. After all, Shem was still alive in the days of Abraham and
didn't die until Abraham was about 150 years old. At the time, no one in the world
was older than Shem, so to many it would seem as if he had lived forever.

And that brings us back to Melchizedek, whoever he was. Paul used him as a
symbol of Jesus. Like Jesus, Melchizedek was called the king of righteousness. He
was a holy man, a priest before God. Like Jesus, Melchizedek was called the king
of peace, because he ruled in Salem, the city of peace, which would eventually be
dubbed Jerusalem, the city of the Great King.

And what if Melchizedek hadn't made choices to be a righteous man? What
if he hadn't been a king of peace? Well, for starters, we would have lost this awesome lesson from ancient history illustrating Jesus as our High Priest in heaven.
We would have never known that, like Melchizedek, we can represent God to the
world. We can be examples of peace and righteousness in this world of sin. As
high priest of Salem, Melchizedek represented Jesus, who represents us before our
Father in the heavenly sanctuary. Jesus offers His righteousness to cover our sins
to make us as spotless as He is. So, then, it doesn't really matter who Melchizedek
was, any more than it matters who we are. In Jesus we are everything. He is our
High Priest, and we are children of the heavenly King.

Methuselah

So all the days of Methuselah were nine hundred and sixty-nine years.
Genesis 5:27

Who's the oldest person you know? Are they ninety-nine years old? One hundred? Today life expectancy for the average man in the United States is seventy-six years. For a woman it's eighty-one. That may sound like a lot of years to a kid, but trust me, when you are an older person looking back on life, it can seem very short.

But let's imagine now that you are an antediluvian living before the Flood. The average person in the Genesis record lived to be 857 years of age. Wow! That's old! In those days the human race was still fairly new, recently created in the image of God through their ancestor Adam. Methuselah, the eighth in line from Eden, lived the longest at 969. Whew! That's almost a thousand years.

Some would say we are getting healthier, that we have better ways to fight disease, and that people are living longer. This is true to a certain degree. Today, in the United States there are more than 53,000 people who are a hundred years old or older. Some scientists think we are on the verge of discovering how to slow down the aging process. Other scientists think cloning your own body organs is the answer. When a liver or heart gets too worn out to function anymore, just take out the old organ and put in a new one you've been growing in a laboratory somewhere. If we could keep doing that, theoretically, it would mean we could live forever—or so they say. Of course, such thinking is foolishness. The wages of sin is death, and since we are all sinners, unless Jesus comes again to take us to heaven, we are all destined to die.

And the good news? Eating and sleeping right can add days to your life. Not smoking and not using alcohol and other drugs will also lengthen your life, as will a life of trust in God. And what if we don't make these lifestyle choices? Then it's likely we'll not live to be a hundred.

Nimrod

Cush begot Nimrod; he began to be a mighty one on the earth.
He was a mighty hunter before the Lord. Genesis 10:8, 9

Nimrod. That's quite a name! He was the grandson of Ham, who was the son of Noah. We don't know exactly how old Noah was when Nimrod was born, but his cousin, Salah, who was also a great-grandson of Noah, was born just thirty-five years after the Flood. So its likely Nimrod could have known Noah personally, for as long as three hundred years. Did he sit around the evening campfires and hear Noah tell stories about the antediluvian world, the fierce giants of that time, and the humongous dinosaurs that roamed the earth? It's likely he did.

As he grew to be a man, Nimrod became well known for his daring adventures. He was a mighty warrior, the first king to set up an empire after the Flood, and the builder of many legendary cities, such as Calah, Nineveh, and the most famous of all, Babel. Nimrod must have been very rich and powerful. He must have lived in a sumptuous palace with lots of servants and fancy food and exotic birds. Did he help design and build the Tower of Babel in the land of Shinar? Probably. The ancient writings of Jewish rabbis called the temple tower "the house of Nimrod." We shouldn't be surprised, then, that Nimrod lived in rebellion of God like his father Cush, and his grandfather Ham, and, of course, he paid for it. Stories from that era tell us he was finally murdered by those who wanted his power and position. And then, strangely enough, after his death he was eventually worshiped as a god.

It was a sad end to the life of a man who could have done so much more. What if Nimrod had not made power and prestige his only goal in life? What if, like Moses, he had chosen to serve God rather than to enjoy the pleasures of sin for a season? If he had, we might be remembering him today as a mighty man before the Lord, maybe even one of the greatest men who ever lived.

Noah

Noah found favor in the eyes of the LORD. Genesis 6:8, NIV

If someone asked you, "Who is the most important person in world history?" what would be your answer—besides Jesus? You might say Adam, or Moses, or maybe even Paul. Me? I'd say Noah. Think about it. If it weren't for Noah, none of us would be here. Well, you say, God could have saved us some other way with the help of someone or something besides Noah and his ark. Yes, He could have, but the short answer to that is, "He didn't." God didn't choose to save the world from a flood through any other means than Noah . . . and his ark. Cool, huh? I think there are going to be a lot of people in heaven who will be lining up to thank Noah for swinging a hammer those 120 years.

Noah spent all his time and money on that ark. Amazing! And why not, you say? The world was coming to an end, so what else could he do? And yet, let's think about how he might have been tempted to stop at any point along the way because of how foolish the whole thing seemed. For one thing, they were building the ark on dry land. Can you imagine how people must have laughed. A boat on dry land? Really! That would be the joke of the century. Every tabloid magazine of the day would be writing about it. And then there was the warning that the world would be flooded by enough water to drown everyone! Even cover the highest hills with water! Start the laugh track. Even harder to grasp, why would God destroy a beautiful world He had created barely fifteen hundred years before?

But, of course, the granddaddy of all questions for you today is a very personal one: "Could you have done Noah's job?" If God had asked you to build the ark, and you had been the only one He could trust, would you have been able to step out in faith and do it?

JANUARY 26

Noah's Wife

"Whoever can be trusted with very little can also be trusted with much."
Luke 16:10, NIV

We don't even know what her name was. We usually call her Noah's wife, or maybe Mrs. Noah. What was she like? What color eyes and hair did she have? Was she a ten-foot giant like other women in her day? Did she have a bubbly personality, or was she more the serious type? Did she have a good relationship with her in-laws? Was she a good mother? Did she have life dreams? A nice house? The truth is, we just don't know.

And what about the ark? Did Mrs. Noah help Noah build it? Did she saw the boards? Did she hammer the wooden pegs that held the ark's giant frame together? Or spread pitchy resin to make it watertight? Did she encourage her boys to support Noah in the amazing project? Did she remind them this ark would end up saving all who believed God's warning to get on board?

And what would you have done for Mrs. Noah if you had spent a day with her at the building site? Would you have helped her make a meal for the workers? Oatcakes and mango pie, maybe? Would you have told her that the story of her faithfulness to God would be shared down through the ages of time? Would you have climbed up on a pile of lumber to tell the people gathered there that they would be crazy not to accept Noah's message of salvation?

Mrs. Noah's example is one for the ages. By faith she accepted God's call to stand with her husband as he built the ark. By faith she ignored the taunts of her neighbors who made fun of her and Noah, calling them all kinds of names. By faith she prayed for 120 years, knowing that when the Flood came, everything in their old world would be gone forever.

Of course, we can't afford to lose the real lesson here. We must be more like Mrs. Noah. Our world is panicking from fear of the coming crisis, and we must help people to prepare. We must show them Jesus. And if we don't? Then many will not get on the ark before it's too late.

Rachel

Now when Rachel saw that she bore Jacob no children, Rachel envied her sister, and said to Jacob, "Give me children, or else I die!" Genesis 30:1

Rachel was the prettiest girl in town. She met her husband-to-be at a city well outside of Haran where her family lived. He fell madly in love with her and then worked for fourteen years to pay the bride price. Aw! That's just about the most romantic story in history. But the odds were against Rachel, and happiness was not to be hers. On the wedding day, her sister took her place in the ceremony through the trickery of their father.

And so the days of the threesome marriage began. It's not likely they had very many happy meals together, because when the family started growing, Leah was having all the babies. Four of them, in fact. The Bible says Rachel was really upset about this and started a contest with her sister in the race for kids. It got so bad that she and Leah told Jacob he needed wives number three and four. Can you believe it? And so their servant girls, Bilhah and Zilpah, became Jacob's new wives and got into the contest. Soon there were seven more sons and a daughter. But Rachel had only one baby of her own to show for all that trouble. What heartaches come from jealousy!

What if Rachel hadn't played that game with Leah? What if she had been satisfied with the number of children God gave her, whether it was one or twenty? Well, for one thing, she and her sister would have been better friends, and so would their two servant girls. And then, of course, there was the end result of the whole baby contest. Rachel died while having baby number two. God sometimes gives us what we think we want because we beg Him so much, but he doesn't always interfere with the end result. Why? Because we are created with the freedom of choice, and the sinful world we live in can sometimes skew the results of those choices out of our control. That's why we should always consult our heavenly Father.

JANUARY 28

Rebekah

And when she had finished giving him a drink, she said, "I will draw water for your camels also, until they have finished drinking." Genesis 24:19

What a nice thing for Rebekah to do! If you have ever watered camels, you know it's a big job! Now, it's likely no one reading this has gotten anywhere near a camel, but if you did, you might be surprised to find that one camel can drink up to fifty gallons of water after a long trek across the desert. Eliezer came with ten camels, so that would be a lot of water! Do the math.

Having a representative from a faraway relative arrive in town must have been exciting, but when Rebekah heard why they had come, she must have gotten really jittery! Isaac was looking for a wife, and Rebekah was it, according to Eliezer, Abraham's chief steward. Wow! To be given as anyone's bride in those days was a big deal, but to become the wife of Isaac, the richest man in Canaan, must have seemed like a wild and crazy dream! She was given a choice, of course. When asked if she would return with Eliezer some four hundred miles south across the wilderness wastelands, she said, "I will go." She knew she would probably never see her family again, and still she went.

And so she arrived in Canaan, and Isaac fell madly in love with her. She was a kind, beautiful young woman, the Bible says, and Isaac knew she was the one for him. She was a miracle wife, after all. Hadn't she showed up in answer to Eliezer's prayer?

But what if Rebekah had not offered to draw water for Eliezer's camels? It was a simple enough gesture, though not an easy task to draw more than five hundred gallons of water to accomplish the feat. If she had not, then, of course, she would have never been asked to return with Eliezer to Canaan, and we know what the results of that would have been. She would have never been privileged to be the ancestor of Jesus, the Son of God, who would die for her sins.

Sarah

Trust in the Lord with all your heart, and lean not on your own understanding; in all your ways acknowledge Him, and He shall direct your paths. Proverbs 3:5, 6

Sarah is one of the most famous women in the Bible, and clearly a brave woman. After all, she traded her sumptuous home in the city of Ur for a tent on the prairies of Canaan. And besides that, she was stunningly beautiful. If she had entered the Miss Universe contest of her day, she would have easily won. It's not a surprise, then, that famous rulers of her day wanted her for a wife. An Egyptian pharaoh made that mistake due to a lie Abraham told him, and so did a king of the Philistines. And the fact that Sarah was sixty-five years old at the time really steals the show. Now, we should probably blame Abraham for such a fiasco. After all, he was a prince in Canaan, one of the richest sheiks of his day, and most important, a worshiper of the one true God. However, we have to remember that it takes two to pull off this kind of deception.

Unfortunately, as Sarah grew older, she continued to make mistakes. It all started because she had no kids. If you had no kids in those days, your family name would disappear forever from the face of the earth. No pressure, right, Sarah? That's when she got the big idea of having her husband take another wife. This way they would have a kid, she could adopt it and call it her own, and everyone would be happy. Wrong. Things didn't go well after that decision, and what a lot of trouble it caused the family down through the centuries!

What if Sarah hadn't slipped up? What if she had told Abraham to cool it, that God had promised them a son and He would deliver. Well, for starters, Ishmael would have never been born, and that means the twelve tribes of Ishmael would have not been around. There would have been no Ishmaelite traders to sell Joseph into slavery, and no wars today between the Arabs and Israelis. Oops! I guess God's ways really are the best ways.

Seth

He hath shewed thee, O man, what is good;
and what doth the Lord require of thee, but to do justly,
and to love mercy, and to walk humbly with thy God? Micah 6:8, KJV

Can you imagine what it must have been like for Adam and Eve to lose two children in one day? Abel was murdered by his older brother Cain, and Cain had to flee from home—never to return.

And now son number three comes along—Seth. That's quite a name! It means "appointed one" or "substitute." Probably his parents hoped he would take Abel's place as the next spiritual leader of the Adam clan. Because of their sin, God told them they and all their descendants would eventually die. However, heaven would one day send a Savior to die for them to pay for their sins, and that gave our first parents hope.

The big question in their minds now was a simple one. Abel obviously wasn't the promised Savior, but might Seth to be the Chosen One? Can you imagine the dread that must have filled Adam and Eve's hearts as they thought about their sons having to pay for their sins?

We know, of course, that Seth was not the Savior of the world, but he did go on to become the head of a godly clan that practiced justice and mercy and walked humbly with God. For more than nine centuries Seth stood for God in a world that became so wicked it would eventually have to be destroyed in a flood. He lived long enough to see his great-great-great-great-great-grandkids to the seventh generation—almost long enough to see Noah, who would build the ark to save mankind.

Now ask yourself this question: "Can I be faithful to God like Seth, standing for what's right though my world collapses around me?" And what if I don't? In the battle between good and evil, God needs young people who will be faithful like Seth. You may not live to be nine hundred years old, but, like Seth, you need to be faithful to God as you watch and wait for Jesus to come.

Achan

And Achan answered Joshua and said, "Indeed I have sinned against the LORD God of Israel, and this is what I have done: When I saw among the spoils a beautiful Babylonian garment, two hundred shekels of silver, and a wedge of gold weighing fifty shekels, I coveted them and took them." Joshua 7:20, 21

The story of Achan is an unusual one because it shows that honesty is the best policy, and it's always better to confess before one gets caught. Achan could have written the book on those two points. Unfortunately he didn't think things through and decided he'd never get caught. Here's how it happened. When the army of Israel destroyed the fortress of Jericho, God told them they must not take any of the spoils or booty for themselves. The silver, gold, brass, and iron were to be put into the treasury of the Lord, but the rest of the city was to be torched because it was such an evil place.

Achan decided he'd do his own thing. While he was invading one of the houses of Jericho, he found a fine Babylonian robe and some silver and gold. He must have sneaked off and hid them, because Joshua's men found them later, after Achan finally confessed to taking them. Unfortunately he waited until after God had instructed everyone to draw lots by tribe and clan and family, and his own name had been drawn.

But what if he hadn't waited so long to confess, and what if he hadn't stolen the forbidden treasures in the first place? Then this whole story would have turned upside down. Israel wouldn't have lost their first battle at Ai. Thirty-six men of Israel would not have died needlessly in the battle, and, of course, Achan himself wouldn't have had to die either. But that's the way it is when we sin against the God of heaven. We can be sure our sins will find us out, because the wages of sin is death.

FEBRUARY 1

Adoni-Bezek

And Adoni-Bezek said, "Seventy kings with their thumbs and big toes cut off used to gather scraps under my table; as I have done, so God has repaid me." Then they brought him to Jerusalem, and there he died. Judges 1:7

So who was this Adoni-Bezek? Sounds like a pretty goofy man to have seventy kings eating under his table. And to make it worse, these kings all had their thumbs and big toes cut off. Why? Well, that's the rest of the story, isn't it?

Adoni-Bezek was a Canaanite king during the time of Joshua, when the twelve tribes of Israel invaded the land of Canaan. His policy of cutting off the thumbs and big toes of those he conquered had given him a reputation, and it came back to haunt him at the end of his life. The practice in courts of the day was to make the punishment fit the crime, and you know what that means. As punishment for the pain he had given those he had conquered, the Israelites cut off his thumbs and big toes before making him a slave. Ouch!

Now, we might be tempted to feel sorry for this mean old king. Can we really blame him for being so cruel, some might ask. After all, he was just being like all the other nations around him. Some of the kings around him acted much worse by executing their prisoners in very barbaric ways—do the research and find out for yourself. But there are no excuses for cruelty. So, let's imagine an Adoni-Bezek who was more humane. What if he hadn't made trophies of these seventy kings' body parts and let them serve him in other ways? Then we would remember him today for his kindness instead of the horrible way that he disfigured his victims. And he would have probably died a natural death in old age, with his subjects around him, sad to see him go—instead of dancing in the streets at his funeral.

Baker and Butler

And they said to him, "We each have had a dream,
and there is no interpreter of it." So Joseph said to them,
"Do not interpretations belong to God? Tell them to me, please." Genesis 40:8

Have you ever had a strange dream and woken up wondering what it meant? Most dreams have no importance at all. Good thing, huh? If we had to live with the reality of our dreams, our lives would become real nightmares.

And that's the way it was for the butler and baker who ended up in prison with Joseph. They had worked for Pharaoh in his palace and considered themselves important, because they had both been directors of their departments. Until one fine day, that is, when they did something to upset Pharaoh, and he locked them up in prison and threw away the key. That's when they had their famous dreams—one about vines, grapes, and Pharaoh's cup, and the other about baskets, bread, and birds. Joseph could see the meaning of the dreams right away, and though he was happy enough to give good news to the butler, he was not anxious to talk about the baker's fate. In three days the butler would be freed from prison and given back his old job as wine taster for Pharaoh, Joseph said. The same timeline applied to the baker, except he would be executed—hung on a tree. And that's exactly what happened.

Now, sad to say, the butler forgot all about Joseph, even though Joseph's interpretations were nothing short of miraculous. But what if he had not forgotten Joseph? What if he had told Pharaoh about the amazing man in prison who could foretell the future with the help of his God? Would it have made a difference and gotten Joseph out of the clink sooner? Maybe, but one thing is sure. When Joseph became prime minister, the butler would have had many chances to eat crow every day, thinking about how he had left Joseph in prison to rot. "But never mind about that," we can hear Joseph telling him. "God rescues us when He is ready. He never makes mistakes."

FEBRUARY 3

Balaam

And Balaam said to Balak, "Look, I have come to you!
Now, have I any power at all to say anything?
The word that God puts in my mouth, that I must speak." Numbers 22:38

Someone should have given Balaam a spanking. Although the Bible considers him a bad person, at one time he had been a prophet of God. That was before he began practicing sorcery and witchcraft and casting spiritualistic spells on unfortunate victims. It was before he agreed to go to Moab and curse Israel, though God told him he must not go. And it was long before his donkey tried to stop his road trip to Moab by running off into a field, crushing his foot against a stone wall, falling down beneath him, and even talking to him. Still, he went ahead and traveled to Moab to accept a handsome bribe, which would bring him bad luck from God indeed. Of course, Balaam had no luck in the venture. Three times he opened his mouth to curse the twelve tribes, and three times, out came blessings instead.

We would think that any one of these setbacks would have convinced him it was time to go home, but not Balaam. He stayed and played with fire. If Israel couldn't be cursed with his magical enchantments, maybe it could be done through apostasy, and that's exactly what happened. King Balak arranged for beautiful young Midianite women to infiltrate the camp of Israel and entice the people to sin. And it worked. Many partied with the pagan girls and even bowed to the strange idols they brought along. And Balaam was there all along to see that it happened. Of course, God wasn't pleased. To prey upon people spiritually like that is satanic! Not long after, He told Moses to destroy the Midianites, and guess who was still among them? Balaam.

What if Balaam had never strayed from his service to God as a prophet? What if he had turned down the money offered to him by kings and princes for his evil incantations? Then he would not have ended up working against the God of heaven or caused 24,000 Israelites to die in a plague. And he himself wouldn't have died in a battle against Israel. What a tragic story about a man who could have been so much more!

Bezalel and Aholiab

*Then Moses called Bezalel and Aholiab, and every gifted artisan
in whose heart the Lord had put wisdom, everyone whose heart was stirred, to
come and do the work. Exodus 36:2*

Can you imagine what it would be like to have a place of worship that has golden furniture and walls of gold? That's what Israel's wilderness sanctuary looked like inside. There was a table for special bread for the priests, a seven-branch candlestick, an altar on which to burn incense, and, of course, the famous ark of the covenant, all covered with pure gold. Then there were the gold-plated walls of the tabernacle. What a sight that must have been, especially when the light of the candlesticks reflected off the gleaming surfaces of the walls!

And, of course, someone had to do all the work. That would be Bezalel and Aholiab, blessed by God with the skills to do the job. And who were these guys? Bezalel was from the tribe of Judah and the family of Caleb, one of the faithful spies who explored Canaan. Aholiab was from the tribe of Dan. The two men did a good job, and God rewarded their hard work by coming to live among the Israelites in their new tabernacle.

But what if these men had not agreed to do the work? Or what if they had cut corners doing a cheap job? Then they wouldn't be remembered as the famous artisans who built the golden furniture that lasted for centuries. Or they might have lost their jobs, and that would certainly have hurt their legacy as a family in the years to come. As it was, when Solomon built his temple 480 years later, he asked the descendants of Aholiab to help in the construction of the temple furniture. God expects us to always do our best when we work, and He is honored when we do that.

Caleb

"But My servant Caleb, because he has a different spirit in him
and has followed Me fully, I will bring into the land where he went,
and his descendants shall inherit it." Numbers 14:24

Caleb was definitely someone you would want on your side if you were fighting in a battle. He was daring and courageous, loyal to his country, and he loved God with all his heart. Best of all, he was a man of great faith. Caleb is best known for his stand as a faithful spy with Joshua when they challenged Israel to face the giants of Canaan. "Let us go up at once and take possession, for we are well able to overcome it!" they shouted as the people began to wail and mourn at the report the other ten spies gave. "Trust God!" they urged the people. "He has done great wonders for Israel, and has never failed us!" Unfortunately, the people didn't listen to Caleb and Joshua. When God punished the nation of grumblers by sending them back into the wilderness for another forty years, Caleb and Joshua had to wander along with them. That must have been very discouraging for them.

But that's not the end of Caleb's story. When Israel finally did arrive in Canaan after miraculously crossing the Jordan, they destroyed Jericho, conquered city-states all up and down the hill country of Palestine, and then divided up the land. At this point we see Caleb doing something very gutsy. He asked for an inheritance in the most difficult part of Canaan—the fortress of Hebron, where giants lived. Wow! What a man, and he did it at the age of eighty-five!

But what if he hadn't been faithful when all the other spies doubted God would help them conquer the giants? To be sure, he would have perished with all the other Israelites in the desert, and, of course, we wouldn't have this inspirational story to remind us that we need to be faithful to God too. And, of course, he would have never lived to actually fight the giants. But praise God he was faithful! Praise God for such a hero!

Deborah and Barak

Then Deborah said to Barak, "Up! For this is the day in which the LORD has delivered Sisera into your hand. Has not the LORD gone out before you?" So Barak went down from Mount Tabor with ten thousand men following him. Judges 4:14

The days of the judges just after the death of Joshua were tough for everyone in Israel. Because the people broke their covenant with God, He allowed them to be enslaved by many of the enemy nations surrounding them. When a Canaanite ruler named King Jabin began oppressing Israel, things looked really hopeless. His general, Sisera, had nine hundred iron chariots, and with these he persecuted Israel for twenty years.

Now, Deborah from the tribe of Ephraim was a judge and prophetess in those days. She was a brave woman and knew that the only answer for Israel was to go to war with King Jabin. So she sent for Barak, a mighty warrior in Israel. "God will help you defeat Sisera and his iron chariots at the Kishon River," she promised. However, strangely enough, Barak refused to go unless Deborah agreed to go with him. She agreed, but she said his lack of faith in God would cost him, because the credit for the victory would be given to a woman. That was a tough thing for a man to hear, but her prophecy came true when General Sisera was killed by a woman.

It's inspiring to see that women have been leaders down through the long centuries of time and that God has been able to count on them during times of great difficulty. However, what if Deborah had refused to lead? During a time when men thought they should be the ones in charge, leading must have been a great challenge for her. And what if Barak had willingly said, "I will lead the army into battle myself"? Then he could have been a partner with Deborah and honored God together with her, and what a dynamic duo they would have been!

Aaron

"And I said to them, 'Whoever has any gold, let them break it off.' So they gave it to me, and I cast it into the fire, and this calf came out." Exodus 32:24

Wow! Is that what really happened? A calf came marching out of the fire? Hmmm. Sounds suspicious, don't you think?

Aaron had been left in charge of the Israelite camp, something he had wanted for a very long time. Unfortunately, when Moses and Joshua didn't return for many days, trouble started in the camp. Some probably thought Moses had died on the mountain. By now it had been nearly forty days, and Aaron was having a hard time controlling the people. Some were suggesting that they choose another leader instead of Moses to lead them on to Canaan.

Things got so bad that Aaron was afraid there was going to be a riot. It's clear the people wanted a god they could see; so Aaron told everyone to give him the gold jewelry they were wearing. Skilled workmen worked to make an image out of gold that looked like a calf. Then the people staged a giant party with a barbecue and liquor, and people running around without much on.

That's when everything really fell apart. Moses came down from the mount, and Aaron told his whopping story about a calf marching out of the fire. Really! We can hardly believe such a story, but we know it's true because we read about it in the book of Exodus.

And what if Aaron had insisted the people behave properly? Then thousands of people wouldn't have died that day because of that wild party! They refused to repent of their horrific sins, and they paid for it. But Aaron had to live with the memory of it for the rest of his life. On that fateful day, he was given much authority, but he took very little responsibility, and that's where he messed up. Not cool, Aaron. Not cool at all.

Shem, Ham, and Japheth

Then the Lord said to Noah, "Come into the ark,
you and all your household, because I have seen that you are righteous
before Me in this generation." Genesis 7:1

What's it like being a preacher's kid? If you are one, you know how hard it can be. PKs are on display all the time, like mannequins in a store window. They have to get up early to go to church and often stay there all day. They have to go to weekend retreats and to camp meeting, not just for the whole week but also for setup and takedown operations of which their father or mother has to be a part. One of the most common expressions a PK has to hear from the family is, "Behave yourself. Don't embarrass the family. Everybody's watching."

Now, maybe it wasn't like that for you as a PK. Maybe your parents were really understanding and didn't put those kinds of pressures on you. But PKs can be hard on themselves too. It's not much fun being different from the other kids in your church and school.

OK, so how hard was it for Shem, Ham, and Japheth as PK kids? Well, they were expected to help build the ark for much of the 120 years. Work, work, work! You think you have chores? And to make things even harder, the boys didn't have all the latest toys and tech gadgets of the day, since all the family's money went into the construction of the ark.

It must have been hard for Noah's kids to be PKs. It must have been embarrassing sometimes to be kids of the "crazy preacher who preaches nothing but the end of the world." And what if the boys hadn't joined their parents and gotten on that ark? Then the world wouldn't exist as we know it today. But they did get on the ark—Shem, Ham, and Japheth, and their brides. Six young people with a boatload of smelly animals—and they lived to tell about it. Next time you're feeling bad about having to be a PK, think again. You've got problems? Try being Shem, Ham, and Japheth, the most famous PKs of all time.

Terah

"You shall have no other gods before Me." Exodus 20:3

Terah is remembered as the father of the most famous man in Jewish history: Abraham. Terah must have done some things right to raise a son who became known as the "friend of God." After all, he did get his family out of Ur, a pagan city of the Chaldees, including Abraham, Sarah, Nahor, and Lot.

But Terah had one weakness of character that doomed most of his family members to obscurity in history. He worshiped idols. Joshua 24:2 says Terah served other gods, probably the local gods of the Sumerians. History tells us the names of some of these gods: Enki, the god of wisdom and magic; Nanna, the moon god; and Utu, the sun god. Terah must have carried these silly little idols of stone with him out of Ur, because his family continued worshiping them. His son Haran and grandson Bethuel must have used them, as did his great-grandson Laban and great-great-granddaughters Leah and Rachel 150 years later.

The second commandment found in Exodus 20:5 warns us that the sin of worshiping idols could reach to the third and even fourth generations. In other words, if men selfishly put things ahead of their heavenly Father, their families would suffer the effects of these sins for generations to come.

But what if Terah had given up his idols? What if he had said, like Joshua centuries later, "As for me and my house, we will serve the LORD" (Joshua 24:15)? In that case the history of God's people might have been very different. Everyone in Terah's family might have been remembered as the "friends of God." They might have all migrated to Canaan and started a nation of believers right away. They might have skipped the years of slavery in Egypt.

What about you and me? What idols are we hanging on to? Our music, our sports, our money? Why not give these things to Jesus today, along with our hearts? That way we can be called "friends of God" too.

Ehud

But when the children of Israel cried out to the Lord, the Lord raised up a deliverer for them: Ehud the son of Gera, the Benjamite, a left-handed man. Judges 3:15

Eglon was a very fat man and the king of Moab during the time of the judges of Israel. He was a nasty man who oppressed the tribes of Israel for eighteen years. God had allowed the nation of Israel to be overrun by enemies like Moab because they had intermarried with pagans and worshiped their idols.

Finally Israel had enough! When they called on God for help, a man named Ehud came to the rescue. How did he do it? He made a special trip to Eglon's palace and smuggled in an eighteen-inch, double-edged sword under his clothing. Since he was left-handed, he strapped it on his right thigh, where it wouldn't be suspected by the king's bodyguards. When he arrived at the palace to pay the taxes Israel owed King Eglon, he told the king he had a secret message for him. And when the two of them were alone in the king's private chambers, Ehud pulled out his sword and killed the king. Then he shut and locked the doors of the palace and escaped before any of the king's bodyguards discovered what had happened.

The servants of the king waited a while for him to unlock the doors. However, as evening arrived they finally took a key, unlocked the door, and found the king lying dead on the floor. Meanwhile, Ehud had made his escape to the hill country of Ephraim, called for an army to fight against Moab, and in God's power defeated the nation of Moab!

What if Ehud hadn't answered God's call to deliver Israel from Moab? What if he hadn't been left-handed? What if he had been caught by the king's bodyguards? All of these things contributed to Ehud's success, and that's the way it is when God asks us to do something that calls for great courage. He will make it happen if we do our part.

FEBRUARY 11

Gibeonites

> But when the inhabitants of Gibeon heard what Joshua had done to Jericho and Ai, they worked craftily, and went and pretended to be ambassadors. . . . And they went to Joshua, to the camp at Gilgal, and said to him and to the men of Israel, "We have come from a far country; now therefore, make a covenant with us."
> Joshua 9:3, 4, 6

This story is a strange one, and the Gibeonites are a very interesting people. They were afraid of the Israelites, and with good reason. The armies of Israel under General Joshua had defeated the fierce Amorites east of the Jordan; the giants of Bashan; and the stout fortress of Jericho. Until now, nothing had stood in their way, not even the Jordan River, which had parted for them mysteriously! And so the Gibeonites lied. They claimed to have come on a "long" journey, showing their old wineskins and moldy bread, their tattered clothes full of holes, and their worn-out sandals tied up with string. With all this they spun a story about being from a faraway country and tricked Joshua into signing a treaty with them. Pretty slick, huh?

So, what would you have done if you were in their shoes? Raised an army to fight the Israelites? Others had tried and failed. Would you have run away to another country? In those days, every man was your enemy. Would you have made friends with Israel and told them the truth? That would probably have been a better idea. Then they could have avoided the shame of having to work like slaves for the Israelites for generations to come.

But what if they had done like Rahab? What if they had said, "Your God is great and mighty. He is infinitely more amazing than our gods of wood and stone, and we would like to surrender to Him so we can live." Now that would have been a real story to tell, and we would be still telling it today. Unfortunately, to make their point, the Gibeonites had to walk around with moldy bread in their pockets. Now that's just nasty!

Jephthah

But above all, my brethren, do not swear, either by heaven or by earth
or with any other oath. But let your "Yes" be "Yes," and your "No," "No,"
lest you fall into judgment. James 5:12

The story of Jephthah is a very disturbing one because it tells us just how devastating the consequences of a foolish act can be. The elders of Gilead had asked Jephthah if he would help them fight against the Ammonites, and Jephthah agreed. However, on his way to battle he made a vow to God and his fellow soldiers that if Jehovah helped him defeat the Ammonites in battle, he would offer a special sacrifice to God. And he was very specific about what the sacrifice would be. "Whatever comes out of the door of my house to meet me when I return in triumph from the Ammonites will be the LORD's, and I will sacrifice it as a burnt offering." Boy, was he in for a surprise! We can be sure Jephthah thought it would be a goat or calf or sheep that met him first on the road to his house, and he would have been content to offer any one of them as a sacrifice to God. However, the thought that his daughter would be the first one to come running out to greet him was the furthest thing from his mind. But that's exactly what happened.

According to the Bible, he went ahead with the vow and offered her as a sacrifice as he would have any other animal. We'd like to think he didn't actually do it, but the Bible doesn't offer any other explanation. So we have to ask ourselves, what if Jephthah hadn't kept his vow to offer a sacrifice? Some would say they understood, for sure, but others would have held it against him. In those days people kept their promises no matter what the outcome, or they were considered to be very bad, dishonest people. If a leader like Jephthah didn't fulfill a vow, no one would ever trust him again. And maybe that's the problem with vows of that kind. We can never be sure exactly what the future holds, so we should be careful about making such promises.

FEBRUARY 13

Jochebed

But when she [Jochebed] could no longer hide him,
she took an ark of bulrushes for him,
daubed it with asphalt and pitch, put the child in it,
and laid it in the reeds by the river's bank. Exodus 2:3

Jochebed was one of the bravest women in history. She gave birth to a son during the most frightening of times, when a Hebrew baby boy's life wasn't worth the blanket he was wrapped in. But she was a godly woman and didn't lack the imagination or the courage it would take for her to do the unthinkable. If her baby son was to live, she would have to take some risks. And that's exactly what she did. She built a little basket boat and set him in it among the reeds of the Nile River. Now, what happened next might seem like an accident, but Jochebed knew exactly what she was doing. That may not be obvious at the start of our story, but it becomes evident later on.

Setting a basket containing a baby on the river might seem like a cruel thing. If the baby didn't cook from the heat of the sun, the crocodiles would surely eat him for breakfast. But, of course, that's not what happened at all. Jochebed put the basket in the reeds along the river's edge near the very spot where Pharaoh's daughter bathed every morning. Did she know the princess would have compassion on her baby? Did she think she would have to give him up? Did she have a clue that he might end up being raised in Pharaoh's royal court?

What if Jochebed hadn't had the unusual courage it takes to pull off such a stunt? What if she had not built that basket boat, and continued to hide her boy from Pharaoh's spies who walked the streets of Goshen? God would have likely found another way to save Moses, but we also know that God helps those who help themselves. And that's exactly what Jochebed did. She helped Moses, and herself, because in the end she was asked by Pharaoh's daughter to be the nanny for Moses until he was old enough to live in the palace. Smart thinking, Jochebed

Joshua

That day the LORD exalted Joshua in the sight of all Israel;
and they stood in awe of him all the days of his life,
just as they had stood in awe of Moses. Joshua 4:14, NIV

Joshua was a faithful leader for God and was honored in many ways for it. Next to Moses and David, he probably had more impact on the history of Israel than any other leader. At age forty he came out of Egypt and quickly became Moses' most trusted man. He helped in the organization of the nation's civil laws, the camping assignments for the twelve tribes, organization for the military, and probably the huge task of deciding where two million people would pasture their vast flocks and herds. Sound like an impossible task? It would have been if he hadn't depended on God for his courage and wisdom.

And God was pleased with Joshua's leadership skills. So much, in fact, that Joshua alone was asked to stay up on Mount Sinai during the weeks that Moses spent so much time there. And that was just the beginning. When twelve spies were chosen to explore Canaan, Joshua was asked to represent his tribe. He and Caleb brought back a good report because they believed they could conquer the giants in the land of milk and honey. When he scolded the other ten spies for their evil report and lack of faith, all Israel wanted to stone him, but God intervened and sent the rebellious nation back into the wilderness to die. For their faithfulness in this incident, only Joshua and Caleb were allowed to enter the Promised Land forty years later. We know Joshua best today for the part he played in conquering the famous city of Jericho and the rest of Canaan.

What if Joshua had not been faithful in his service to God? What if he had not stood firm with Caleb? What if he had told God to get someone else to lead Israel into Canaan after Moses died? Then he would not be remembered today as one of God's greatest champions for truth. And we would not be singing "Joshua fought the battle of Jericho!"

Korah, Dathan, and Abiram

They gathered together against Moses and Aaron, and said to them,
"You take too much upon yourselves, for all the congregation is holy,
every one of them, and the Lord is among them. Why then
do you exalt yourselves above the assembly of the Lord?" Numbers 16:3

Korah, Dathan, and Abiram probably caused more trouble for Moses and Aaron than anyone else on the forty-year trip from Egypt to Canaan. Korah and his buddies didn't like the idea of being peons, and they made no bones about it. Since he was a Levite, Korah and his family helped to transport all the sanctuary furniture whenever the nation pulled up stakes and moved, but that wasn't good enough for him. He wanted to be the high priest, and he set out to make his wish come true. First he got his two closest friends, Dathan and Abiram, involved, and then 250 other princes joined them. "We're just as good as you," they whined to Moses and Aaron. "We deserve to be leaders too!" At that point God decided things had gone far enough and called all the elders to the tabernacle so He could tell them who would be the leaders in Israel. But Korah and his followers were not interested in what God had to say.

Moses said, "Back away from the tents of Korah, Dathan, and Abiram!" and quicker than a wink, the ground split open and swallowed the three rebels, their tents, and all their families. Then the 250 princes were destroyed in a fire! Wow! That's scary! How sad, because it didn't have to end in disaster.

But what if these men hadn't grouched against Moses? What if they had not defied God and His law? Well, for starters they would not have been swallowed up in the pit. That's a no-brainer! The 250 princes who had followed their lead would not have been burned up with the glory of God's presence, and their descendants would still be with us today. That's a lot of responsibility for three men who set a bad example. Very sad, but true.

Ephraim, Manasseh, and Company

It had a great, high wall with twelve gates, and with twelve angels
at the gates. On the gates were written the names of the twelve tribes of Israel.
Revelation 21:12, NIV

Jacob had twelve sons who later became twelve tribes of Israel. Some of them became famous, others developed a bad reputation. Some dropped into obscurity down through the ages. Strangely enough, two of Jacob's grandsons also became tribes in Israel. Joseph's two sons, Ephraim and Manasseh, inherited the birthright because their uncles, Reuben, Simeon, Levi, and Judah, all disqualified themselves. Benjamin, the youngest brother, remained one of the smallest tribes in Israel and had some shameful times down through the years. However, after the kingdoms of Judah and Israel split during the reign of Rehoboam, Benjamin was the only tribe that remained loyal to Judah.

Zebulun, Issachar, Dan, Gad, Asher, and Naphtali, the six middle tribes, are not so well known in the history of Israel. Dan was later taken out of the tribe lineup, and so was Ephraim. Why? Both tribes became fascinated with pagan idols instead of worshiping Jehovah, the God of their fathers. Not only did they eat pigs and bats and mice, but they also became corrupt and made sacrifices to pagan gods like Molech and Chemosh.

What if the northern tribes of Israel had been faithful to God? What if they hadn't become so corrupt and immoral and eaten all those disgusting things? What if they hadn't given sacrifices on altars to pagan gods? Then the world would have been more ready for Jesus when He came to this earth as the Son of God. But there's good news for the sons of Jacob. The book of Revelation tells us the names of the twelve tribes will be written on the twelve gates of the New Jerusalem. All's well that ends well.

Job's Friends

Now when Job's three friends heard of all this adversity that had come upon him, each one came from his own place—Eliphaz the Temanite, Bildad the Shuhite, and Zophar the Naamathite. For they had made an appointment together to come and mourn with him, and to comfort him. Job 2:11

If you lost everything that was precious to you in the world, wouldn't you want your friends to come and stay with you? Wouldn't you want them to sit with you and cry a bit? Most people would, and that's what Job's friends intended to do for him. He had lost everything—his livestock, his children, and his health. He was so sick, in fact, that when his closest friends came to comfort him, they didn't even recognize him. They intended to mourn with him over his losses, but that's not how it turned out. By the time they were done with their little charade, they were doing just the opposite. "God isn't happy with you," they said. "He's punishing you for your sins," and, "You're too proud, Job, and God is waiting for you to become humble."

Job listened humbly and politely, but in the end he had to give them all a piece of his mind. And so did God. "My wrath is aroused against you and your two friends, for you have not spoken of Me what is right, as My servant Job has." Those are pretty strong words from the God of heaven. These "friends" had come with a misunderstanding of who God is, and they tried to convince Job that God was probably more interested in punishing him for his sins than comforting him in his time of great sadness. The truth is, because of the battle between good and evil all around us, innocent people sometimes become casualties.

But what if Job's friends had just come and cried with him over his losses? What if they had just sat with him and prayed for him? Like Job, we all need sympathy when disasters come our way. Words don't help much when we are grieving, but shared tears do.

Joseph

And Pharaoh said to his servants, "Can we find such a one as this,
a man in whom is the Spirit of God?" Genesis 41:38

Joseph is one of the most amazing characters in the Bible. He was a legend in his time, everybody's hero, and an icon for God's people down through the ages. But things didn't start out that way. Growing up, he was a spoiled child and drove his ten older brothers crazy with his superior ways. They hated him for being their father's favorite, and the multicolored coat Jacob gave to him. In the end they did the unthinkable by selling him to slave traders who doubled as traveling salesmen in Egypt.

Joseph was overwhelmed with grief and terror at the thought of being a slave for the rest of his life, but he promised God that he would be faithful. He would not become one of the Egyptians and worship their pagan gods. Within ten years, he had risen to the highest position of trust in the household of Potiphar, captain of the king's guard. Unfortunately, his boss's wife found him attractive, and when he refused her attentions because of his love for God, she reversed the engines and angrily got him sent to prison.

In prison he did not let go of his confidence in God, and before long he was asked to manage the prisoners. During that time he interpreted dreams for a baker and butler who had been imprisoned for supposed crimes against the royal household. This paved the way for Joseph to ultimately interpret Pharaoh's dreams for him, prophesy that Egypt would have seven years of famine, and be appointed prime minister of Egypt.

But what if he hadn't been true to his convictions about worshiping the one true God while in Egypt? What if he hadn't been honest and hardworking in everything he did? What if he had given in to the temptations offered to him by Potiphar's wife? Then, of course, he would have never landed in prison, never interpreted the dreams for the butler, baker, or Pharaoh, and never had a chance to save millions of lives. And so we see that all things work together for those who love God. Without doubt, being faithful pays big dividends.

FEBRUARY 19

Miriam

Miriam was shut out of the camp seven days, and the people did not journey till she was brought in again. Numbers 12:15

Miriam was a born leader and one of the most honored women in history. As a young girl of thirteen she helped save her brother from certain death on the Nile River. As a 93-year-old on the shores of the Red Sea, she led a praise team of women. Clearly she was honored to be one of three siblings who were hand-picked to lead Israel out of Egypt. But she had her ugly side too, and we're not talking about facial features. She had a selfish, mean streak, and Moses was at the short end of it now and then. For example, there was the time when she and her brother Aaron accused Moses of selfishly hoarding the leadership privileges for himself. That didn't go over real well with God, and He called Miriam and Aaron to the sanctuary to set things straight for them.

"If there is a prophet among you, I, the Lord, make Myself known to him in a vision, and I speak to him in a dream," said God. "Not so with my servant Moses. He is faithful in all my house. I speak with him face to face." That was quite a rebuke for Miriam. And we understand there was something else going on here too. She didn't like Moses' wife, Zipporah. Why? We don't know everything about the situation, but it's clear she was prejudiced against Zipporah because she was not an Israelite.

It's too bad Miriam treated her sister-in-law like that, but what if she hadn't? What if she had been a model example of how a leader should act? What if she had been kind to Zipporah and made her feel welcome in the camp? Then things would have turned out quite differently. Moses wouldn't have had so many headaches, and everyone would have complained less. And who knows, Zipporah and Miriam might have even ended up as best of friends.

Moses

Moses was very humble, more than all men who were on the face of the earth.
Numbers 12:3

Historians say that Moses was one of the greatest men to ever walk the face of the earth. He was a statesman, a general, and a religious giant who helped change the course of history. As a young man he was given the opportunity to become Pharaoh—leader of the most powerful nation at that time. He could have chosen fame and fortune, but instead he decided to "suffer affliction with the people of God, [rather] than to enjoy the pleasures of sin for a season" (Hebrews 11:25, KJV).

And that's where the story of Moses gets really interesting, because if he thought he was going to be shortchanged somehow in the adventure department, he was in for a surprise. Yes, he did have to bring the people of God out of Egypt in the aftermath of the ten plagues. He did have to lead the frantic, screaming Israelites through the Red Sea with Pharaoh and his army of charioteers right behind them. He did have to listen to the whiners grumble about having to eat food from heaven every day. But there was an upside to Moses' life too. He got to spend forty days in the presence of God on Mount Sinai. He had the privilege of meeting with God every day in the tabernacle sanctuary to learn patience about how to deal with the ornery, free-loading, along-for-the-free-ride mixed multitude. And though he did die before entering the Promised Land, he was buried by the angels on Mount Nebo, and later was raised by Jesus Himself. Wow! That's a pretty good payoff for forty years of wandering in the wilderness with the unthankful and the unholy.

But what if he hadn't chosen to stake his claim with the people of God? What if he had said, "I'd rather hold a scepter in my hand and rule Egypt"? Then today he would be a dried-up, shriveled mummy somewhere in an ancient Egyptian tomb, if we could even find him and prove that he lived. Without God, that's as good as it would have been for Moses.

Mrs. Potiphar

"How then can I do this great wickedness, and sin against God?" Genesis 39:9

Joseph was a good-looking young man. Maybe he was tall, dark, and handsome, with six-pack abs. But he wasn't a show-off. He just went about his business every day, minding his own business, doing work for Captain Potiphar, keeping the kitchens, gardens, shops, stables, and armory running smoothly.

But Mrs. Potiphar wasn't satisfied just having Joseph bring prosperity to her household. She wanted more from him. Maybe she was lonely because her husband was away a lot, or maybe he seldom told her she was beautiful, or that he loved her. We don't know much about her, but the Bible tells us that she tried to persuade Joseph to do wrong one afternoon, and that's where all the trouble started. The Bible says Joseph refused her advances. Good plan. He took the high road. Unfortunately, for this he received a prison sentence. But that was proof enough he was innocent, because if Potiphar had thought otherwise, he would have had Joseph executed on the spot. And the fascinating story doesn't end there. Within two years, Joseph became the most powerful ruler in Egypt next to Pharaoh. The slave would now become the master. Oops! Guess Mrs. Potiphar's plan backfired. We don't know what became of her, but we can imagine Captain Potiphar felt ashamed for the part he had played in the fiasco.

What if Mrs. Potiphar had not tried such a stunt? For sure she would have been blessed many times over for the loyal service Joseph brought them. And who knows, she might have been remembered as a Ruth or Queen Esther who maximized her God-given opportunities. Maybe she would have accepted Joseph's God and made Him Lord of her life. Instead she disappeared into obscurity, identified for the bad she did—not the good she could have done.

Nadab and Abihu

Then Nadab and Abihu, the sons of Aaron, each took his censer
and put fire in it, put incense on it, and offered profane fire before the Lord, which
He had not commanded them. Leviticus 10:1

Nadab and Abihu were preacher's kids, but not just any PKs. They were the high priest's PKs, and that makes this story even sadder. They were spoiled, rebellious kids, no doubt, but we can guess why that might be. Their father was the number-two guy in the camp of two million Israelites, so it's no surprise that his two oldest sons might be tempted to get a little rowdy from time to time. The fact that they had met with God on Mount Sinai didn't seem to make much of an impression on them. Even though they saw Jehovah standing on a pavement of brilliant sapphire blue with flames of glory washing over it, they soon forgot.

And this is where the story gets crazy. One day they did something sacrilegious. They went to church drunk. What? That's right. Grabbing up the special censers they used to conduct prayer services in the golden tabernacle, they put "strange" fire in them and danced their way into the sanctuary. And that's when a brilliant burst of glory came shooting out of the mercy seat in the Most Holy Place and killed Nadab and Abihu. Wow! What a shameful pity, and what a traumatic day for their family! The sad thing is that Aaron could have raised them to be more respectful. Unfortunately, he had problems himself with reverence. After all, he did make a golden calf for the people to worship.

But what would have happened if Aaron had told Nadab and Abihu to smarten up when they were young? What if he had told them to "shape up or ship out"? Then we probably wouldn't be telling this story. They might have gone down in history with honor as great leaders like their uncle Moses. But that's the way it is when we are not respectful of holy things. Sooner or later this attitude will take us down. No good ever came from being a brat.

Og

For only Og king of Bashan remained of the remnant of the giants.
Indeed his bedstead was an iron bedstead. . . . Nine cubits is its length
and four cubits its width. Deuteronomy 3:11

When the twelve spies invaded the land of Canaan two years after leaving Egypt, they saw many giants in the land. In the southern part of Canaan they encountered the giant sons of Anak, and east of the Jordan they saw giant Amorites. "They were huge, and we felt like grasshoppers next to them!" the spies said.

Roll the clock forward forty years, and again Israel met fierce enemies when they neared Canaan. Among them were the giants of Bashan, a cruel and violent nation who lived in sixty fortresses built with huge black stones. Their leader was King Og, a giant among giants. In fact, he was so big that his bed was thirteen feet long! King Og usually fought his battles in the rocky canyons of the high country, but confident of success against Israel, he brought his army of giants out on the open plain. And wonder of wonders, he lost. Why? Because God fought for His people.

It's possible Og may have even been one of the giants the twelve spies saw forty years before when they explored the land. If this is true, he should have known better than to attack Israel. He knew the stories about the ten plagues in Egypt and the Red Sea crossing. Unfortunately, he had also seen what cowards the Israelites were when they refused to face the giants of Canaan the first time around. It's this lack of faith that made Og so bold the second time around.

But it didn't have to be this way. King Og could have surrendered to Moses and the armies of Israel. If he had, his people might have lived, a nation of super giants, to honor God and serve Him. As it is, they are only a memory of a lost race that tried to defy the God of heaven.

Othniel

When the children of Israel cried out to the LORD, the LORD raised up
a deliverer for the children of Israel, who delivered them:
Othniel the son of Kenaz, Caleb's younger brother. Judges 3:9

The days of the judges in ancient Israel were a very turbulent time for God's people. The Israelites worshiped pagan gods, such as Baal, Chemosh, and Molech, so Jehovah allowed them to be overrun by enemy nations. Raiders from these nations would come through the tribes of Israel to rob and plunder. Sometimes they stole their grain or cattle, and often they captured young women and children to make them slaves.

God wanted to protect Israel, but He could not because they had broken their covenant with Him by worshiping other gods. However, when they repented, God would raise up a leader from among them who would inspire them, bring them back to God, and lead them against their enemies.

Othniel was just such a leader during the days of Cushan-Rishathaim, king of Mesopotamia. This pagan king oppressed Israel for eight years, but when they called to the Lord in their trouble, Othniel was sent to deliver them. With God's help, Othniel defeated Cushan-Rishathaim, and then he became their judge. What a relief for Israel, because under his leadership Israel then had peace for forty years.

But what if Israel had not been weak spiritually? What if they had followed God's commandments that told them not to intermarry with pagan worshipers? What if they had not sacrificed to the gods of wood and stone? Then they would have been blessed by God and would not have needed Othniel. And wonder of wonders, the surrouding nations might have even been led to serve the one true God who is Creator of heaven and earth. That's what happens when we are faithful to God as He has asked us to be.

Pharaoh I

So Joseph answered Pharaoh, saying, "It is not in me;
God will give Pharaoh an answer of peace." Genesis 41:16

It's hard to guess what Pharaoh was thinking when he first saw Joseph being brought up from the prison to interpret his dreams. Did he know this slave was the son of a wealthy sheik? Not likely. He knew his dreams were unusual, but did he know they would in fact become legends in their time? Again, probably not. "I saw seven plump heads of grain grow up out of the earth," said Pharaoh, "and then seven wilted heads of grain, and the withered grain consumed the good grain so there was nothing left. In the second dream I saw seven fat cows come up out of the Nile, and then seven scrawny cows, and the seven skimpy cows ate up the fat, sleek ones. What do these strange dreams mean?"

And you know the story. Joseph explained to Pharaoh that his dreams had been given to him by the God of heaven as omens of days to come. The rest was history. Seven good years of abundant crops would come to the Mediterranean countries, and then seven years of famine. Everyone not prepared for the coming famine would starve to death. Pharaoh was so impressed with Joseph's insight and ability to interpret dreams that he immediately promoted him to second in command over all Egypt. Quite a turn of events for a Pharaoh who came close to never meeting Joseph.

What if he hadn't allowed Joseph to help him? What if he had been too proud to ask a slave from prison to do something as important as interpreting a royal dream? After all, Pharaoh was considered to be a god. If he had not gotten Joseph's help, he wouldn't have received the warning God intended. Joseph wouldn't have become his prime minster to manage the coming harvests, and the famine would have killed millions. What a blessing for Pharaoh!

Pharaoh II

And Pharaoh said, "Who is the LORD, that I should obey His voice to let Israel go? I do not know the LORD, nor will I let Israel go." Exodus 5:2

Pharaoh of the Exodus was very different from Pharaoh in Joseph's day. He was a proud man and enjoyed the free labor of two million slaves. But there is more to the story than meets the eye. This Pharaoh remembered the dark stories of genocide eighty years before, when Hebrew babies had been murdered. He knew Moses had escaped that decree and was adopted by Pharaoh's daughter. He knew Moses had been raised to be Egypt's next Pharaoh and that he worshiped only Jehovah.

Of course, everything changed when Moses killed an Egyptian overseer and fled the country to save his skin. After forty years he had returned to Egypt and was public enemy number one. "Let Jehovah's people go!" he demanded, but Pharaoh refused, as we know, on grounds that he didn't know who Jehovah was. Really? Actually, he and his priests did know about Jehovah, the one true God. They knew that if they let the twelve tribes go to worship God, they would never again be satisfied with being slaves. But ignoring Jehovah was a gamble, and it cost Pharaoh dearly. In quick succession came ten horrible plagues, each one more disastrous than the one before it. The Nile became like blood; frogs and flies and gnats swarmed over the land; disease, storms, and locusts devoured everything; and, of course, there were the days of impenetrable darkness. But the worst of all God's judgments to come was the death of Egypt's firstborns.

God always provides a way of escape, though Pharaoh in this case didn't choose that option. What if he had? What if he had let Israel go, as God asked? Then Egypt would have escaped an annihilation that affected the country for generations to come. All their crops and livestock would not have been destroyed, and our memory of Pharaoh would be very different.

Pharaoh's Daughter

And the child grew, and she brought him to Pharaoh's daughter,
and he became her son. So she called his name Moses, saying,
"Because I drew him out of the water." Exodus 2:10

Who was this daughter of Pharaoh who came to bathe at the Nile River each morning? Do we know her name? Is her life recorded anywhere in history, or on the temples and ancient tombs of the Pharaohs? Biblical and archaeological experts think she may have been a woman named Hatshepsut, who lived during the time of Moses, and ended up co-ruling Egypt with her brother when her father died. Ancient records tell us she had no children, so it is in fact possible she was Moses' stepmother, and she fits the profile in the Exodus story.

What was she thinking when she fished Moses out of the Nile that morning some 3,500 years ago? Did she understand he was a Hebrew baby? Did she think Moses had been sent from Hapi, who the Egyptians believed to be the god of the Nile? Maybe. He had been taken out of the Nile, after all. This kind of legend was part of Egyptian folklore. One thing is sure. Angels of heaven had directed Pharaoh's daughter to that spot. Clearly God had His eye on this baby, who would one day deliver Israel from slavery and change the course of history.

And so it was that Pharaoh's daughter rescued Moses from the river, from being executed by her father, who called for the death of all Hebrew baby boys. This wretched mass genocide would come back to haunt Pharaoh of the Exodus eighty years later, but for now the princess' act of compassion had saved at least one baby.

What if Pharaoh's daughter had not rescued Moses? What if she hadn't had compassion when she heard his pitiful cries in the basket? Then God would have had to save Moses some other way, and she would have missed out on raising one of the Bible's most famous heroes.

Captain Potiphar

The LORD was with Joseph, and he was a successful man. . . .
And his master saw that the LORD was with him,
and that the LORD made all he did to prosper in his hand. Genesis 39:2, 3

Joseph was a good luck charm as far as Potiphar was concerned. "Everything Joseph touches turns to gold," we can almost hear the captain saying. And it was true—because Joseph was a hard worker, honest, and obedient to the laws of his Creator, God could bless him. In the world of business, that's almost as good as owning a goose that can lay golden eggs. The Bible says Captain Potiphar "left all that he had in Joseph's hand, and he did not know what he had except for the bread which he ate" (Genesis 39:6). He favored this young man who was smart beyond words, who knew how to read and write and was evidently a great accountant. It was clear to Potiphar that Joseph was no ordinary young man. His character and pedigree showed that he was from a fine family of sophisticated stock. It must have touched his heart to see Joseph doing his work faithfully as a household slave, though he would have much rather been back home in the hills of Canaan. Unfortunately, the good times were not to last, but not because Potiphar wanted it that way. He would have wanted the blessings to go on forever.

It was his wife who opened the can of worms, so to speak, and Potiphar allowed her to do it. But what if he hadn't listened to the accusations she was making against Joseph? What if he hadn't put Joseph in jail? He knew the charges against Joseph couldn't be true. In that case Joseph would have no doubt missed a two-year prison sentence and all that went with it. But then again, God never makes mistakes. If we trust in Him, He will never allow us to go through with something that is bad for us in the long run. The story of Joseph is living proof.

MARCH 1

Puah and Shiphrah

But the midwives feared God, and did not do as the king of Egypt
commanded them, but saved the male children alive. Exodus 1:17

Their names were Puah and Shiphrah, and we know almost nothing about them, except that they disobeyed Pharaoh. Why? Because they were compassionate. Here's how it went. Pharaoh saw that the number of Hebrews in Egypt was rapidly increasing. To him they looked as numerous as the sands of the sea, something that sounds very familiar when we think about the promises God made to Abraham. Anyway, he got very worried. "If we have a war, they may join our enemies and fight against us!" he said. And so he ordered that all Hebrew baby boys be thrown into the Nile River. What a demonic thing to do! Of course, he couldn't expect the Hebrew mothers to kill their own babies, so he hired two Hebrew midwives to do it for them. The midwives were supposed to make sure the executions were carried out, but they refused. They obeyed God rather than man. Then, too, the Hebrew women were healthy because of all the work they were accustomed to as slaves, and when it came time to give birth to their babies, their labor and delivery were quick. At least that is what Puah and Shiphrah told Pharaoh.

We can be sure God blessed these two women for the part they played in saving the lives all those baby boys. But what if they had said, "It's our necks on the line, and we're not taking any chances by disobeying the orders of Pharaoh." Then, many babies would have died. We can't imagine all the good those two women did by being compassionate. Yea! Puah and Shiphrah!

Abinadab of Kirjath–Jearim

Then the men of Kirjath Jearim came and took the ark of the Lord,
and brought it into the house of Abinadab on the hill,
and consecrated Eleazar his son to keep the ark of the Lord. 1 Samuel 7:1

When the ark of the covenant was sent back to Israel by the Philistines, it sat in a field for a while near Beth-Shemesh in the tribal territory of Judah. No one knew what to do with it. Hophni and Phineas, the caretakers of the ark, were dead, and so was Eli the high priest; likely Samuel had to help make a decision about where to take it, young though he was. The ark couldn't be returned to the town of Shiloh, where the tabernacle sanctuary had been pitched since the time of Joshua some three hundred years earlier. Archaeological evidence tells us Shiloh was destroyed about 1100 B.C., probably by the Philistines, which fits perfectly into our story timeline.

While everyone debated where the ark of God should be taken, the people in the town of Beth-Shemesh tried to take a sneak peek inside, an act that was forbidden by God. And fifty of them died. As a result, the people of Beth-Shemesh were sure they didn't want the ark to stay with them. To them it represented death.

But not to Abinadab. He understood that the mercy seat of the ark was the place where God's presence dwelled in Israel. And he knew exactly what he was doing when he invited a group of priests to bring the ark of God to his home in Kirjath-Jearim. He was humbled with awe and reverence that God would come to dwell in his home. For twenty years the ark stayed with him, and God blessed him and his son Eleazar.

What if Abinadab had refused to keep the ark? What if his family had been too afraid? Then they would have missed the blessings of having God's holy ark come live in their home. As far as we know, it was the only time in history that someone had that privilege.

Abner

Then the king said to his men, "Do you not realize that a prince
and a great man has fallen in Israel this day?" 2 Samuel 3:38

General Abner was the most powerful man in Israel. More powerful than the tribal chieftains or the high priest or maybe even the king himself. What he said carried weight and influence among the twelve tribes of Israel. Abner had served King Saul well, helping him win many battles. He also helped the king chase David all over Israel to exterminate him like some kind of pest or parasite. In return, David had embarrassed the veteran general on many occasions when God helped him evade Abner's clutches. And more than once David had the chance to kill King Saul while the army was in hot pursuit of him. Abner should have been protecting the king, but obviously he had slipped up on his security measures.

But when Saul was killed in battle, Abner knew things would change. The new king of Israel, Saul's son Ishbosheth, was a weak ruler, and his days were numbered. A major argument between Abner and King Ishbosheth erupted, and finally the general decided to defect to the service of David, who was now king in Judah. Not surprisingly, David's nephew and general, Joab, didn't trust Abner and plotted his death by assassination. King David knew nothing of the plot and afterwards mourned Abner's death.

Did Abner have to die like that? Maybe not. Would it have been possible for him and General Joab to serve King David together in the royal army? Possibly, if Abner had been more humble and willing to serve under Joab as commanding officer. But that wasn't likely. Long before, Abner had made an enemy of Joab when he killed Joab's brother, Asahel. Remember, what goes around comes around. If we treat others kindly, they will likely do the same for us. If we don't, our chickens will eventually come home to roost.

Achish

And David arose, and he passed over with the six hundred men that were with him unto Achish, the son of Maoch, king of Gath. 1 Samuel 27:2, KJV

Could it possibly be true? Would David actually be willing to go and live among the people who had been Israel's enemies for generations? And why would King Achish want him there? After all, David had killed Goliath, the Philistine champion!

Well, for starters he came with six hundred of the fiercest warriors in the land, among them a troop of thirty legendary fighting machines called "David's mighty men." Achish was no dummy. He was probably actually quite gratified. These warriors in exile were all being hunted by King Saul, the archenemy of Achish, king of Gath. If you've ever heard the expression "The enemy of my enemy is my friend," you get a pretty good picture of why Achish might welcome David.

So, King Achish invited David to move right into Gath and its surrounding villages. But, of course, David was smarter than that. He feared the pagan influence of the Philistine culture on his men and their families—idol worship, for one thing, and all kinds of detestable things at their feasts, for another. Honestly, he didn't really want to be a Philistine. He just wanted a safe place to live for a while. That's when David suggested an alternate plan. His men needed a town of their own, so King Achish gave him the town of Ziklag.

What if King Achish had insisted that David go with him into battle against Israel? What would David have done in that event? He couldn't fight against his own people, so God intervened. Thankfully, it saved his neck, and probably his political career too. King Saul died at the hands of the Philistines during that famous battle, but David wasn't there to be a part of it.

Agag

Then Samuel said, "Bring me Agag king of the Amalekites."
Agag came to him in chains. And he thought, "Surely the bitterness of death is
past." But Samuel said, "As your sword has made women childless,
so will your mother be childless among women." And Samuel put Agag to death
before the Lord at Gilgal. 1 Samuel 15:32, 33

This is a pretty gruesome story, but when we hear the details of who Agag really was, we get a different picture of why things turned out the way they did. The Amalekites were a cruel, ruthless people who made their living by running raids on neighboring nations. They thought nothing of stealing cattle and crops and children, torturing and killing anyone who got in their way. Even worse, they would disfigure those they defeated in battle, cutting off various body parts, or disemboweling pregnant women, killing their unborn babies.

God finally told Samuel the day of judgment had come for the Amalekites and that King Saul should raise an army to destroy the warring tribes living in southern Judah. "Take no hostages," God said, "and bring back no spoils of war." Samuel gave the order, but King Saul did not carry it out properly. His soldiers brought back the best of their captured livestock to be used as offerings, and Saul brought back King Agag as a war trophy. This was a common practice of the day, but in this case forbidden by God. And as the story goes, Saul was told his disobedience would cost him the kingdom, after which Samuel executed King Agag himself.

Now, what if Agag had not been so cruel? What if he had remembered that he should treat others as he would want to be treated? Then, of course, he would have lived. He would not have been executed and maybe even enjoyed the blessings of serving the God of his great-great-great- (many more times great) grandfather Abraham. That's right, Abraham was Agag's relative too.

Ahimelek

David went to Nob, to Ahimelek the priest. Ahimelek trembled when he met him, and asked, "Why are you alone? Why is no one with you?" 1 Samuel 21:1, NIV

Ahimelek was Israel's high priest in the days of King Saul. He was a descendant of Eli, probably a grandson of the famous priest under which the ark of God was captured by the Philistines. The tabernacle sanctuary was now in the little town of Nob. One day David showed up at the sanctuary alone, and Ahimelek was suspicious right away. "What are you doing here?" he asked, and the Bible says David trembled. Why? As a part of the king's bodyguard, David never went anywhere alone. Maybe Ahimelek had heard rumors that things weren't going so well between David and the king.

And then David did a very bad thing. He lied. "The king sent me on a secret mission, and I was in such a hurry that I left without my men or my weapons," he said, knowing it probably sounded pretty hokey.

Unfortunately, David's lie would later get Ahimelek in a lot of trouble. He didn't really mean any harm by his dishonesty, but his blunder helped set up the high priest for a fall. The high priest unwisely gave David some holy bread from the sanctuary, along with Goliath's sword, of all things. Later this would be reported to Saul, giving the crazed king every reason to believe what he wanted to believe—that Ahimelek had conspired against him to help David.

What could Ahimelek have done to protect himself from this predicament? Not much. As a priest, his job was to help people. The question should be rather, "What if David had not told his big, fat lie?" Quite likely then, Ahimelek would not have been implicated and incriminated, and eighty-one priests of God would not have been martyred.

MARCH 7

Rahab

By faith the harlot Rahab did not perish with those who did not believe,
when she had received the spies with peace. Hebrews 11:31

What a story! A woman in Jericho hides two Israelite spies to keep them from being found by the king's soldiers and goes down in history as a woman of faith. She was a pagan, and though she had done many bad things in her life, when it really mattered, she came through with shining colors.

"I know that the Lord will give you the land of Canaan," she said. "We have heard how Jehovah dried up the Red Sea, destroyed the giants across the Jordan, and then stopped the waters of the Jordan. Our hearts have melted within us for the Lord your God is ruler of heaven and earth. Now promise me that you will show compassion to my family, since I have shown kindness to you."

The spies were impressed with her sincerity and her loyalty to the God of heaven. They were also grateful for her help in hiding them, and they promised to spare her life. When the king's soldiers had gone, she came up with a plan for them to escape. For all this, she gets her name in the hall of faith in the book of Hebrews.

But what if she had not helped the spies? What if she had not believed that Jehovah was the only true God? As a reward for her help and her loyalty to God, she was saved with her family when the walls of Jericho fell. Then she was accepted into the nation and made a citizen of Israel, and best of all, she got herself into the lineup of Jesus' ancestors. That's right, she became the great-great-great-great-grandmother of Jesus thirty-three generations before He arrived on earth as a baby.

Shamgar

Shamgar the son of Anath . . . killed six hundred men of the Philistines
with an ox goad; and he also delivered Israel. Judges 3:31

Shamgar must have been one of the toughest characters in ancient Israel. In those days he would have been comparable to David, or "David's mighty men," or possibly even Samson himself! Why? Well for starters he was a great warrior who led God's people to victory during a time of crisis, and for another he brought them back to the worship of the one true God.

He probably lived at the time of Deborah and Barak, two famous judges who helped deliver the northern tribes of Israel from the Canaanites. Shamgar is best known for the battles he fought against the Philistines, a warlike people who had migrated from the western Mediterranean to invade Palestine. He appears to have been a foreigner originally, or maybe his father was, because the name Shamgar is not an Israelite name. It is thought his father may have been a Hittite and his mother an Israelite, a common marriage arrangement in those days.

Shamgar became famous as a national hero when he defeated six hundred Philistines in battle all by himself with nothing but an ox goad. An ox goad was a wooden staff about eight feet long with a metal tip on the end, for guiding an ox while it pulled a plow. The other end of the goad usually had a chisel-shaped blade for scraping the blade of a plow.

What if Shamgar hadn't answered God's call to deliver Israel from their enemies? Or what if he had not been someone God could call for the task? Then Israel would have had to look elsewhere to find a man to do what Shamgar could do. We don't know whether Shamgar was an especially strong man, but he must have been very quick, a good fighter, and a man of faith and courage that God could call on. What a man! What a leader! What a story!

MARCH 9

Sisera and Jael

And then, as Barak pursued Sisera, Jael came out to meet him, and said to him, "Come, I will show you the man whom you seek." And when he went into her tent, there lay Sisera, dead with the peg in his temple. Judges 4:22

The story of Israel's battle with Sisera in the days of the judges is not a pretty story, but then again, General Sisera was not a nice person. In this story we also find a woman who fills a rather gruesome role in a remarkable drama.

Without a doubt General Sisera had all the modern weapons of the day—including nine hundred chariots of iron! That was pretty scary for Israel—if they had *one* chariot they were lucky. The story tells us Deborah and Barak bravely led Israel out to battle against Sisera's evil hordes and that God helped them win. The enemy turned tail and ran, and even Sisera jumped out of his chariot and headed for the hills. When he arrived, exhausted, at the tents of a man named Heber, he relaxed a bit because the man was an ally of King Jabin. "I'm very weary!" he told Heber's wife, Jael. "Guard the tent door so I can get some sleep." Unfortunately, he failed to ask Jael if she was an ally of the king also. She was not, and that brings us to the climax of this story. When General Sisera was fast asleep, she took a large tent peg and drove it through his head into the ground.

Quite a story, isn't it? Jael was a very brave woman to take such a chance, but what if she hadn't had the courage to execute him? Sisera would have gone home and raised up another army to come back and kill many more thousands of Israelites. He would have likely captured hundreds more children and women on his raids and made them all his slaves. The nation was saved by a heroine with nerves of steel and a tent peg, no less.

Zipporah

Who can find a virtuous wife? For her worth is far above rubies. . . .
"Many daughters have done well, but you excel them all." Proverbs 31:10, 29

Ladies, what would you do if a handsome Egyptian prince came out of the desert, rescued you from bully shepherds that were pushing you around, and then asked you to marry him? OK, that sounds a bit on the fairy tale side of things when it comes to stories, but it actually did happen just like that to a girl named Zipporah. She was one of seven daughters, and the prince who married her was none other than Moses.

Following this marriage, she settled into a shepherd's life with Moses for the next forty years while he worked for her father. However, that peaceful life came to a screeching halt when Moses turned eighty. To everyone's surprise, he was called by God at the burning bush to go back to Egypt and free the Israelites from slavery.

Some might think it would be wonderful being married to the most famous man in Israel's history, but, of course, it wasn't all peaches and cream for her. After all, she and her husband sacrificed everything to serve God as they led those two million people around in the desert. And living in a tent for forty years and cooking over an open fire with sand blowing in your face every day wouldn't be much fun.

Plus, her sister-in-law, Miriam, didn't make it easy for Zipporah either. When someone makes fun of your nationality or skin color, it can hurt, and that's exactly what Miriam did. As the story goes, God wasn't happy about the way Miriam acted. In fact, He felt so strongly about it He gave Miriam leprosy as punishment. Ouch! It's a shame that there should be fighting in a family like that. The Bible doesn't say how Zipporah reacted personally, but we do know her husband took the insult with patience.

Now, Zipporah could have avoided all these troubles if she had never agreed to marry Moses in the first place. After all, he was a fugitive in exile. And what if she had? Then she wouldn't have become one of the most famous wives of all time.

Reuben

"Reuben, you are my firstborn, my might and the beginning of my strength, the excellency of dignity and the excellency of power. Unstable as water, you shall not excel." Genesis 49:3, 4

The first part of the Bible passage above is a pretty good resumé for a firstborn son, and then comes the second part. "Unstable as water, you shall not excel." It sounds like Jacob was calling Reuben wishy-washy in the verse, and that's exactly what he intended to do. Rueben had his good points, but his weaknesses of character were so great that they would affect him for the rest of his life. He was supposed to get the family birthright, which was the spiritual leadership role in the family, and twice as much inheritance money as his brothers. But Jacob passed him by, and here's why.

Reuben had an affair with Bilhah, one of Jacob's wives. Say what? This was considered a serious crime in those days, even by the pagan nations around them, as it still is today. Why would he do such a thing? Reuben had a rebellious streak in him, it appears, something we see in many firstborn biblical children. Maybe he thought his father expected too much of him. Maybe Jacob was constantly reminding him to behave and grow up since he was the oldest and scheduled to be the next spiritual leader of the family. Anyway, none of this excused him. What he did was sinful, and the whole family was shamed for what he did.

What would have happened if Reuben had not been such a scoundrel? What if he had been more like his grandfather, Isaac? For starters, his descendants four generations later would have had a better example. We read that his great-grandchildren, led by Dathan and Abiram, revolted against Moses during Israel's wanderings, and many in the tribe of Reuben died in the earthquake, fire, and disease epidemic that followed. Let's remember, the sins we cherish will condemn us, but if we confess those sins, Jesus will heal us of all unrighteousness.

Barzillai

Now Barzillai was very old, eighty years of age. He had provided for the king during his stay in Mahanaim, for he was a very wealthy man. 2 Samuel 19:32, NIV

Barzillai was one of the most respected men of his day, and the Bible says he was very wealthy too. He had many cattle and sheep and servants, but nobody resented him for it. The Bible says he was kind, good, and unselfish, and near the end of his life he became the symbol of what we all should be when hard times come to others.

When civil war broke out in Israel and Absalom threatened to take the throne, Barzillai was a man King David could count on. He and his servants brought everything David and the other refugees might need when they arrived in the city of Mahanaim, east of the Jordan. Food, grape juice, blankets, and extra clothes were just a few of the supplies he so generously provided. David was touched by Barzillai's loyalty and compassion and thanked him for it. But the most amazing part of this story was the fact that Barzillai was eighty years old and was still actively doing good deeds. And even though it seemed everyone was in support of Absalom taking the throne from David, Barzillai was still loyal to the king.

But what if Barzillai had not been willing to help David out? It wasn't a very popular thing to do at the time. In that case David would have had to make it on his own with the help of the few supporters he had with him when he fled Jerusalem. As it was, Barzillai's friendship and support cheered the heart of David, who felt he had come to the end of the road.

After it was all over and David was on his way back to Jerusalem, he invited Barzillai to come live with him at the royal court. Barzillai thanked the king but declined his offer, saying he was too old to travel that far from home. Jesus reminded us that when we are kind to others, it is as if we are doing these deeds for Him.

Bathsheba

"You shall not commit adultery." Exodus 20:14

A woman's influence over a man can be deadly if she uses that influence to bring him down spiritually. Intentional or not, that's exactly what happened when Bathsheba took a bath on the roof of her house—within sight of the king's palace. Now, of course, David was even more to blame, since he was the powerful king and the Lord's anointed. He had many wives and didn't need to steal one that belonged to another man. We all know the story: Bathsheba was the wife of Uriah, one of David's most loyal soldiers. But even after David knew who she was, he still sent for her and invited her to his house. That was bad enough, because they both knew they had stepped over the line.

Not surprisingly, David tried to cover it up. After all, adultery called for the death penalty in their day. A few weeks later, Bathsheba let David know that she was pregnant—and things went from bad to worse. David panicked and planned a strategy that would bring grief and treachery to the royal house for the rest of his days. The plan? Bring Bathsheba's husband back to Jerusalem so he would think the baby was his. That scheme backfired, however, when Uriah refused to go home, and the rest is history. Afraid that his shameful deed might become public, David ordered the death of Uriah on the battlefield. That's how bad things can go when we want a little pleasure at the expense of godliness.

But what if Bathsheba had declined David's invitation? Saying no to a king in those days could bring the death penalty, but what if she had found the courage to do it? She would have saved the kingdom of Israel a national scandal. She wouldn't have had David's baby, it wouldn't have died, and her husband Uriah wouldn't have been unjustly executed. Wow! What an outcome that could have been!

Boaz

And when she rose up to glean, Boaz commanded his young men, saying, "Let her glean even among the sheaves, and do not reproach her." Ruth 2:15

Boaz was tall, dark, and handsome. Well, we're not sure about all that, but he was rich, and he was an eligible bachelor in Bethlehem, and that's where the story gets interesting. He owned large parcels of land and was just getting started with the barley harvest when he noticed a beautiful young woman gleaning in his fields.

When he asked his field supervisor about her, he was told it was Ruth, Naomi's Moabite daughter-in-law. Boaz knew Ruth was a widow and that she and Naomi needed food, so he invited her to work in his field until the harvest was done. He also told her she could eat with his workers at break time, and he asked his harvesters to leave extra grain stalks and sheaves of barley lying around for her to pick up. Boaz said he knew all about her loyalty to Naomi. Then he asked God to bless her. "The LORD repay your work," he said, "and a full reward be given you by the LORD God of Israel, under whose wings you have come for refuge" (Ruth 2:12).

Well, the story gets better, because Naomi realized there was a budding romance between Ruth and Boaz. She set up a date for the two of them, where Ruth dropped him a hint that she wouldn't mind being his wife. If he agreed, this meant he would also have to buy Naomi's land and eventually give it to the children he and Ruth might have. Of course, you know the rest of the story. He agreed to her "proposal," they were married, and they lived happily ever after.

Now, what if Boaz had not been so kind to Ruth and Naomi? What if he had said no? Ruth was a pretty young woman, but the money he gave for the land was a gift. It would never really be his. In any case, he said yes, and because he did, he became the great-grandfather of King David and the ancestor of Jesus the Messiah. Wow! That's cool! Good choice, Boaz!

David

"I have found David son of Jesse, a man after my own heart." Acts 13:22, NIV

David rose to an important place in Israel at a very young age. While still a teenager, he challenged the most fearsome giant in the land, killed him with only a sling, and became a national hero. Handsome, dashing, and yet humble, he won the heart of a princess, married into royalty, and then fled when rumors were leaked that he had been anointed the next king of Israel.

Later, as God had promised, he did become king. After years of being in exile, David was finally crowned king. He developed prominent trade with surrounding nations, extended the boundaries of Israel, and finished the Philistines off once and for all. Unfortunately, he did have some dark spots in his life, and the episodes were not pretty. For one thing, he had too many wives and too many children. As a result of lack of discipline and his own poor choices, his family became dysfunctional and corrupt. For example, son number one raped his half sister and then was murdered by son number two in retaliation. Son number two fled the country but later staged a coup to steal his father's throne. Tragically, he died in a battle during his coup. Son number three also tried to crown himself king illegally but was upstaged in the nick of time by Solomon, a son born to David by a woman with whom he had had an affair. Shortly after this fiasco, son number three was executed by Solomon for trying to steal the throne.

That's a lot of turmoil for one man, and yet David was called a man after God's own heart. Why? Because he always came back to God after his shenanigans. No matter what he did, he never stayed away from God. And what would have happened if he had not done this? He would have died a broken man—without hope, without forgiveness, and without God.

David's Mighty Men

And the three mighty men brake through the host of the Philistines,
and drew water out of the well of Bethlehem, that was by the gate, and took it, and
brought it to David: nevertheless he would not drink thereof,
but poured it out unto the LORD. 2 Samuel 23:16, KJV

David is probably best known for his battle with the giant Goliath. But did you know he had thirty legendary warriors who fought beside him in battle? Everybody called them "David's mighty men"—fierce, battle-hardened men who could fight the enemy in hand-to-hand combat and win every time. And they did it under impossible odds. One of them, named Adino, killed eight hundred men single-handedly in a battle. Abishai, Adino's nephew, could also fight like a machine and proved it one day when he fought three hundred Philistines with only a spear in his hand. And then there was Benaiah, a ferocious warrior who was known for killing two lion-like heroes of Moab, an Egyptian giant, and a lion in a pit on a snowy day.

But one of the most heroic deeds "David's mighty men" did for him was to break through enemy lines at his hometown of Bethlehem and bring him back a drink of water from the village well. David was touched. "I can't drink this!" he said. "These men risked their lives to get it for me!" And we can imagine it must have brought tears to his eyes.

It's a shame David didn't show such gratitude to all his mighty men for their service. One of them, Uriah the Hittite, he ordered to be put on the front line of battle to die so that David could marry his beautiful wife. That was a scandal that became known to all Israel, and David paid for it the rest of his life as his sons committed one act of treachery after another. What if David had called on God to deliver him in that one moment of weakness? Surely he would have avoided that dark spot in his life, and he and his mighty men would have gone down in history as a symbol of the most valiant and loyal band of warriors the world has ever known.

MARCH 17

Delilah

So Delilah said to Samson, "Tell me the secret of your great strength and how you can be tied up and subdued." Judges 16:6, NIV

Can we think of a story more treacherous than Samson and Delilah? These two were a classic duo in history, as couples go. We don't know much about Delilah, except that Samson liked her and spent a lot of time in her town. What it would have been like to date the strongest man in the world is anybody's guess. Sadly, it is doubtful that she truly loved him—in the end she sold him out for money. How much? Eleven hundred pieces of silver from each of the five ruling lords in Philistine territory. That was fifty-five hundred pieces of silver, enough money to buy 275 slaves at the going rate. Wow! That's a lot of money! No wonder she betrayed him!

And so the game was on. Could she trick him into revealing the secret of his strength? Would he actually tell her his secret? We all know the story, and it just goes to show how far a person will go if the price is right. Four times she begged Samson to tell her everything, and three times he lied. Unfortunately, each answer brought him closer to revealing the truth.

What if Delilah had said no to the Philistine lords? What if she had refused to help them in their desperate scheme? Would they have burned her with fire as they had Samson's first wife? Maybe, but she would have died knowing she was doing the right thing. Then again, maybe God would have found a way to honor this woman who wouldn't help others destroy His chosen judge. One thing is sure: If we do things God's way, the end is always good.

Egyptian Priests

The Egyptian magicians also did the same things by their secret arts:
Each one threw down his staff and it became a snake.
But Aaron's staff swallowed up their staffs. Exodus 7:11, 12, NIV

Who were these guys that advised Pharaoh during the days of Moses just before the mass exodus of Israel from Egypt? They were the fortune-tellers, the astrologers, and mystic magician priests who practiced the black arts of the satanic cults in the land. Whenever Pharaoh wanted advice from the spirit world, he called them in. And of course, when Moses came asking Pharaoh to release the Israelite slaves, the magicians were invited to the palace to give their two cents' worth. That's when Aaron threw down his rod and it became a serpent—probably a king cobra, since that was the most sacred of Egyptian serpents. And then the story gets really interesting. When the Egyptian magicians threw down their special diviner's rods to show their supernatural authority, Satan was allowed to simulate the appearance of serpents from their rods. But the Bible says Aaron's serpent began to systematically eat up all the phony serpents. And now, of course, the priests had no more diviner's rods, which was their only proof of authority in the supernatural world. Bingo! God wins again.

We later see them trying to duplicate plagues one and two, However, God shut them down during the destruction that came with the eight final plagues. In the end the magicians told Pharaoh, "Let the Israelite slaves go free, or we will all be dead men!"

And what would have happened if the magicians had told Pharaoh from the start that they were no match for Jehovah? Then Pharaoh might have let Israel go free earlier. Egypt would have avoided all the horrible plagues of disease and destruction and death. Unfortunately, by the time they all realized this, there was nothing left in Egypt to save. Too late they admitted, "Now we know Jehovah, and we will let Israel go."

Eli

Then Eli said, "He is the LORD; let him do what is good in his eyes."
1 Samuel 3:18, NIV

If you ever have kids, will you discipline them? Will you punish them if they lie, cheat, or steal? If you haven't thought that far ahead, or just don't want to answer the question, read the story of Eli and his sons in the book of 1 Samuel. It's a chilling reminder of what happens when we ignore our God-given responsibilities as parents.

Eli was the high priest of Israel, but he was also considered a judge or political leader for his people. It's likely he knew Samson because the two of them probably lived in Israel during the same time frame. Eli was famous in Israel, but the trouble was, he didn't discipline his boys, and the country paid for it. He let them do whatever they wanted, and it was a disaster.

Case in point, his boys developed horrific habits while they were growing up because Eli never punished them. And when they became priests in the tabernacle, they kept right on doing all those nasty things. But here's the clincher! Eli never took them out of office! He never brought them before a court of justice to convict and punish them for all the bad things they had done to dishonor God.

Years earlier, a man of God had warned Eli that his family was going to pay a price if their act was not cleaned up—and still Eli refused to take action. Then God came to Samuel in the night and gave him another warning for Eli. The old priest believed Samuel's message, but it was too little and too late. The million-dollar question is, What if Eli had obeyed the voice of the Lord? What if he had punished his boys? One of the greatest tragedies in Israel was the loss of God's sacred ark of the covenant, and that would have never happened if Eli had disciplined his boys. Shame, shame, Eli!

Eliab

Eliab's anger was aroused against David, and he said, "Why did you come down here? And with whom have you left those few sheep in the wilderness? I know your pride and the insolence of your heart, for you have come down to see the battle."
1 Samuel 17:28

Eliab was not a very nice brother. We don't know why for sure, except that his brother David was the youngest, and the keeper of the sheep, and sometimes that's just the way big brothers treat their little brothers. But there seems to be something else going on here too. It could be that Eliab was jealous of David. After all, getting to go to the royal palace to play for the king was no small matter for anyone, let alone the youngest in the family. In those days, big brothers were supposed to be honored over little brothers. And when Samuel chose David over Eliab for a secret job, that probably didn't sit too well with Eliab either. Did Eliab know David was going to be king? We don't really know, but Eliab likely thought that whatever Samuel had in mind for David was probably something he'd wish to have for himself.

The big showdown came when David showed up at Goliath's battlefield with provisions for his brothers. David's father had sent him with food and other supplies and also to see how his brothers were doing. But Eliab didn't welcome him at all! "What are you doing here?" he demanded. "You should have stayed home with the sheep. You just want to be a show-off!"

What if Eliab had been a nice big brother? What if he had treated David with kindness and love? It would have encouraged David as he prepared to fight Goliath and made Eliab a better person. As it was, after this story, Eliab's name disappears, and we never hear of him again, except when his daughter marries David's son. How's that for the fame and fortune Eliab hoped to gain for being the eldest brother in the family? Being kind to others is definitely the best-kept secret for happiness, but unless we learn that lesson we can never really expect life to be peachy.

MARCH 21

Giants

"There we saw the giants . . . and we were like grasshoppers in our own sight, and so we were in their sight."
Numbers 13:33

Giants are some of the most amazing creatures on earth. Fairy tales have been told about them, and storybooks are full of them. At some time or other in our lives, many of us have probably even wished we could be one. But did you know that once upon a time, everyone on earth was a giant? That's right. From the days of Adam until Noah's flood, the earth was filled with them. They were a super race of people that could outthink, outrun, and outlive you and me by hundreds of years.

Centuries later, when the Israelites were ready to enter Canaan, they faced the remnants of the antediluvian world. That's right, the giants were still hanging around—lots of them. It scared the twelve tribes so badly that they wimped out of the fight and God sent them back into the desert to die.

Roll the clock forward 350 years and we find giants again, this time in the days of David. David killed Goliath, of course, but his mighty men killed four more of them. Read about it in 2 Samuel 21:15–22 and 1 Chronicles 20:4–8. There was Ishbi-Benob, Saph, Goliath's brother Lahmi, and a giant with six fingers on each hand and six toes on each foot.

Now, there have probably been a fair share of good giants in the history of the world, but most of them have not been so nice. Most could be described as pagan monsters that were evil and cruel and sadistic. But what if these giants had devoted themselves to the service of God? What if they had been godly leaders in their generation? Surely God would have blessed them. They would have been considered legends in their own time and helped change history for sure.

One day soon when we arrive in heaven, we will be given a crown of life, a harp, a robe of righteousness, and the body of a giant. Wow! I can hardly wait! How about you?

Gideon

When the angel of the Lord appeared to Gideon, he said,
"The Lord is with you, mighty warrior." Judges 6:12, NIV

We've all heard the story of how Gideon fought the Midianites with only three hundred soldiers who were carrying what seemed like very strange weapons. They all had swords, no doubt, but it was the pitchers, torches, and trumpets that must have turned the most heads the night they went out to fight the Midianites. The enemy wasn't expecting such a small army, but if they had known it had been reduced by God from 32,000 soldiers to 300, they would have been even more surprised. But that was the hand Gideon dealt them. Whether or not God gave him talking points for success, we don't know, but attacking the enemy in the dead of night was a stroke of genius. That much you probably already know, but did you know that Gideon came from a well-to-do family in the town of Ophrah, from the tribe of Manasseh? Did you know he was the youngest of several brothers, all of whom had been killed by two Midianite kings named Zebah and Zalmunna? It's why Gideon complained to the Angel of the Lord when he met Him at the winepress where he was threshing wheat to keep it hidden from the raiding enemy soldiers. It's why he asked where the God of Israel was at a time like this. We can understand a little bit about why he doubted whether God still cared about Israel.

But what if Gideon hadn't been faithful to do all God asked him to do? What if he had said, "Enough men have died already in my family"? Then Israel wouldn't have gained a victory over 135,000 Midianite and Amalekite soldiers, and the enemy would have gone on raiding, pillaging, and capturing people in Israel. The odds were 450 to one, but with God on Gideon's side, how could he fail?

Goliath

And a champion went out from the camp of the Philistines, named Goliath, from Gath, whose height was six cubits and a span. 1 Samuel 17:4

We all know this name. He's probably the most famous giant of all time, and David the shepherd boy was the one who made him famous. For forty days Goliath came out to taunt the Israelite soldiers and curse their God, Jehovah. That's when David showed up. He was very upset when he heard Goliath shouting all kinds of obscenities at God and vowed he would fight the giant himself.

This would be no easy task. Goliath was nine and half feet tall (about three meters). That's a tall man, two feet taller than our tallest basketball players today, and a lot bigger since he must have been built proportionately. In today's standard weights of measurement he would have weighed about seven hundred pounds, or 320 kilograms. His metal-plated chest armor weighed at least 125 pounds, and his spear head fifteen pounds. He wore greaves of brass on his shins, a type of armor imported by the Philistines when they came from the Greek Isles in the western Mediterranean.

As the story goes, Goliath died in battle at the hands of a young man named David. How did he manage to get himself killed like that? Well, for starters he was too arrogant for his own good. Second, he underestimated the skill set of a shepherd boy with a sling. And saddest of all, Goliath did not know the God of heaven. David was right. The armies of heaven came to fight along with him that day, and no one can win a battle against those odds.

But what if Goliath had recognized the fact that David had something he didn't possess? What if he had surrendered to David's God right there on the spot? No doubt his life would have been spared. And if oversized bullies like Goliath could do it, then so can you and I. It's called giving our hearts to Jesus.

Hannah

> "For this child I prayed, and the Lord has granted me my petition
> which I asked of Him. Therefore I also have lent him to the Lord;
> as long as he lives he shall be lent to the Lord." 1 Samuel 1:27, 28

This is a most unusual story, and probably one that only women will truly understand! Hannah had no children, and her frustration at not being able to have a child was making her grow desperate. Some days she was so depressed she could hardly eat, and then she would cry her eyes out until there were no more tears. After all, her biological clock was ticking, and time was not on her side. Every year when she went up to worship at Shiloh, she would go to the sanctuary to lay her petition before God. "Please, Lord, give me a son!"

Now, for some reason God did not give her a son right away. Maybe it was because He was testing her faith in His promises. Or maybe He just wanted her to love the little guy to pieces when he finally did arrive. We know that God needed a boy who would grow into a man that would lead His people as a judge and priest and prophet. If Hannah had known what was coming, she might not have prayed so hard and made such a promise.

However, when God finally told her she would have a son, she was ecstatic. Then she dedicated him to God before he was born. Now that was a strange thing to do—most people dedicate their babies *after* they are born. Not Hannah, and God blessed her for it! When her baby Samuel was born there was great rejoicing, we can imagine, and when he was weaned, Hannah took him to the sanctuary at Shiloh to live with the priest Eli.

But what if Hannah hadn't dedicated Samuel to God? What if she had changed her mind and decided to keep him home? Well, he would have never gone to work for Eli. He would not likely have become a judge in Israel, or a priest, or a prophet. Way to go, Hannah!

Hophni and Phineas

Eli's sons were scoundrels; they had no regard for the Lord. 1 Samuel 2:12, NIV

Hophni and Phineas were rascals of the worst sort. The Bible writer called them scoundrels, and that's exactly what they were. They probably started out just like other boys. They probably loved to run and jump and play games, but as they grew they became real brats. Lots of kids do that, but their father Eli did nothing to make them behave. "That's the proper way to raise kids," some psychologists have claimed in the past few decades of American society. Let the kids experiment and make choices and find out what is right and wrong on their own. But if Eli were here today, he would tell these psychologists to go jump in a river. He learned his lesson the hard way.

By the time they were grown-ups, there was no changing Hophni and Phineas. They lied, cheated, and stole from God's people whenever and wherever and however they wanted. But the worst thing of all was what they did to the ark of God's covenant. When Israel went to war against the Philistines, their army was beaten badly in battle. To energize the soldiers and guarantee a win, Hophni and Phineas took the holy ark into battle on the second day of fighting. But it backfired. Israel's army was beaten again, Hophni and Phineas were killed, and the ark of God was captured by the enemy! What a disaster! What a tragedy!

It didn't have to end that way. What if Hophni and Phineas had decided they were going to be honest men and not cheat people? What if they had decided they were going to behave and not go to wild parties? What if they had honored their father, Eli, and obeyed God in all things? Then the judgment of God would not have come on their family. The ark of God would not have been stolen by the Philistines, and they would be remembered today as good boys, honorable men who pointed people to the God of their fathers.

Ishbosheth

Ishbosheth, Saul's son, was forty years old when he began to reign over Israel, and he reigned two years. 2 Samuel 2:10

Ishbosheth was Saul's fourth and youngest son. His older brothers had died with their father, King Saul, in battle against the Philistines. Some, like General Abner, assumed King Saul's dynasty would go on, so they crowned Prince Ishbosheth as king over Israel. God had promised that David would be king, but at the time he was only ruling over the tribe of Judah.

So the kingdom was split in its allegiance, and the inevitable civil war everyone knew would come, finally did. David and his general, Joab, went to battle against Abner and Ishbosheth's cronies, and David prevailed more often than not. And as the months passed, David grew stronger—much stronger. Ishbosheth should have had all the advantages because he had the majority of Israel on his side, and the royal army as well. There is an unwritten rule that says, "Whoever has the army wins the war," so Ishbosheth's victory should have been secure.

And then Ishbosheth accused Abner of having an affair with one of King Saul's wives. Was it true? Maybe, but the accusation, true or not, spelled the end of Ishbosheth's reign as king. Abner got angry and defected to King David. Not long after that, two of Ishbosheth's army officers murdered him while he was having a noontime siesta. Wow! What a way to go!

What would have happened if King Ishbosheth had not made such an accusation against Abner? He might have lived, but he would have certainly lost some respect, and possibly even his throne to Abner. In that event he would have also been murdered so that Abner could be king over Israel. We may never know, but at least Ishbosheth died with some self-respect, and that is something no one could take away from him.

Jesse

Now the LORD said to Samuel, . . . "I am sending you to Jesse the Bethlehemite. For I
have provided Myself a king among his sons." 1 Samuel 16:1

This is the story of a rich old man who got the surprise of his life. He had eight sons, all of them handsome, gallant, and potential leadership material, but only one was to be chosen for a very special job. It happened this way. Samuel came to Bethlehem on a secret mission, and everyone who was anyone in town must have guessed something was up. The prophet revealed nothing about his plan since he knew King Saul had spies everywhere. From the day Samuel had announced God was going to give the kingdom to one of Saul's neighbors, the king had been watching all his neighbors. Samuel didn't want innocent blood to be shed, so he came to hold a big feast—and to find the next king.

You know the story. The seven oldest sons were observed by Samuel and turned down because God didn't give him the green light on any of them. It's unclear whether Jesse or any of his sons knew why Samuel had come, and it's likely Samuel wanted it to stay that way, for the time being at least. David was still out in the fields tending sheep, but he was called in when Samuel insisted on seeing him. And of course, that's when God told Samuel that David was the one. We don't know who was actually present at David's anointing, but if Samuel's arrival in Bethlehem had raised eyebrows, it's likely the prophet wanted to keep everything secret, for the time being at least. Likely David was anointed in secret, just as King Saul had been.

What if Jesse hadn't brought David in from the fields? Guarding sheep wasn't high on anyone's career options, and that left David the most unlikely of candidates for king. If Jesse had known Samuel was choosing David for king, he would have probably been shocked. But it all worked out. In the end, son number eight did become king, and a very good one at that.

Joab

> "Moreover you know also what Joab the son of Zeruiah did to me,
> and what he did to the two commanders of the armies of Israel,
> to Abner the son of Ner and Amasa the son of Jether, whom he killed.
> And he shed the blood of war in peacetime." 1 Kings 2:5

When David became king, many of his relatives received high offices in his kingdom. His nephew Joab became the most powerful man of them all. As general of David's army, he made many decisions that helped Israel prosper and grow in peace.

But all was not well in David's kingdom, because although Joab served David well, he did many things that were not right. He killed Abner, King Saul's ex-general, after a party given by King David. He tricked David into bringing his son Absalom back from exile, only to have Absalom then stage a coup to steal the throne. And if that wasn't enough, when Absalom was found alive hanging by his hair in a tree during the ensuing battle, Joab was the one who killed him. Not surprisingly, David had had enough of General Joab's treachery, but when he tried to replace him with Amasa, another nephew, Joab murdered Amasa while giving him a kiss of peace.

What a mess! It's no wonder David advised Solomon to have Joab executed for all the crimes he had committed during David's reign. But what if Joab had been an honest man? What if he had always done what God wanted him to do? What if he had helped Absalom be the son King David wanted him to be, and what if he hadn't murdered the officers in David's army? Then he would be remembered as one of the great leaders in Israel's history, and we would be saying only good things about him today. As it is, we're not sure he will even be in heaven someday. He wanted the best for King David, but he always managed to include himself in those plans.

Joash (Gideon's Father)

But Joash replied to the hostile crowd around him,
"Are you going to plead Baal's cause? Are you trying to save him?
Whoever fights for him shall be put to death by morning! If Baal really is a god,
he can defend himself when someone breaks down his altar." Judges 6:31

The story of Gideon is a great one, but it might never have gotten started if his father hadn't stepped into the line of fire. Here's how it happened. When God called Gideon to do battle with the Midianites, Gideon had no idea how he would pull it off, but he knew he had to do something, and quick. Calling together ten of his friends, he headed to the town square late that night to make a statement in favor of the God of heaven. And what did they do? They brought along a yoke of oxen and pulled down the town altar to Baal.

Wow! Did that ever start a firestorm! The men of Ophrah were angry the next morning when they discovered what Gideon had done. The shocking thing was that they were not only worshiping Baal instead of God, but they were also willing to execute someone for desecrating the altar to Baal.

Now, there's no doubt Joash was afraid to lose Gideon. After all, Gideon was the only son he had left after all their wars with the Midianites. But he must have also have been a bit disgusted when he realized what this was all about. He and his fellow elders of Ophrah were guilty of worshiping the pitiful idol of stone, and now this crazy obsession with Baal might cost him his son's life. And that's why he was brave enough to threaten anyone who tried to defend Baal, as the verse says above.

But what if Joash hadn't defended Gideon? Might God have allowed Gideon to become a martyr? Maybe. Of course, with Gideon's death, gone was any hope Israel had for defeating the Midianites, for the time being. Without a doubt, Gideon was the man of the hour.

Joel and Abijah

When Samuel grew old, he appointed his sons as Israel's leaders. . . .
But his sons did not follow his ways. They turned aside after dishonest gain and
accepted bribes and perverted justice. 1 Samuel 8:1, 3, NIV

Samuel's two sons, Joel and Abijah, were the ultimate preacher's kids. They grew up in a home with a father who was a priest, prophet, and judge. In other words, he had a lot to do and was never at home. That was a real problem for his sons, because they didn't have him around much. Everybody loved Samuel because they knew he was a godly man, but they didn't care much for his sons. The boys must have had real character issues as kids, because when they grew up they were dishonest, dishonorable men. In his old age Samuel asked them to help him govern Israel, but they were irresponsible, and this brought a real crisis to Israel. "We want a king," the tribal elders told Samuel. "We can't trust your sons to help us like you do. They accept bribes and don't deal fairly with the people."

Samuel was shocked and didn't know what to say, but God wasn't surprised. "Go ahead and do as the people have asked," He said. "It isn't you they have rejected, but Me. Give them a king, but warn them of all the bad things that will happen if they go through with this."

That's how the history of having kings in Israel got started. Samuel's sons ruined a good thing for everyone, and what came next was going to be a disaster for sure! Up until then, no one in Israel had to pay taxes. No one had to work for the king like slaves. No daughters had to go live in the palace as part of a king's harem.

What if Joel and Abijah had been honest boys? What if they had been more like their father? Then the elders in Israel might not have demanded a king, at least not then. What a shame! Like Samuel's sons, we need to remember that our actions can have long-lasting effects.

Jonathan

Jonathan said to his young armor-bearer, "Come, let's go over to the outpost of those uncircumcised men. Perhaps the LORD will act in our behalf. Nothing can hinder the LORD from saving, whether by many or by few." 1 Samuel 14:6, NIV

Jonathan was a courageous kid. He was always listening for the voice of God, and because of this, the Lord was able to use him to win a great victory for Israel. This is how it happened. The Philistines were camped at Michmash, just a few miles from where Saul had set up his military headquarters. Everyone was really scared, and Saul had almost no soldiers left. All but six hundred had deserted him, and the ones who were still with him had no iron swords or spears to fight with. But Jonathan, the king's son, thought they could win.

"This is my plan," he told his bodyguard. "We will go across the canyon and show ourselves to the Philistine sentries up on the edge of the cliff. If they say, 'Wait there until we come down to you,' then we will hold our position and get ready to fight. However, if they say, 'come up to us,' then we will know that God has given the garrison into our hands." It was perfect. God must have inspired Jonathan to say such a thing, because that is exactly what happened.

"Look! The Hebrews are coming out of the holes where they have been hiding!" the Philistine sentries shouted when they saw Jonathan and his bodyguard. "Come up here and we will show you a thing or two!" That was the signal Jonathan had been waiting for! He and his bodyguard scaled the cliff, took out the first twenty Philistine soldiers, and rallied Israel's troops to win the battle that day! What courage Jonathan had, and what faith in God!

But what if he hadn't dared to stand up against the Philistines? What if he had said, "There's nothing I can do!" Then the Philistines would have probably won the battle and completely overrun the land, and the history of Israel might have been much different.

King Hanun

> Then David said, "I will show kindness to Hanun the son of Nahash,
> as his father showed kindness to me." 2 Samuel 10:2, NIV

Today we would call this good foreign policy, but in those days nations didn't send condolences when an enemy died. Instead, they rejoiced.

But then we learn the rest of the story. Evidently Hanun's father, Nahash, had been kind to David when he was on the run, fleeing from King Saul and his military posse. And so David sent his ambassadors to Nahash's son to express sadness for the loss of his father. Unfortunately, instead of telling the messengers "thank you" for their kindness, King Hanun took the bad advice of his counselors, who were inept in the art of diplomacy. He accused David's men of being spies and did the unthinkable! He cut off half their beards and the bottom half of their outer tunics from the waist down, leaving them to return home in their underwear. Talk about embarrassing!

David was very unhappy about the treatment his ambassadors received. King Hanun might as well have declared war, because that's exactly what he got. Call it what you will, but it sounds like a death wish to me. Now Hanun had to hire 33,000 mercenary soldiers from surrounding nations to help protect him. Sadly his plan backfired. By returning evil for good, he ended up fighting a war that annihilated his armies.

What if Hanun hadn't been so mean and suspicious? What if he had accepted the offer of sympathy that David's ambassadors brought? For starters his country would have kept its independence. There would have been no war, lots of people would have lived, and he could have been friends with the most famous king in Israelite history. To make a long story short, Hanun should have learned from the mistakes his father and grandfather made. Read the story in 1 Samuel 11.

APRIL 2

King Nahash

And Nahash the Ammonite answered them, "On this condition I will make a
covenant with you, that I may put out all your right eyes,
and bring reproach on all Israel." 1 Samuel 11:2

What a guy! What a deal! This man was a nasty despot who cared for no one
but himself and for his cruel military campaigns to conquer his enemies.
Here's the background for the story.

Nahash went up against his neighboring city of Jabesh-Gilead to attack it and
demand its surrender. The people in the city were frightened nearly to death and
offered to make a treaty with him. He accepted their proposal with one additional
clause: that he be allowed to gouge out the right eye of every man, women, and
child in the city.

Sounds like quite an offer, but we shouldn't be surprised to find that pagan
kings of his day often offered their enemies such an option in exchange for letting them live. And the people of Jabesh-Gilead were willing to accept his offer!
But they asked that he give them one week to see if anyone would come to their
rescue—they had few other options.

To make a long story short, the newly crowned King Saul in Israel gathered
an army when he heard the cry for help. Then he marched overnight, met Nahash
and the Ammonites in battle, and totally destroyed them. That's how it happened,
and so, of course, Nahash never got to carry out his threat.

What if Nahash had decided to be civilized toward the citizens in the city of
Jabesh-Gilead? He could have conquered the city just the same and then levied a
heavy tax upon them. He could have required them to work for him as servants
or even slaves. He could have done any number of things to show his power over
them, but gouging out their right eyes was just plain sadistic. And that's when God
called upon Saul to teach Nahash a lesson.

King Saul

Samuel said to all the people, "Do you see the man the Lord has chosen?
There is no one like him among all the people." 1 Samuel 10:24, NIV

Samuel wasn't pleased that the elders of Israel wanted a king, and neither was God. However, sometimes the Lord lets us have our way to show us what happens when we don't follow His advice. God chose the best man He could find for the job—knowing exactly what would happen. His name was Saul. He was tall, handsome, and a shy sort of guy, at first anyway. They crowned him king, and when he led an army into battle to fight against the Ammonites, he and his men whipped 'em! Everyone was so proud of Saul for his bravery and leadership that they started saying all kinds of nice things about him.

As time passed, things changed. King Saul got proud and started doing things he shouldn't, like disobeying God's instructions when he went to war, offering sacrifices to God when only priests were allowed to do that, and chasing after David to kill him even though David was a good man and a national hero for killing Goliath. By now Saul was a mean old guy, with few friends. He trusted no one, and whenever he thought someone might be plotting against him, he killed them. And then the Philistines got on the warpath again and came looking for a fight. Saul didn't know what to do, so he went to a witch to ask her advice about the coming battle. That was King Saul's last mistake. God left him to his own devices, and the next day he died in battle.

What if King Saul hadn't gone to see the witch? What if he hadn't been so suspicious of people and killed everyone who disagreed with him? What if he hadn't been proud and disobedient to God? Then God would have blessed him, and he would have been a good king. Unfortunately, it was a lesson he learned too late.

Mahlon and Chilion

Now they took wives of the women of Moab: the name of the one was Orpah, and the name of the other Ruth. And they dwelt there about ten years. Then both Mahlon and Chilion also died. Ruth 1:4, 5

We don't know much about these two except that they moved from Judah to Moab with their parents and lived there about ten years. Their names were Mahlon and Chilion, and they probably liked to play sports, go fishing, and watch girls from the rooftop of their home in Moab.

But there was one thing that was very wrong about this story. The family was not living in the land of Canaan, where God intended them to be. Nations outside of Israel worshiped pagan idols, and God knew this might eventually be a temptation to them. In Moab everyone worshiped Chemosh, a god that required the sacrifice of children. How could Mahlon and Chilion's parents keep them in Moab, where the people worshiped a god like Chemosh? And what were the chances the boys would fall in love and marry Moabite girls who worshiped such a god? The chances were very high, and that's exactly what happened. Mahlon married a young woman named Ruth, and Chilion married Orpah. Unfortunately, both boys died, and this tragic event left the girls as young widows with no children.

What if the boys hadn't moved to Moab with their parents? They wouldn't have married girls who grew up in a culture that offered children as sacrifices, that much is sure. And who knows, maybe God didn't give Mahlon and Chilion any children because He knew they would be in danger in Moab. And Mahlon's death? Could it be that Ruth needed to go to Judah, but that wouldn't have happened if Mahlon hadn't died? Fortunately God saved Ruth, and someday Mahlon will find out just exactly how He did it.

Mr. and Mrs. Manoah

Now there was a certain man from Zorah, of the family of the Danites, whose name was Manoah; and his wife was barren and had no children. Judges 13:2

What would it be like to be the parents of Superman or, let's say, the Incredible Hulk? Well, there was such a couple once upon a time, and the Bible tells us the story. We know them as Mr. and Mrs. Manoah. Our story starts one day with Mrs. Manoah out working in the field when Jesus dropped by for a visit. He didn't appear in all His glory, of course, or He would have frightened her away. Instead He appeared as a Man in ordinary clothes. He told her she was going to have a son, and this shocked her because, physically speaking, she couldn't have children.

He gave her details about things she and the baby shouldn't eat or drink. No pork, no fish without scales, no meat that still had the blood in it. Alcohol was off-limits, and besides all this, the boy's hair was never to be cut. "This will be the special sign between him and God," Jesus told her, "because he is going to deliver Israel from the Philistines." When He finished speaking, a very excited Mrs. Manoah ran home to tell her husband. What was his reaction? He wanted to talk to Jesus himself. Not a surprise for a man who now knew his boy would become a champion. To their great joy, Jesus came again to tell them exactly how they should raise the boy, and they both agreed to follow the instructions.

What if Mrs. Manoah had later decided that it wasn't important to eat the way God had asked? She might have contracted a strange disease and died like so many people did in those days. What if she decided she wanted a little wine with her meals? Maybe Samson would have been born with issues like the babies who suffer from fetal alcohol syndrome. One thing was sure, Samson's future was dependent on her promise to obey God, and she knew it. Looks like Mrs. Manoah is the real hero in our story.

Micah and His Mother

When he returned the eleven hundred shekels of silver to his mother,
she said, "I solemnly consecrate my silver to the LORD for my son
to make an image overlaid with silver." Judges 17:3, NIV

This story takes place in the days of the judges, a time when every man and woman did what was right in his or her own eyes. In other words, it was a time in Bible history when there seemed to be no standard, no rules about right and wrong. Hmm. That would be very dangerous!

Micah, a young man from the tribe of Ephraim, lived during this era, but his story is not one we would envy. For starters he stole eleven hundred pieces of silver from his mom, and she was worried sick about it, thinking someone had broken into her house to take them. When Micah confessed to the deed, she was so relieved that she took two hundred of the silver pieces and made an image to be used in the worship of God. Can you imagine that? The Israelites were forbidden to make idols for worship, and yet she thought she was doing a good thing. Go figure.

Next, Micah made a shrine and set up his son to be its priest, even though they weren't from the tribe of Levi. More big mistakes, since these things were forbidden by God. The only shrine allowed in Israel was God's holy tabernacle sanctuary in Shiloh. When a young Levite from Bethlehem came traveling through town, Micah convinced him to stay and be his personal priest. And then, later, when soldiers from the tribe of Dan came calling, they stole the silver image and kidnapped the young Levite to be their personal priest, leaving Micah with nothing.

Micah was mixed up, to be sure, because, like many people in his day, he did only what was right in his own eyes. For this he lost out on God's blessing. But what if he had worshiped God as the commandments required? What if he had skipped the idol thing and moved on up to Shiloh? Then this story would have turned out quite different, and a lot of people wouldn't have died. Judges 17, 18 tells us all about it.

Michal

Now Saul's daughter Michal was in love with David,
and when they told Saul about it, he was pleased. 1 Samuel 18:20

This sounds like a clip from a happily-ever-after fairy tale. A brave young man steps up in service of his king, becomes a national hero, and catches the eye of the princess. But that's where the story turns south—the young couple didn't live happily ever after, thanks to the king. It's true David was a champion because he killed the giant, Goliath. It's true Michal fell in love with him. What young woman wouldn't have, under these circumstances?

Michal married David, and the problems started right away. David served King Saul well when he fought against the Philistines, and that made the young maidens sing his praises. It's not surprising that the king resented him for that. One night Saul's soldiers came to arrest David at his house, but he escaped and went into hiding. For years he had to flee from place to place to avoid Saul and his henchmen, and somewhere in there Michal was married off to another man. That's quite a finish to a storybook fairy tale that never really got started.

Now, what if Michal had stood up to her father and told him to keep his hands off David? What if she had refused to marry another man? King Saul was all-powerful, but she was his daughter, and it appears he had a soft place in his heart for her (1 Samuel 19). David was a man destined for greatness, and she could have been part of it. Let's face it, she blew it! For this she lost God's blessing, never had any children, and disappeared into history without a trace.

Elimelech and Naomi

Now it came to pass, in the days when the judges ruled, that there was a famine in the land. And a certain man of Bethlehem, Judah, went to dwell in the country of Moab, he and his wife and his two sons. Ruth 1:1

So, what's the rest of the story about Elimelech and Naomi? Why did they go to Moab? Why would they take their two boys to live in a pagan country, where worshipers were required to offer child sacrifices to gods like Chemosh? Why would they leave the land of their fathers that God Himself gave them as an inheritance? We don't know all their reasons. There was a famine in the land, but they lacked faith in God that He would provide for their needs.

Whatever their reasons for going to Moab, their two boys, Mahlon and Chilion, grew up to love pagan women, and each of them married one. Then they and their father died tragically. We don't know from what, or why, but when they were gone, they left three widows behind: Naomi, Ruth, and Orpah. Naomi decided to return to Judah, and Ruth went with her. Everyone in Bethlehem was glad to see Naomi return, but she was very bitter over how things had turned out for her while in Moab. "Don't call me Naomi anymore," she said. "Call me Mara. I'm very bitter, because God has punished me while we were in Moab."

We can understand her pain; but what if Naomi hadn't gone to Moab with her husband? What if they had stayed in Judah in their house on the land their family had owned for hundreds of years? The famine would have passed eventually. Her boys would have been raised in a country where the Creator of heaven and earth was worshiped and loved. They would have married girls from Judah. Then, too, Elimelech, Mahlon, and Chilion wouldn't have died in Moab, leaving behind their wives. Like Naomi and Elimelech, we may not always understand why God allows bad things to happen to us, but if we wait patiently and trust Him, He will bless us.

Orpah

"Look," said Naomi, "your sister-in-law is going back to her people
and her gods. Go back with her." Ruth 1:15, NIV

What a contrast between Orpah and Ruth. Both were married to sons of
Naomi and Elimelech. Both lost their husbands and became widows while
still young. Both decided to leave Moab and return to Judah with their widowed
mother-in-law. But that is where the comparison ends.

Orpah was married to Chilion, the younger son of Naomi and Elimelech.
She was heartbroken when he died, but, like Ruth, her situation was even worse
than we might think. Widows in her day would be destitute if there was no man in
the household to support them, and Naomi's family into which Orpah had married had lost all three of their working men. And now the three women were on
their way to Bethlehem to try to eke out a living together, and the outlook looked
bleak indeed. But part way home Naomi stopped to reconsider their plan. The
girls should not return with her to Bethlehem, she said. She was grateful for their
loyalty, but she had nothing more to offer them. Her sons were gone, and she
had no more sons to give them. Go back to your father's household, Naomi told
the girls. And after weighing her options, Orpah decided to do just that. She was
young and could easily marry again. She wanted children, which was the best gift
any girl could give her family and husband-to-be.

What if Orpah had stayed with Naomi? What if she had gone to Bethlehem
like Ruth and made a life for herself there with her mother-in-law? Who knows,
she might have become famous like Ruth. She might have been remembered for
what she did instead of what she did not do. Today we know nothing more about
her except that she disappeared into obscurity. Instead of worshiping the God of
heaven and earth, she returned to a country that worshiped Chemosh, the Moabite
god that demanded the sacrifice of children. Wow! That is really sad!

Abiathar

> Now one of the sons of Ahimelech the son of Ahitub, named Abiathar,
> escaped and fled after David. And Abiathar told David that Saul
> had killed the Lord's priests. 1 Samuel 22:20, 21

Abiathar grew up in the peaceful town of Nob as part of a family of priests, but all that came crashing down one terrible day when his whole family was executed by order of the king. It started when David came to the tabernacle at Nob looking for something to eat. He spun a tale about being on a secret mission for the king, and Abiathar's father unwittingly gave him some food and a weapon. To everyone's shock, King Saul came into town a few weeks later and accused the high priest of conspiring against him. Abiathar's father protested, but his words fell on deaf ears. In short order he was condemned to death, and Doeg the Edomite led a bloody rampage that killed everyone in the town of Nob. Everybody except Abiathar, that is, who miraculously escaped and fled for his life. He found refuge with David, who was hiding out in a cave near the town of Adullam. David was devastated when he heard the news and blamed himself.

Through this tragic experience, the two of them became best of friends and supported each other for years. Abiathar became David's personal priest. And then, near the end of their lives, Abiathar seemed to turn against King David when he supported Prince Adonijah, who staged a coup to get himself anointed king of Israel. The attempt quickly failed, and David banished Abiathar from the priesthood in Jerusalem.

What if Abiathar had not helped Adonijah's scheme to become king? What if he had supported David to the end as God's anointed one? Then Adonijah might not have died prematurely, and Abiathar would have kept his job. Wow! That is a lot that went wrong when Abiathar should have been on the side of right.

Doeg

Then answered Doeg the Edomite, who was set over the servants of Saul, and said, "I saw the son of Jesse going to Nob, to Ahimelech the son of Ahitub. And he inquired of the LORD for him, gave him provisions, and gave him the sword of Goliath the Philistine." 1 Samuel 22:9, 10

What a troublemaker! Did Doeg ever really understand what he had done when he tattled on the high priest at the sanctuary in Nob and got him in trouble? He was an Edomite and not an Israelite, so it isn't likely. Let's take a look at how the story developed.

When David suddenly showed up in Nob one day, he took the priest Ahimelech by surprise and asked for food and weapons. The priest was suspicious about why David would come to Nob alone, but unwisely he gave him some bread and Goliath's sword. Doeg, King Saul's royal shepherd, happened to be there that day and later reported the incident to King Saul. It's not surprising that Saul left immediately for Nob, where he grilled Ahimelech and charged him with treason. His suspicion? That the priest had aided David in his getaway, giving him food and weapons. Really? Sounds like something the local tabloids and media networks would like to get their hands on today, doesn't it?

Then King Saul did the most horrific thing possible. He ordered his soldiers to kill Ahimelech. But they refused. One man, Doeg, stepped in and killed him. He was a violent man who didn't respect Jehovah or the high priest. He carried out King Saul's orders. He also killed all eighty-five priests in Nob, and their families, and all their livestock. Wow! That sounds crazy!

What if Doeg had refused to do it? Would King Saul have gone through with it himself? We'll never know, but the stain of this atrocity falls directly on Doeg himself, and he will have much to answer for on the judgment day.

Peninnah

*Because the Lord had closed Hannah's womb, her rival [Peninnah] kept provoking
her in order to irritate her. This went on year after year. 1 Samuel 1:6, 7, NIV*

Elkanah had two wives, and Peninnah was wife number two. That's the way
many men did things in those days. They married a second wife if their first
wife couldn't have children. Hannah was Elkanah's favorite wife, as the story goes,
so Peninnah tried to make life miserable for wife number one.

She did it in many ways, as we can imagine. She probably teased Hannah
about her hair, her weight, her teeth, or if she burned the evening meal. But mostly
she razzed her about not being able to have children. Ouch! That's gotta hurt. It's
bad enough if a woman taunts another woman about her kids, but to taunt her for
not being able to have children is sick.

We can guess that Elkanah scolded Peninnah for her incessant mocking of
Hannah, but what he said to Hannah didn't help much. "Why are you down-
hearted? Don't I mean more to you than ten sons?" (1 Samuel 1:8, NIV)

So why did Peninnah treat Hannah so badly, and what would it have been like
if she hadn't? Well, she was jealous, and that made all the difference in the world—
Elkanah loved Hannah more than Peninnah, even though she was childless.

What if Peninnah hadn't been so mean to Hannah? What if she had been kind
instead? In that case it's likely she would have been loved by Elkanah too. No one
likes a bully, and it's even harder to love one. Then, too, it's possible she would have
found a friend in Hannah. After all, Hannah was in the same boat. She must have
felt bad that Elkanah wanted a second wife at all. It's not fun to have to compete for
someone's love. Just ask Peninnah. She was an expert.

Ruth

*"Entreat me not to leave you, or to turn back from following after you;
for wherever you go, I will go; and wherever you lodge, I will lodge; Your
people shall be my people, and your God, my God." Ruth 1:16*

Who was this amazing woman who came out of nowhere to be a player in one of the most famous love stories of all time? She was a Moabite woman, which would have made it very difficult for her to live in the city of Bethlehem. She was not rich, so she would have to glean in the harvest fields. She was a widow, and her husband had no brothers whom she could marry to carry on the family name, as was the custom in her day. Those were pretty tough odds for a girl!

Of course, we know what happened when she came to Bethlehem. Though she was a foreigner, people admired her for supporting Naomi after all the men in their family had died. Every day during the harvest, Ruth went to the fields to pick up any stray stalks of grain she could find, so she and Naomi could survive. And when Boaz, a relative of Naomi, noticed Ruth, he took a fancy to her. In due time, they married and lived happily ever after. How else could the story end?

That's a good question. What if she hadn't gone to Bethlehem with Naomi? To be sure, things would have turned out much different for her. How different? She might have given up her worship of the one true God and gone back to her pagan gods. She wouldn't have married Boaz, because she wouldn't have met him. And that means she wouldn't have had her son Obed, who was the father of Jesse, who was the father of King David. That's right, she would have never become the great-grandmother of King David. Wow! What a girl! What a great story describing what can happen when a girl commits herself to Jesus!

APRIL 14

Samson

Then Samson said, "Let me die with the Philistines!"
And he pushed with all his might, and the temple fell on the lords
and all the people who were in it. Judges 16:30

So who was this Incredible Hulk that God called to be a deliverer for Israel? He sounds like some kind of superhero! Samson is by far the most celebrated strongman in human history, and if he had done exactly as God had asked, next to Jesus he might have been the most famous character in biblical history. But that's where he messed up, and though his story resembles something you might see in a movie, it has a sad ending.

Born miraculously to Israelite parents in the tribe of Dan, Samson quickly rose to a position of leadership. Unfortunately, it doesn't appear that he cared much for the older folks in his nation, and they didn't seem to have much faith in him either. Maybe that's because he was always running down to party in Philistine cities like Timnah and Gaza. And so it was that one by one he gave up the promises he had made to Jehovah about lifestyle, friends, and loyalty to the worship of the one true God. Eventually he broke every part of the covenant he had made with God.

But what if he hadn't learned to love alcohol and the company of lewd pagan women? What if he had made his covenant with God the most important thing in his life? Then Satan clearly wouldn't have been able to prey upon these weaknesses, which eventually brought him down to ruin in the temple of Dagon. The saddest thing about this whole story is that Samson felt secure with all the benefits his strength could give him. He probably thought he could go back to the safety of his country and his God whenever he wanted. But that's not the way it is when we dabble with the devil. He reaches into our lives with his tentacles of sin until we are bound tight in his grasp, and then we cannot get away. Why? Because we have broken our covenant with God. Samson was oblivious to this reality. By God's grace, don't let it happen to you.

Samson's Wife

Then Samson's wife wept on him, and said, "You only hate me!
You do not love me! You have posed a riddle to the sons of my people,
but you have not explained it to me." Judges 14:16

Samson was a strong man in every sense of the word, but when it came to women he was the weakest of the weak. His fiancée from Timnah was living proof. Of course, his parents were dead set against the marriage, but he wouldn't listen. When he asked for the girl's hand, she thought it might work, but, boy, was she wrong! The whole thing turned out very bad for both of them—especially for her.

It all started when she begged him to tell her the answer to a riddle he told his friends at their wedding feast. He finally gave in, she turned around and told his friends, and he lost the bet. So he killed thirty Philistines, stripped off their clothes, and gave them to the winners of the bet to fulfill his part of the bargain. Samson went off in a huff but came back a few weeks later to find his wife married off to the best man at their wedding. Now Samson was really mad, so he caught three hundred foxes, tied firebrands between their tails, set them off running through the fields, and burned thousands of acres of Philistine grain, olive orchards, and vineyards. The Philistines came looking for Samson, but he grabbed up the jawbone of a dead donkey and killed a thousand of their warriors. Wow! That's a lot of trouble just because two people from enemy nations tried to marry.

Now, what if Mrs. Samson hadn't tried to trick Samson into giving her the answer to his riddle? She was caught between a rock and a hard place because she was married to an enemy of her people. When she tricked him, he was angry, but if she hadn't tricked him, the thirty guests at her wedding feast would have killed her—which is exactly what they did later after Samson destroyed all their crops. Her own people treacherously burned down her family's house with her and her family inside. What's the lesson for us here? Don't be unequally yoked in marriage.

Samuel

The boy Samuel ministered before the LORD under Eli. In those days the word of the LORD was rare; there were not many visions. 1 Samuel 3:1, NIV

Who was this wonder boy that came to live with Eli when he was little more than a child? He was a prayed-for miracle baby, to be sure. He was raised at his mother's knee to memorize Scripture, to love God with all his heart and soul and mind, and to listen to the Holy Spirit. And it's a good thing he had this good start in his life! The things he would see and hear at the tabernacle in Shiloh when his mother took him to live there would have been enough to turn anyone from the worship of the one true God.

The sons of Eli were the worst kind of example for Samuel. They cheated the worshipers at Shiloh every chance they got. They stole money and sacrificial meat from the Lord's offerings. They drank alcohol and partied with women who served at the gate of the tabernacle. And still Samuel remained pure before God. Evidently, he was the only one God could trust, because the Lord came to him one night to tell him about all the bad things that were going to happen to Eli and his family. Because of Eli's sons' great wickedness, eventually all the children and grandchildren in the family would die.

Samuel went on to become one the most respected prophets in the history of Israel and a man of great power and influence. He performed miracles, led armies, took down kings and set them up. Without a doubt Samuel was a man of God, because he knew the voice of his Creator. But what if he had refused to go to Shiloh to live with Eli? What if he hadn't loved to study the Scriptures as a boy? What if he hadn't loved God more than anything? He would not have become a prophet and priest and judge in Israel. He would not have set up the schools of the prophets and trained a whole generation of young men to serve God faithfully. Good thing he listened to God's voice!

Uriah

"Why did you despise the word of the LORD by doing what is evil in his eyes? You struck down Uriah the Hittite with the sword and took his wife to be your own. You killed him with the sword of the Ammonites." 2 Samuel 12:9, NIV

What a mess! The man after God's own heart committed the crime of the decade, and one of his mighty men paid the price for it. Who was this man? Uriah the Hittite was a foreigner who had joined David's band of fugitives years before, when he was on the run. It's quite a story. How could such a thing happen during the reign of a godly king, and what was the senseless act of treachery that took Uriah down?

For starters, his beautiful wife was in the wrong place at the wrong time, and it shamed both her and the king when they spent an afternoon together in his palace. But Uriah didn't know anything about this. He was out on maneuvers across the Jordan River, laying siege to the Ammonite city of Rabbah. When he received an order from General Joab calling him back to Jerusalem, he must have been a bit confused about why he was called. The king told Uriah to go home and see his wife. "Get some R and R," the king ordered. But wouldn't you know it, Uriah declined the offer. "How can I take time off when your soldiers and officers are on duty, camping in tents out under the open sky?" he asked David. "I can't, and I won't." And so David did the unthinkable. He ordered the execution of Uriah, battlefield style, by putting him in the hottest spot of the skirmish against Rabbah. It was a cold-blooded thing to do, but it worked—Uriah died. Later, when the fiasco was revealed by Nathan the prophet, both David and Bathsheba paid a heavy price.

What could Uriah have done different? Not much. He was a faithful soldier for David and didn't deserve to die. We might ask instead, what if David and Bathsheba hadn't spent that afternoon together? That, of course, would have fixed everything.

Witch of Endor

Saul then said to his attendants, "Find me a woman who is a medium, so I may go and inquire of her." 1 Samuel 28:7, NIV

Can you imagine that? The first king of Israel had started out so well, and now he was asking to get advice from a witch. Why? Because he felt he had nowhere else to turn. He had killed all the priests of God, rejected the prophet Samuel's words of warning, and he was hunting his champion David, who now lived in Philistine territory.

And now he must lead the armies of Israel to fight the Philistines. The eve of the battle had come, but he didn't have the heart for it. If he could just find someone to give him courage, he felt he could go on. Finally he thought of going to a spiritualist medium to find out what the next day might bring.

He found the woman living in a cave and asked her to contact Samuel the prophet, who had recently died. Of course, the witch could do no such thing. Samuel was resting in his grave waiting for the resurrection morning. What Saul did get, however, was a visit from Satan himself, who gave him no words of comfort. "You are doomed," Satan told him, "and you will die in battle tomorrow with your three sons!" Wow! What a scary message for sure!

The witch should have known better than to serve Satan like that. What if she had decided she was not going to do Satan's bidding? She could see how far the king had fallen. What if she had told Saul to pray to the God of heaven and ask His forgiveness for all his sins? Then God would have saved the king and given him victory the next day over his enemies. There's a lesson in this for all of us. No matter how rough things get, don't turn to Satan for help. Ask your heavenly Father.

Zebah and Zalmunna

And he said to Zebah and Zalmunna, "What kind of men were they whom you killed at Tabor?" So they answered, "As you are, so were they; each one resembled the son of a king." Judges 8:18

This is a story full of treachery and war. It was the days of the judges in ancient Israel, and the Midianites had invaded the northern tribes of Israel like a plague of locusts. The really sad part in this story was the fact that the Midianites were long-lost relatives of Israel. That's right. The Midianites were descendants of Abraham's son Midian. They were relatives of Israel and now were treating them as the worst of enemies. Leading the charge were two Midianite kings named Zebah and Zalmunna. They were notorious for their cruelty and had killed all Gideon's brothers when they invaded the northern tribes of Israel on a previous raid.

We know the story of how Gideon attacked the camp of the invaders in the middle of the night with pitchers, torches, and trumpets. He and his three hundred men totally demoralized the Midianites, sending them packing in a hurry. All night and the next day, Gideon chased the Midianites east into the desert, destroying them along the way. By sunset, all that was left of the original 135,000 who had invaded the land was 15,000 enemy soldiers. And when Gideon finally captured Zebah and Zalmunna, they knew they deserved to die for how badly they had treated God's people.

Now, what if Zebah and Zalmunna had treated Israel with the respect and honor due to God's people, and their family members? What if they had not invaded the land every few months to steal crops and livestock and children? Then they could have lived in peace together and shared the fruits of the land. They could have enjoyed the blessings that the God of their father Abraham had intended for them. What a loss! What a tragedy! It was a lesson they never learned.

Absalom

Now in all Israel there was no one who was praised as much as Absalom
for his good looks. From the sole of his foot to the crown of his head
there was no blemish in him. 2 Samuel 14:25

Absalom was the most eligible bachelor in Israel, though most girls would have been foolish to want him as a boyfriend, fiancé, or husband. He was self-centered, arrogant, and vain. And he was far from honorable. As a young man he must have had his sights set on his father's throne, because when his half brother Amnon raped his sister Tamar, he took his chance to begin clearing a pathway to the throne. It's not surprising that he executed Amnon and then fled the country to hide out with the king of Geshur, who happened to be his grandpa. Three years later he was allowed to come back to Israel through the efforts of David's general Joab. But Absalom never did become reconciled to his father, King David, and that only made it worse.

He began to pave his way to the throne by being sneaky. Every day he sat at the gate and told the people how sorry he was that there was no justice in Israel, and how wonderful it would be if he were the king of Israel. Then he would race through the streets of Jerusalem in a chariot with fifty men running ahead of him. Finally, he staged a coup against his father and marched on Jerusalem to take the throne. He rode out to battle against his father, King David, but died when his hair got caught in the branches of an oak tree while he was escaping on his mule. King David mourned Absalom's death, but no one else did.

All in all, Absalom was one messed-up kid. What if he hadn't murdered his brother Amnon? God could not bless Amnon with the throne of Israel after he raped his sister Tamar. In that case, Absalom was the next in line, and he wouldn't have had to steal the throne. If he had developed a character that was good and kind and true, God might have decided he was the best man for the job. Unfortunately, we will never know.

Adonijah

Then Adonijah the son of Haggith exalted himself, saying, "I will be king";
and he prepared for himself chariots and horsemen,
and fifty men to run before him. 1 Kings 1:5

Adonijah foolishly followed in the fateful steps of his brother Absalom, oblivious to the consequences if he should fail. The Bible says he set his sights on the throne of Israel and paraded himself in Jerusalem with chariots, horsemen, and men to run ahead of him wherever he went. As in the case of Absalom, King David didn't reprimand Adonijah for all this, though it was clear what the prince was up to.

Then Adonijah took the final step and invited all his supporters to a big feast, where he pronounced himself the next king of Israel. Joab, David's general, was there. Abiathar, David's personal priest, was there, and so were most of King David's sons. Nathan was the first one to sound the alarm about Adonijah's treachery. Quickly Nathan and Bathsheba roused King David to do something about it. Immediately David's supporters paraded Prince Solomon through the streets of Jerusalem and crowned him king of Israel.

Now it was Adonijah's turn to scramble. Within five minutes of hearing the news about Solomon's coronation, all of Adonijah's supporters had disappeared. Before the day was done, he had asked for pardon, and amazingly it was given to him by Solomon.

What if Adonijah hadn't tried to take the throne by force? What if he had asked his father who God wanted to place on the throne of Israel? Such humbleness might have appealed to God and King David. But Solomon was no dummy and realized his older brother was up to no good. When Adonijah later asked for one of David's wives to become his own, he set a trap for himself. Such a thing was considered treason, because it would bring Adonijah one step nearer the throne. In those days that was a no-no, and Solomon ordered his execution. What a waste!

Ahimaaz and Jonathan

"Indeed they have there with them their two sons, Ahimaaz, Zadok's son,
and Jonathan, Abiathar's son; and by them you shall send me everything you hear."
2 Samuel 15:36

Ahimaaz and Jonathan were in the right place at the right time in history, and they came away with one of the most exciting adventures in all the Bible. When Prince Absalom tried to steal the throne, many Israelites remained loyal to King David. The families of these two boys, Ahimaaz and Jonathan, were faithful supporters of the throne. In fact, it turned out they were more helpful than they could have imagined.

When messages needed to be sent to David, who had left Jerusalem and was on his way to the Jordan River, Ahimaaz and Jonathan were the ones to do it. No one would be watching them, since they were just boys. The two teenagers could run, and that's exactly what they did. Their fathers, Zadok and Abiathar, were priests, and when they got word that Absalom was gathering an army to follow David and fight him, the boys sneaked out of Jerusalem secretly with the message. Unfortunately, another boy saw them, and the two boys had to run for it. They managed to make it to the town of Bahurim, and with the help of a woman, they hid in a well. God kept them from being discovered, and they escaped to the Jordan, where they notified David—just in time. He and the people with him crossed the Jordan and fled to the town of Mahanaim, where "David's mighty men" prepared for war.

What if Ahimaaz and Jonathan hadn't been loyal to King David? What if they had sided with Absalom? He was a handsome young prince, and the boys must have admired him. They might have found themselves following Absalom, a cruel, vain man who thought of no one but himself. Too late they would have discovered that serving a selfish man like him was no picnic.

Ahithophel

Now the advice of Ahithophel, which he gave in those days,
was as if one had inquired at the oracle of God. So was all the advice of Ahithophel
both with David and with Absalom. 2 Samuel 16:23

Ahithophel was the wisest of the wise in the days of David. Whenever anyone wanted government advice, Ahithophel was the go-to man. The Bible says Israel's elders respected his words of wisdom so much that they viewed it as if they had consulted God Himself. But there was a problem. Ahithophel was not a godly advisor and was in fact a very bad man. We see this playing out at the time of Absalom's coup against King David.

Ahithophel served David well for much of his reign, but when it looked like Prince Absalom was going to pull off the heist of the century, Ahithophel rebelled with him. The Bible says Ahithophel was Bathsheba's grandfather, so we can understand his dislike for David after the way he treated Bathsheba and her husband Uriah.

When Absalom entered Jerusalem, Ahithophel set the wheels in motion to see that the prince was successful in stealing the throne of Israel. For starters, he advised Absalom to go sleep with all David's concubines who had not already left Jerusalem. Wow! That was the custom in those days, but it was a very evil thing to do against David and against God. Then he told Absalom to immediately take an army of twelve thousand and pursue his father David before he had a chance to cross the Jordan. Ahithophel knew David and his supporters would be unable to win a battle while fleeing. Clearly this was an act of treachery and treason!

What if Ahithophel had given his allegiance to David instead of Absalom? Maybe then he could have survived the coup. As it was, Absalom took another advisor's advice instead of Ahithophel's, and that spelled the end for him. He knew the jig was up and went home to commit suicide. What a way for Ahithophel to go! Without peace, and without the blessing of God!

APRIL 24

Ancient of Days

"I watched till thrones were put in place, and the Ancient of Days was seated; His garment was white as snow, and the hair of His head was like pure wool. His throne was a fiery flame, its wheels a burning fire; a fiery stream issued and came forth from before Him. A thousand thousands ministered to Him; ten thousand times ten thousand stood before Him. The court was seated, and the books were opened." Daniel 7:9, 10

Wow! That's quite a picture! The Ancient of Days! A glorious Being shining with the brilliance of lightning. A throne with wheels streaming flames of fire on a sea of glass. One hundred million angels singing their hearts out in an awesome courtroom, and books are opened. Which books? The book of life with names of everyone who have ever been sealed by God's grace. A book of remembrance that records the good done by all the saints. The book of death that shows all the evil deeds done by those who refused to repent. The Book of God's Law, more commonly known as the Bible.

Amazing! Mind-boggling! Super-neato, peachy keen! A courtroom that looks like this ought to turn heads, and we can be sure it will because that day represents Judgment Day in heaven. Who is the Ancient of Days? None other than God the Father. Whew! In the presence of God Almighty! Such a sight is enough to take your breath away!

You see, this is God's chance to clear the air once and for all about right and wrong, good and evil, Christ and Satan. Was it fair for Satan to stage a reign of terror on earth for six thousand years? No! Was Jesus' agonizing crucifixion an act of mercy to save you and me from eternal death? A thousand times, yes! But what if the Ancient of Days hadn't called for that massive court session in the heavenly court? What if He had said, "Sinners have had their chance. We're done here!" Then you and I would have never known how incredibly good—and yet absolutely fair—He is to put an end to sin. What a story for the ages! Breathtaking! Heart-stopping! A day to end all days!

Gad

> So Gad . . . said to him, "Shall seven years of famine come to you in your land? Or shall you flee three months before your enemies, while they pursue you? Or shall there be three days' plague in your land? Now consider and see what answer I should take back to Him who sent me." 2 Samuel 24:13

How would you like to be the prophet to ask such a thing? That was the job of Gad, a prophet during David's reign. "Don't be putting your stock in horses or armies," God had told David. "It will make you proud and lead you to forget all the times I saved your skin." But David did it anyway. He ordered his general Joab to count the men in Israel to see how big an army he could raise. And that's where Gad the prophet entered the picture. "Thus says the Lord," Gad began, "because you have ignored my warnings and despised the blessings of protection I offer you every day, I am going to withdraw my protection from you for a while. Maybe then in your pride you will humble yourself and truly understand all that I have been doing to protect Israel and keep everyone alive. Now take your pick of how you think it should happen. Do you want famine in the land, or invasion by enemy armies, or a disease epidemic?" It's hard to imagine Gad asking such a thing of David, but the king wasn't the only guilty one. The people of Israel had grown proud and were not living lives of gratefulness for God's blessing of protection either.

"Make your choice," Gad said. In other words, "Pick your poison." It could be that this was a test for David to see how truly unselfish he was, in spite of his mistake in numbering Israel. As it turned out, David chose an epidemic because he felt there was more chance for God's mercy under such circumstances.

What if God hadn't sent Gad to David to give the warning? Was it possible all three judgments might have come? If enemies had invaded the land they would have stolen all the crops, and then people would have suffered from malnutrition and contracted all kinds of diseases. And so we see God in His mercy was kind after all.

Ittai the Gittite

> But Ittai answered the king and said, "As the LORD lives, and as my lord the king lives, surely in whatever place my lord the king shall be, whether in death or life, even there also your servant will be." 2 Samuel 15:21

Ittai's conversion to the worship of the one true God is one of the most unusual stories in the Old Testament, and the fact that he brought six hundred warriors with him is worth telling. So how did such a thing happen? Well, we might say Ittai himself was a trophy of war, because that's what it looks like. In those days, conquerors usually came back with spoils of war like gold and silver and horses, but when you come back with six hundred warriors as trophies, that's pretty good. The Bible says Ittai and his men asked if they could migrate to Israel and become worshipers of Jehovah. The answer was yes, and that made David one of the most successful missionaries in the Old Testament. The fact that Ittai and his friends were from Gath is really quite amazing! That was the city Goliath the giant was from! Quite possibly some of Ittai's warriors were there the day David killed the Philistine champion. Ittai must have admired David a lot, and from that day forward he became one of David's most loyal supporters.

Fast-forward to the day Prince Absalom staged a coup against King David. As David's supporters hurried out of Jerusalem to flee with him, Ittai came along too, with his six hundred warriors. What a testimony to his loyalty! When David's men went out to fight Absalom's forces a couple of days later, Ittai was one of the three commanding generals to lead the charge.

What if Ittai hadn't moved to Israel and brought his men with him? Then he might not have become a worshiper of God. What if he hadn't been so loyal to David and supported him in the war against Absalom? Then he would have missed out on serving one of the greatest kings in Israel's history.

Nabal

Now there was a man in Maon whose business was in Carmel,
and the man was very rich. He had three thousand sheep and a thousand goats.
And he was shearing his sheep in Carmel. 1 Samuel 25:2

Once upon a time there was a grouchy old rancher named Nabal who lived in the southern hills of Judah. He was a rich man who owned lots and lots of sheep and goats, and that somehow gave him the idea he could be mean. Unfortunately he lived up to his reputation when David sent ten of his men to ask him for a favor.

David was on the run, hiding out in the hills around Nabal's estate. It took a lot of food to feed the warriors who traveled with him from place to place, but food was scarce in the desert where they were camping out. He paid Nabal a visit to ask for food. This was a common thing to do in Israel, and people generally shared what they had, even if complete strangers were asking for it.

But not Nabal. When he heard what David wanted, he sent the messengers packing in a hurry. "Who is this David?" he scoffed, as though he hadn't heard a word they said. "Why should I take my food and give it to men I don't know?"

David was shocked when his men told him what had happened. "Get your weapons!" he ordered. "We're going to kill this man and all the men who work for him!" But he never got to wreak vengeance on the old man. Nabal's farmhands told his wife, Abigail, all that had happened, and she sent a large gift of food as a peace offering. David calmed down and was spared the guilt of killing Nabal.

What if Nabal hadn't been such a nasty man? What if he hadn't refused to give David and his men food? Then he would have saved everyone a lot of grief, and maybe he wouldn't have had a stroke and died ten days later. Sad, but true.

Solomon

"Therefore give to Your servant an understanding heart to judge Your people, that I may discern between good and evil. For who is able to judge this great people of Yours?" 1 Kings 3:9

Solomon was the wisest man on earth, and when people came to see him for themselves, they left in astonishment. There was nothing he didn't know or couldn't explain.

God had asked what Solomon wanted, and when Solomon said, "Just wisdom to lead Your people," God gave him that and more—riches, honor among the nations, peace, prosperity for everyone, and long life. Palaces with servants galore, thousands of horses and chariots to put all armies to shame, silver as plentiful as stones in the streets of Jerusalem, a throne of ivory covered in pure gold, and twelve carved lions on the six steps to the throne.

Though Solomon was blessed by God, he had a huge weakness—he loved many foreign women from pagan countries. God had told the Israelites not to intermarry with foreigners because He knew their hearts would be turned away after false gods. But Solomon ignored these warnings and married them anyway, and in the end they were his downfall. God was not pleased with Solomon for such shenanigans. He appeared to Solomon twice, warning him specifically not to worship other gods, making the king's sin worse. "Because you have not kept My covenant and My statutes, I will allow enemy nations to overrun you, and in the end I will tear the kingdom away from you and give it to your servant," God said.

At the end of Solomon's life, he repented with bitter tears for all the wicked things he had done. But what if he had never turned away from God? What if he had been true and faithful to obey God's commandments? Then he would clearly have been the most famous king in world history, and Israel would have joined him in being true to the God of all the earth.

Uzzah

Uzzah put out his hand to the ark of God and took hold of it, for the oxen stumbled. Then the anger of the Lord was aroused against Uzzah, and God struck him there for his error; and he died there by the ark of God. 2 Samuel 6:6, 7

This is one of the saddest stories in the Bible—sad because he died while still a young man, and sad because it didn't have to happen. His name was Uzzah, and his father was Aminadab, a Levite priest in the city of Kirjath-Jearim.

King David decided he wanted to bring the ark of God to Jerusalem, and he did it with fanfare and music and dancing. Uzzah and his brother Ahio attended the ark as it made the nine-mile trip to Jerusalem, but they brought it on a wooden cart, something that was forbidden by God—mistake number one. If they had read the Law of Moses they would have realized it must be carried by two poles that ran through four rings on the sides of the ark. While the cart with its precious cargo was bumping along on the rocky road, it suddenly tipped dramatically. A wheel must have hit a hole in the road, because the oxen lurched forward, and Uzzah reached out to steady the ark—mistake number two. The punishment was swift, and Uzzah dropped dead instantly. Everyone was shocked!

Uzzah should have known better. Why? His family had cared for the ark of God when the Philistines brought it back to Israel. It had been in his house in Kirjath-Jearim for at least twenty years, and God had blessed his family for it.

God was trying to show the irreverent Israelites that salvation is a gift and that they should be grateful for His holy presence, which had come to dwell among them. What if Uzzah hadn't touched the ark? He would have showed us that when God asks us to do something specific, we need to obey. He knows best under all circumstances and wants us to live long and prosper. Unfortunately, if we think we know better, we may have to suffer the consequences of disobedience.

Asa

In the twentieth year of Jeroboam king of Israel,
Asa became king over Judah. . . .
Asa did what was right in the eyes of the LORD,
as did his father David. 1 Kings 15:9, 11

Asa was the third king of Judah after the two kingdoms split under his grandfather Rehoboam. He was a good king for most of his life and did his best to remove all forms of idolatry from the kingdom. The queen grandmother at that time was Maachah, Absalom's daughter, and Asa sent her packing because she tried to corrupt Judah with sun worship. He also removed all the temples used for male prostitution. And when Cush and Libya invaded Judah, Asa called on God for help and was miraculously delivered from the million-man African army.

In later years, however, he failed to trust God when other nations invaded his space. Baasha, king of Israel to the north, attacked Judah's borders, and Asa shook in his boots. Instead of asking God to get him out of the jam, he gave Ben-Hadad, king of Syria, a call and offered him huge sums of money to come rescue Judah. Ben-Hadad did just that, but God wasn't pleased. He didn't want Asa making political deals with pagan nations. God sent the prophet Hanani to scold Asa for making this alliance with Syria, and to everyone's surprise the prophet was jailed for it. Evidently Asa didn't like people telling him what to do—even God! From that point forward, things began to go downhill for him. His health deteriorated, and he could hardly walk after he got a strange disease in his feet.

What a shame! He had started out so well, but somewhere along the way he must have forgotten who he was. What if he had kept on trusting God to help him be a good king as he had when he was younger? He wouldn't have had to give all his money to foreign nations; his people wouldn't have been influenced by pagan worship; his health would have been better; and he wouldn't have ended up so mean and grouchy. Very sad.

Athaliah

When Athaliah the mother of Ahaziah saw that her son was dead,
she arose and destroyed all the royal heirs. 2 Kings 11:1

Athaliah did a lot of bad things. Though we don't know much about her early years, her mother was Queen Jezebel of Israel, and that's enough to help us fill in all the blanks. While still a young woman, she married Jehoram, king of Judah, and, like her mother, promoted the worship of Baal, the god of lightning and thunder. Under her influence, Judah sank to new depths of evil.

She was the only queen to sit on a throne in Old Testament history, and the story of how she got there is not a nice one. For starters she and her husband killed his brothers and the remaining royal princes who might be rightful heirs to the throne. After only eight years on the throne, her husband died, and her youngest son, Ahaziah, became king. Sadly, he himself was murdered less than a year later. That left Athaliah in a pickle, because she and her dead husband had many enemies. To keep from being demoted, or maybe even executed, she murdered all of Ahaziah's children who could one day grow up to be king of Judah. Wow! That's quite a trail of blood—all because Athaliah craved the power that comes with a throne.

What if Athaliah hadn't been such a violent person? What if she hadn't been an avid worshiper of Baal? Baal's followers believed he was a violent god, so Athaliah's behavior shouldn't really surprise us. That she could stand by and let all her husband's brothers be murdered, and then kill all her grandkids as well sounds like something out of a nightmare. Unfortunately, it was all true, and in the end she paid the price for it. In her seventh year as queen, her subjects rebelled against her rule and executed her. And who took her place on the throne of Judah? Little Joash, her grandson who survived because the high priest's wife hid him when he was a baby.

Uzziah

But when he was strong his heart was lifted up, to his destruction,
for he transgressed against the Lord his God by entering the temple of the Lord to
burn incense on the altar of incense. 2 Chronicles 26:16

Uzziah was one of Judah's most successful kings since the days of David and Solomon. He ruled for fifty-two years, longer than almost any other king in Judah's history. Uzziah was best known for strengthening Judah's army, increasing his country's agricultural exports, and fortifying Jerusalem, as well as the cities and garrisons where the army resided. He won several very important victories against the Philistines, Arabians, and Ammonites, forcing them all to pay heavy tribute money. This made him very wealthy and extremely powerful.

He was generally considered a good and righteous king, but he must have been somewhat of a people-pleaser too. The Bible says he started allowing people to worship their pagan idols in the gardens and parks located on all the high places in Judah. Then Uzziah's fame and fortune really went to his head. He decided he was important enough to go into the temple of God to offer sacrifices as a priest. This was unheard of. The presence of God dwelt in the temple over the mercy seat of God's holy ark, and to enter His presence was considered suicide. It's not surprising that eighty priests of God followed him into the temple to tell him he had to leave. But he got mad and started shouting at them. Bad decision. At that moment the Lord struck him with leprosy—the worst disease of the day—and he had it for the rest of his life.

What if he hadn't been so proud and haughty before the Lord? Well, for one thing he wouldn't have gotten leprosy, and he might have reigned much longer, honoring God by his example. Such a waste for a man who got such a good start!

Ben-Hadad

Then Elisha went to Damascus, and Ben-Hadad king of Syria was sick; and it was told him, saying, "The man of God has come here." And the king said to Hazael, "Take a present in your hand, and go to meet the man of God, and inquire of the LORD by him, saying, 'Shall I recover from this disease?' " 2 Kings 8:7, 8

Ben-Hadad was king of Syria in the days of Elisha, and what a lot of trouble he caused Israel and Judah. If he wasn't at war with one, he was battling the other.

It was this king who was hopping mad when he discovered the prophet Elisha was reporting the battle strategies he was making in his own secret war rooms. In retaliation he sent an army to Dothan to capture Elisha. His soldiers were blinded by heavenly angels, led meekly to Samaria to be held at spear point, and then kindly released after they received their eyesight back. Amazing! How is it that King Ben-Hadad thought he could capture a man whom God was telling everything he was going to do? Not to forget that Elisha was the man who had healed Naaman—Ben-Hadad's army commander—of leprosy just a short time before!

But what goes around comes around. If you're not so nice, you can expect that people will treat you badly too, and that's exactly what happened to King Ben-Hadad. When the king got sick, he sent Hazael, his chief of staff, to ask Elisha if he would recover. The prophet told him to tell the king that he would get well. But he also said that the king would die. It all came true just as Elisha said it would, except Hazael was the one who fulfilled it when he himself assassinated the king.

What if Ben-Hadad had practiced being a kind ruler? It's true, most kings didn't do that sort of thing in those days; but he should have tried it. Being kind can have its benefits—like having people love you, and not having ulcers, and living to a ripe old age. That's not something Ben-Hadad knew anything about, because he was murdered by his most trusted servant. What a way to go—without hope and without God.

MAY 4

Hazael

Hazael said, "Why is my lord weeping?" He [Elisha] answered, "Because I know the
evil that you will do to the children of Israel: Their strongholds you will set on fire,
and their young men you will kill with the sword; and you will dash their children,
and rip open their women with child." 2 Kings 8:12

Hazael acted horrified when the prophet Elisha made this prophecy about him.
"Am I a dog, that I would do such a thing?" he demanded. "How can you
make such an accusation?"

But Elisha was serious because he knew Hazael was already making plans.
"The Lord has shown me your future," he told Hazael. "You will become king of
Syria."

That was quite a speech, but sure enough, as soon as Hazael arrived back in
Damascus, he began to fulfill Elisha's prophecy. He started by assassinating King
Ben-Hadad, using a thick cloth dipped in water to smother him. Then he set himself up as king and became one of the cruelest, most treacherous rulers to ever
sit on the throne of Syria. His reign lasted about thirty-seven years. He invaded
Israel and the southern kingdom of Judah, killing women and children without
mercy, and then took the strongest men away to become slaves. He also attacked
the Philistine cities along the coast, and even battled the Assyrians.

However, things didn't go so well for him in his later years. Assyria invaded
Hazael's capital city, Damascus, and took away trophies of war, such as golden
furniture and sculptures made of ivory. In fact, archaeologists have found a piece
of an ivory bed with Hazael's name carved on it in the ruins of ancient Assyria.

What if Hazael had decided he wasn't going to be such an evil man? Did
he have to fulfill Elisha's prediction? Of course not. It's what we call conditional
prophecy. Like Jonah, Hazael could have helped God rewrite the future, and what
a blessed, God-fearing future that would have been!

Hezekiah

He trusted in the LORD God of Israel, so that after him was none like him among all the kings of Judah, nor who were before him. 2 Kings 18:5

That pretty much says it all, because Hezekiah was the ultimate king. Here's a list of the things he did during his reign. He was a righteous king (unlike his father). He repaired and cleansed the temple, reorganized the religious services, and celebrated a great Passover to which he invited the ten tribes of Israel in the north. He removed the parks on all the high hills where people worshiped pagan idols (called the high places). He destroyed all forms of idol worship in Judah, including the bronze serpent Moses had made in the wilderness, to which people were now offering incense. He collected Solomon's unpublished proverbs and made them available to the people. He conquered the Philistines once and for all, built store cities, and strengthened the gates and walls of Jerusalem. His most amazing accomplishment was to cut a 1,700-foot tunnel through solid rock to bring water into Jerusalem in case of an enemy siege. However, Hezekiah is best known for his faith in God when Sennacherib tried to attack Jerusalem and God miraculously delivered Judah by destroying the Assyrian army—all 185,000 of them.

Unfortunately, there was one dark spot in Hezekiah's life, and it changed the history of Israel. When he was healed miraculously from a fatal illness, visitors came from Babylon to hear the story of why Jehovah made the sun go backward in the sky. Instead, Hezekiah spent most of their visit showing them the riches of his kingdom. For all the good in his life, he messed up big time on this one. But what if he hadn't? What if he had told them how blessed he was to worship God? Then the Babylonian ambassadors would have gone home praising God for His amazing wonders, and ninety-five years later they might not have come back to Jerusalem to clean out the city.

Isaiah

"Woe is me, for I am undone! Because I am a man of unclean lips,
and I dwell in the midst of a people of unclean lips;
for my eyes have seen the King, the LORD of hosts." Isaiah 6:5

What a guy! Isaiah was considered the greatest of the Hebrew prophets—more famous than Daniel, and more celebrated than John the Baptist. His book has been quoted more often than any other to show that Jesus was indeed the Savior of the world. He was eloquent, educated, and cultured, and he served Judah for more than fifty years under kings Uzziah, Jotham, Ahaz, and Hezekiah. He was considered a royal prophet, because he was an advisor to these kings, and also a member of the royal household. Hebrew tradition tells us that he was a cousin to King Uzziah.

At a young age God called him to be a prophet. "I can't do this!" he told God. "I'm not good enough!" But God insisted, and the rest is history. In his later years as a prophet, Jerusalem was threatened by the armies of Assyria, but Isaiah didn't waver in his faith that God would deliver Judah from the enemy. "Sennacherib won't come into this city or even shoot an arrow here," he told King Hezekiah, and when 185,000 Assyrian soldiers died, his prophecy came true.

What if Isaiah had decided he wasn't going to answer God's call to be a prophet? What if he had said, "Nope! This job's bigger than me. Find someone else"? He would have saved himself those fifty years of giving messages to kings who didn't want to hear them. And he would have saved himself from a martyr's death. Ancient Hebrew writings tell us he was brutally murdered when he was sawn in two by Hezekiah's son, King Manasseh.

Was he afraid to die? Probably not. In vision he had seen God on His judgment throne with glorious fire streaming from Him, thunder and smoke surrounding Him, and seraphim (angels) hovering nearby in worshipful adoration. Wow! That's enough to inspire anyone. Don't you wish we could all see what he saw? Absolutely, and we will one day very soon, when Jesus comes again.

Jehoiada

> Then Jehoiada made a covenant between the LORD, the king,
> and the people, that they should be the LORD's people,
> and also between the king and the people. 2 Kings 11:17

Jehoiada was the kind of guy who was always doing the right thing at the right time. He was the high priest at the temple in Jerusalem. His wife saved little Joash from certain death when Queen Athaliah went on her rampage to kill all the royal children. With God's help they managed to keep the boy hidden for six years, until they were finally able to proclaim him king of Judah.

But that's only part of the story. After Jehoiada crowned Joash king, he asked all the people of Judah to make a covenant with God to keep His commandments. Then, with Jehoiada leading the way, they all went to Queen Athaliah's temple of Baal and tore it down, stone by stone. They smashed the altars and idols to pieces, and they also executed Mattan, the evil priest of Baal who had been scamming everyone with the foolish worship of Baal. The Bible says everyone was relieved now, because the city was quiet, the wicked queen Athaliah was gone, and a godly little boy was on the throne of Judah.

Unfortunately, the story didn't end very well. Jehoiada lived a long, productive life of 130 years. The Bible says all the years he was alive he was able to mentor Joash and make sure the young man was obedient to God. But things changed after Jehoiada died. To Joash's shame and disgrace, he turned to idol worship and even killed the high priest's son.

What would you have done differently if you had been Jehoiada? Who knows, maybe the high priest was making all the decisions while he was alive, not giving Joash any chances to make choices for himself. You can't be in charge forever. The bad parts of this story were not his fault, however. Today we remember him for the revival he started in Judah. The rest is on Joash.

Jehoshaphat

Jehoshaphat the son of Asa had become king over Judah
in the fourth year of Ahab king of Israel. . . . And he walked in all the ways
of his father Asa. He did not turn aside from them,
doing what was right in the eyes of the LORD. 1 Kings 22:41, 43

Jehoshaphat was one of the best kings ever to sit on the throne of Judah. He obeyed the commandments of the Lord and did much to make Judah a good place to live. He wasn't in office very long before he decided to make some real changes in the kingdom. First, he sent princes, Levites, and priests throughout the country to teach people about the Law of God. Then, he set up a supreme court of judges in Jerusalem to help make laws and settle legal disputes. The Lord blessed him for it, and he had a peaceful reign during most of his years on the throne.

When he did have to fight, he usually asked God for guidance and was a smashing success at it! One famous war story tells of a battle he had to fight against the Ammonites, Moabites, and Edomites. The enemy army was huge, but God told him not to worry. Jehoshaphat went out with his army singing all the way to battle, and when they got to the battlefield, the enemy soldiers were already dead, their bodies strewn everywhere. All Jehoshaphat and his soldiers had to do was collect the spoils of war. The fact was, it took three whole days to carry home the weapons and other valuables they found on the battlefield.

There were the times when Jehoshaphat didn't consult God. He arranged a marriage between his son, Jehoram, and Ahab's daughter Athaliah. She brought the worship of Baal to Jerusalem and ended up killing all the royal heirs to the throne after her husband was assassinated. What if Jehoshaphat had asked for God's advice on this one? Well, for one thing it would have stopped the worst marriage of the century from taking place, and for another it would have kept the royal family from being slaughtered! Whew! That's what you get when you don't check with God before you make heavy-duty decisions.

Nadab, Baasha, Elah, Zimri, and Omri

The ungodly are not so, but are like the chaff which the wind drives away.
Therefore the ungodly shall not stand in the judgment,
nor sinners in the congregation of the righteous. Psalm 1:4, 5

After the kingdom of Israel split, things began to go downhill fast for the northern nation of Israel. Jeroboam reigned for twenty-two years, but after that it was like musical chairs. During the reign of King Asa in Judah (forty-one years), six different kings ruled Israel. The ten tribes to the north were in chaos during that time because, like Jeroboam, the five kings who followed him were all wicked. Their names were Nadab, Baasha, Elah, Zimri, and Omri.

Nadab reigned in Israel only two years, until Baasha, one of Israel's army commanders, assassinated him. Then Baasha killed everybody in Nadab's family, just as God had said would happen because his father, Jeroboam, had been so wicked. And there was war between the king of Judah and Baasha, the king of Israel. After twenty-four years of violence Baasha died, and his son, Elah, reigned for two years. He was assassinated by General Zimri, his commander of the charioteers, who crowned himself king and then murdered everyone in Elah's and Baasha's families. But that didn't last—when the soldiers in the army heard what Zimri had done, they sent Omri, the army commander, after him. When Zimri heard they were coming, he committed suicide by burning the citadel of the king's palace down upon himself. Omri became king and ruled Israel for the next twelve years, and like those before him, he was very evil.

And so we see a sad tale of treachery and murder in the line of kings that reigned in the northern kingdom of Israel. What if these kings had decided to serve God instead of themselves? What if they had been good, fair rulers that people could look up to? Then the history of Israel would have been quite different. Our lesson today? Plan ahead. If you make bad choices, you may not like what's coming tomorrow.

Hiram

So it was, when Hiram heard the words of Solomon,
that he rejoiced greatly and said, "Blessed be the Lord this day,
for He has given David a wise son over this great people!" 1 Kings 5:7

Hiram was one of the most successful men of his day. He was the king of Tyre in Phoenicia, north of Israel. He and his men built amazing ships and then partnered with King Solomon to sail the seven seas and transport all kinds of exotic things from Africa and Arabia and Asia. Who knows? They may have gone as far as North America. Once every three years, the ships came back to their home ports bringing precious woods, gold, silver, ivory, and apes. And the kings became fabulously wealthy doing it. On one trip alone the ships came back with 450 talents of gold. That's a lot of gold!

King Hiram was a good friend of David and helped him build his royal palace. Then he helped David's son Solomon build a palace that was even more grand. It was half the length of a football field and had forty-five pillars, each of them forty-five feet tall. But Hiram's most amazing contribution to the kingdom of Israel was the temple of God in Jerusalem. It was one of the wonders of the ancient world with its walls and ceiling made of cedar and cypress wood that came from King Hiram.

Those were good years of peace and prosperity for everyone in both Phoenicia and Israel. Unfortunately, all the money Solomon made in the partnership with Hiram was the beginning of a terrible curse for Israel. The sailors and craftsmen from Phoenicia brought with them the worship of the pagan gods Baal and Ashtoreth.

What if David and Solomon hadn't gone into business with Hiram? Money is nice to have, but Israel would have saved themselves the temptations brought to them by Hiram's pagan gods. And they lost God's promise that the kingdom of Israel would stand forever.

Huram

"And now I have sent a skillful man, endowed with understanding, Huram my master craftsman (the son of a woman of the daughters of Dan, and his father was a man of Tyre), skilled to work in gold and silver, bronze and iron, stone and wood, purple and blue, fine linen and crimson, and to make any engraving and to accomplish any plan which may be given to him." 2 Chronicles 2:13, 14

Huram was a very talented man. He was a skilled worker in precious metals, but he was even more than that. When we first read of him in this story, we find he is already famous. His father was from Tyre, and his mother was from the tribe of Dan. Huram was a descendant of the one-and-only Aholiab, master craftsman who helped design the furniture for the tabernacle sanctuary in the wilderness—including the ark of the covenant.

Among the first things Huram made were two giant, thirty-five-foot-tall bronze pillars to stand at the entrance of the temple. They were made in the Jordan valley and then hauled by wagon up the steep, winding roads to Jerusalem. Then he made a humongous bronze sea (basin) to be used for ritual baths by the priests. Actually it looked more like a swimming pool, because it held more than eleven thousand gallons of water. It was fifteen feet across, seven and half feet deep, and forty-five feet in circumference. Underneath the sea were twelve bronze statues of oxen, three on each side. Huram also made an altar of gold for Solomon's temple, a table of gold for the shewbread, and ten golden lamp stands. As a grand finale, he carved two giant angels out of olive wood and covered them with pure gold. These stood guard over the ark of God's covenant in the Most Holy Place.

There is no doubt that Huram was a master craftsman, but what if he had been too busy to do the work? He was already a wealthy man and probably had plenty of contracts for work in Tyre. In that case he would have missed out on the joy of helping Israel design one of the wonders of the ancient world. Best of all, we remember him today as blessed by God.

Hushai

So Absalom and all the men of Israel said, "The advice of Hushai
the Archite is better than the advice of Ahithophel."
For the LORD had purposed to defeat the good advice of Ahithophel,
to the intent that the LORD might bring disaster on Absalom. 2 Samuel 17:14

We don't know how many royal advisors King David had, but Hushai was one of them, and on at least one occasion his advice saved David's kingdom. This is how it happened.

Prince Absalom had stolen the royal throne in Jerusalem, and the first thing on his agenda as king was to call in his advisors. He knew that as long as his father was alive, there was a danger he would try to retake the throne. Ahithophel, another advisor of King David's, had sided with Absalom in the rebellion, and he offered to take twelve thousand men and go after David immediately. It was the only plan that would work, he said.

Hushai knew Ahithophel was right. The man rarely made mistakes when it came to strategy. Any chance they had of surprising David would have to be done before David could escape across the Jordan. Hushai knew this was his one chance to save David. When Absalom asked for his advice, he took a chance on the vanity of the young prince. "Don't go after David tonight," he said. "You know your father is a brave man and will be hiding in a cave somewhere with his mighty men. Instead, you should gather an army like the sands of the sea and lead it yourself. With such an army you will overwhelm him and kill him." Absalom took Hushai's advice, and while he was preparing for battle, Hushai sent two boys to take a message of warning to King David. And David's life was spared.

What if Hushai had decided it was too risky to give Absalom counsel contrary to that of Ahithophel? He would have been safer temporarily, but his life wouldn't have been worth much serving a man like Absalom. God honors us when we do what is right.

Jeroboam I

Then Ahijah took hold of the new garment that was on him, and tore it into twelve pieces. And he said to Jeroboam, "Take for yourself ten pieces, for thus says the Lord, the God of Israel: 'Behold, I will tear the kingdom out of the hand of Solomon and will give ten tribes to you.' " 1 Kings 11:30, 31

How would you like to be the one to stage a coup against the royal throne of Israel? Sound scary? God had pronounced judgment on the throne of Solomon for his wicked ways, and now the nation was about ready to split. He sent the prophet Ahijah to find Jeroboam, an officer for one of King Solomon's construction crews. "You are going to be the king of ten tribes in Israel," he told Jeroboam, and to make his point, he tore a tunic into twelve pieces and gave Jeroboam ten of them.

The next part of the story is insane! Jeroboam became king over Israel, but, like Rehoboam, he made some really foolish choices. For one, he decided to start his own system of worship in the ten northern tribes. He set up two golden calves and told everyone, "Here are your gods, O Israel, which brought you up from the land of Egypt!" (1 Kings 12:28) It's not likely anyone really believed him, but he made the worship service a real temptation for those who were spiritually weak. And how did he do that? By setting up the worship services to be a time for feasting and drinking. How disgraceful for a man anointed by God! What a foolish man he must have been!

What if he hadn't made that fateful choice? What if he had been more like David than either Solomon or Rehoboam? Then he would have saved his country from the horrible apostasy into which it would fall. In the years to come, every Bible writer would compare future rulers to him for wickedness! Worst of all, a mere two hundred years later, Jeroboam's kingdom would be totally destroyed by the Assyrians, never to rise again. That's what bad choices did for Jeroboam.

MAY 14

Jeroboam II

Jeroboam the son of Joash, king of Israel, became king in Samaria, and reigned forty-one years. And he did evil in the sight of the LORD. 2 Kings 14:23, 24

We often call him Jeroboam the Second, and he was probably the most successful king in the history of northern Israel for all the things he did right. He reigned forty-one years, and he conquered Damascus in the north to subdue the Syrians like no one had done since the days of David. By the end of his reign he had regained all the territory lost since Solomon was king.

Unfortunately, he did much the same as former kings of Israel had done when it came to spiritual things. The Bible says he did evil in the sight of the Lord just like Jeroboam the First had done twelve kings earlier. He continued to lead Israel down the road of apostasy through the worship of Baal and Ashtoreth, pagan gods borrowed from the Phoenicians to the north.

God was not able to bless King Jeroboam or his son because of their wicked ways. The prophet Jonah foretold that Jeroboam would be successful in gaining back lost territory, but Amos prophesied that Israel would lose it all again in the days of judgment to come.

And sure enough, just six months after Jeroboam's death, it all began to unravel when his son Zechariah was assassinated. This brought an end to his family dynasty that had been in power since Jehu, the wild chariot driver, three generations before.

What if Jeroboam the Second had been faithful to God? What if he hadn't followed the habits of his namesake, Jeroboam the First, some 150 years before? Then God would have been able to bless Jeroboam. The king would have helped his people worship the Creator instead of earthly creatures and idols of wood and stone. In that case, the kingdom of Israel would not have crumbled and fallen to the Assyrians fifty years later. Unfortunately, the handwriting was on the wall. In 722 B.C., Sargon II, king of Assyria, conquered Samaria, the capital city of Israel, and with it the nation collapsed.

Mephibosheth

*And Mephibosheth lived in Jerusalem, because he always ate at the king's table;
he was lame in both feet. 2 Samuel 9:13, NIV*

Mephibosheth is one of the unique characters in the Bible. He was the son
of Jonathan and grandson of King Saul. He was only five years old when
his father and grandfather died in a battle against the Philistines. When his royal
nurse heard the news, she feared for their lives and fled the country, accidentally
dropping Mephibosheth as they went. Unfortunately, he injured both feet and became lame for life.

Years later, David wanted to honor any remaining descendants of King Saul,
and was told by Ziba, Saul's personal servant, that there was one named Mephibosheth. David brought him to the royal court, but Mephibosheth was afraid. His
grandfather King Saul had hunted David for years, trying to kill him, so Mephibosheth expected to be killed. But that's not what David had in mind at all. In fact,
he felt just the opposite.

"Don't be afraid," he told Mephibosheth. "I have brought you here to show
you kindness for your father Jonathan's sake. I will restore to you all the land that
belonged to your grandfather Saul, and you will always be a guest at my royal table
like one of my own sons."

Mephibosheth didn't know what to say. "Who am I that you should be so
kind to me?" he finally asked. But David assured Mephibosheth that he and his
father Jonathan had been good friends, and he wanted to honor that friendship.
Amazing!

What if Mephibosheth had not trusted David? What if he had run away and
hid instead of coming to the royal palace to talk with the king? Then he would
have been afraid the rest of his life. He would have missed out on being honored
at the royal court, and he wouldn't have received the property of his grandfather
Saul. Good move, Mephibosheth.

Nathan

Then Nathan said to David, "You are the man! . . . Why have you despised the commandment of the Lord, to do evil in His sight?" 2 Samuel 12:7, 9

Nathan was a royal scribe, a prophet of the Lord, and one of David's most faithful friends. He was the one who helped David make plans for a new temple to be built in Jerusalem and the one who warned David that his son Adonijah was staging a coup against the throne. But probably the most unpleasant task he ever had to do was condemn King David for his affair with Bathsheba. It went something like this. Nathan the prophet came to the palace one day to tell David a story. "There were two men in a certain town, one rich and the other poor," said Nathan. "The rich man had many sheep and cattle, but the poor man had nothing except one little lamb that was like a daughter to him. Now, a traveler came to the rich man, but the rich man wouldn't take from his own flocks to prepare a meal for the traveler. Instead, he took the lamb that belonged to the poor man, killed it, and gave it to the rich man to eat."

David was very angry when Nathan finished the story. "The man who did this should die!" he growled.

"You are that man!" Nathan replied, looking straight at David. "Why have you done this wicked thing to murder Uriah and take his wife to be your own?"

It wasn't much fun for Nathan to give such a message to the king. What if he had been too afraid to do it? King David had already ordered the execution of Uriah to cover up the scandal. Would one more execution add much to the crimes he had already committed against God and man? But Nathan delivered the message to David anyway. The king repented with bitter tears, as the story goes, and Nathan assured him his sin was forgiven. However, the consequences of David's actions would eventually result in the death of four princes, all of which Nathan would witness. When God asks us to speak for Him, like Nathan, we should do it.

Queen of Sheba

Now when the queen of Sheba heard of the fame of Solomon concerning the name of the LORD, she came to test him with hard questions. 1 Kings 10:1

The Queen of Sheba was beyond curious by the time she got to Jerusalem. And why not? She came all the way from Arabia to see and hear incredible things about a man she felt couldn't possibly exist. There is an old expression that says "Don't believe anything you hear, and only half of what you see." Well, the Queen of Sheba was pleasantly surprised on both counts. Her mouth dropped at the sumptuous palaces and extravagant luxury in every phase of Solomon's royal life. She was astonished at the food on his tables, the proper decorum of his servants, the service of his waiters and their apparel, his cupbearers, and the grand staircase to God's temple. And she tested Solomon with questions on many topics, to see if he was as smart as everyone said he was. She probably asked him about how bees communicate, and what makes flowers smell so good, and what the square root of 132,564 is, and why Jehovah is the one and only true God. And amazingly, Solomon had an answer for every question she asked! The Bible says she was so overwhelmed by all she saw and heard that there was no more spirit in her. "The half wasn't told me," she said, and today we still use that expression when we see something that defies the imagination. "Happy are those who serve you, and blessed is the Lord your God who has set you over Israel," she added. And then she gave Solomon many gifts, as was the custom in those days. The gifts included more than four tons of gold, spices in great quantity, and lots of precious stones.

What if she hadn't come all that way to see Solomon? Travel was difficult in those days. What if she hadn't asked him all those hard questions? Then she would have never met the wisest man who ever lived or been introduced to the God of heaven. How blessed she was!

Sheba

*And there happened to be there a rebel, whose name was Sheba
the son of Bichri, a Benjamite. And he blew a trumpet, and said:
"We have no share in David, nor do we have inheritance in the son of Jesse; every
man to his tents, O Israel!" 2 Samuel 20:1*

Sounds like scary times for King David. As soon as he returned to Jerusalem from his war with Absalom, new problems came up when Sheba, a tribal chieftain, revolted against the crown. It was now clear to David that God's judgments for his shameful sin against Uriah and Bathsheba was coming full circle. "The sword will never depart from your house because you have despised Me by killing Uriah and stealing his wife," God said.

Nathan told him he would pay the price, and the story about Sheba's revolt is proof enough. Sheba's call to arms caused quite a stir in Israel, and soon everyone was defecting to his side. Only the tribe of Judah remained loyal to King David, and he was worried. "We've got to stop this man or he's going to do us more harm than Absalom did," he told Amasa, his newly appointed general. "Take the army now and go after him before he escapes to some fortified city. If he does that, we'll never catch him." But Amasa failed to raise the army, so General Joab took charge. Meanwhile, Sheba had indeed escaped to the fortified city of Abel in northern Israel, and Joab made a beeline for that city too. When he got there, Joab's army laid siege to the city and began to batter down the walls. However, a wise woman inside made a deal with Joab. "If you'll turn Sheba over to us, we'll go away," Joab told her. Sheba's end was a violent one, because the woman killed him and threw his head over the wall.

Wow! That's quite a story! What if Sheba hadn't revolted against David? He knew what had happened to Prince Absalom when he tried such a thing. If he had listened to God's still small voice, he would have remained loyal to the king and spared thousands of men from dying in battle.

Shimei

And as David and his men went along the road, Shimei went along
the hillside opposite him and cursed as he went, threw stones at him
and kicked up dust. 2 Samuel 16:13

Shimei was a despicable man during the days of David. He was from the tribe of Benjamin and a relative of King Saul. When David had to flee Jerusalem because Prince Absalom was marching on the capital city, he passed the city of Bahurim on his way to the Jordan River. Guess who came out to curse and throw rocks at him? That's right, Shimei. Prior to this he gave the king lip service, because he felt he had to. But when David was on the run, escaping for his life, Shimei showed his true colors. "Get out of town, you bloodthirsty man!" he shouted. "The Lord is punishing you because you stole the kingdom from Saul, and now your son Absalom is giving you your just rewards." Everyone was horrified that Shimei would talk this way to King David! Abishai, one of "David's mighty men," offered to have him executed. "Why should this dead dog curse my lord the king?" he said. "Please, let me go over and take off his head!" (2 Samuel 16:9) Amazingly, David declined his offer.

What if Shimei had been kind to King David instead of mocking him? What if he had helped him instead of cussing him out? Well, one thing is sure, he would have lived longer. Years later, when Solomon became king, he brought Shimei in and gave him the business. "I can't trust a man like you after the way you treated my father," he said. "Stay in Jerusalem where I can keep an eye on you, or I'll have you executed." Shimei agreed, but he broke the agreement three years later when he went looking for two slaves that had escaped. And, true to the customs of the day, Solomon kept his part of the bargain too. Such was the end of a man who cared more about himself than anyone else.

Ahaz

But Ahaz said, "I will not ask, nor will I test the LORD!" Isaiah 7:12

Wow! That's a brazen thing to say! Who was Ahaz, and what was his problem? He was king of Judah in the days of Isaiah. The prophet had come to encourage Ahaz because Syria and Israel were going to attack him from the north. "Don't lose any sleep over this," Isaiah said. "Those two countries are toast and will soon be weaker than weak. God can take care of them. You don't believe it? Why not ask Him for a sign?"

But Ahaz stubbornly ignored the prophet's advice because he already had a plan. "I'll just ask Assyria for help," he said, and he promptly sent King Tigleth-Pileser all the gold and silver to be found in Jerusalem. Tigleth-Pileser kept his part of the bargain. He whipped Israel and Syria in a battle. Ahaz then went up to meet the Assyrian king to pay him homage while he was in Damascus. In other words, he drooled all over him. Even worse, he brought home blueprints for a pagan altar like the ones they used in Assyria. But wait, there's more. Where do you think Ahaz set up the altar? That's right, in the temple of God. And he removed the sacred altar used for burnt offerings to God. This was the ultimate slap in God's face. How ungrateful! The kingdom of Judah was founded on the worship of God the Creator, but Ahaz chose to worship idols of wood and stone. The sacred lamb sacrifices that represented Jesus could not be offered on Ahaz's pagan altar, but he set it up anyway.

What more could God have done to help Ahaz? It's amazing that Ahaz didn't take God's offer of help, but what if he had? Well, he would have had God's protection. He would have saved himself a bunch of money. He would have avoided desecrating God's holy sanctuary, and history would remember him as a king who took God at His word. After all, God is the One doing all the work. All we have to do is wait for the answer.

Ahaziah of Israel

Now Ahaziah fell through the lattice of his upper room in Samaria, and was injured; so he sent messengers and said to them, "Go, inquire of Baal-Zebub, the god of Ekron, whether I shall recover from this injury." 2 Kings 1:2

Ahaziah missed the boat on two counts. First, he didn't watch where he was standing (he probably had one too many glasses of wine). Second, he wasn't smart enough to ask the God of heaven for healing. Elijah was still a prophet in Israel at the time, so there would have been no shortage of miracle power available. But that's how things go when we don't make God first in our lives. We don't see the forest for the trees. One disaster leads to another, and we end up without hope or healing.

Here are the details. Ahaziah, son of Ahab, was king of Israel at the time, and he had a bad fall. The Bible says he fell through a lattice wall in an upper chamber of his palace and hurt himself quite badly. We don't know how far he fell, but it was far enough for him to wonder if he would even recover. Internal injuries, no doubt. In keeping with the pagan habits of his mother, Jezebel, and his father, Ahab, Ahaziah sent messengers to the city of Ekron. The mission? To consult Baal-Zebub, the god of flies, to see what Ahaziah's prognosis was. It all looked good on paper until the messengers ran into Elijah, whom God had sent to intercept them with a message of His own. "Are you telling me there is no God in Israel that you must consult a heathen god who can't see or hear or speak?" Elijah said. And then came the bad part. "For your insolence and lack of faith, you will not come down off your deathbed, and there you will die!"

Wow! What a way to go! And what if King Ahaziah had asked God for help? Surely the Lord would have helped him if he had stepped out in faith. Many people during that era gave God a chance. Unfortunately, Ahaziah wasn't one of them.

Amaziah

Therefore the anger of the Lord was aroused against Amaziah, and He sent him a prophet who said to him, "Why have you sought the gods of the people, which could not rescue their own people from your hand?" 2 Chronicles 25:15, 16

This is another one of those stories that started out so well but ended very badly. Why? Because King Amaziah of Judah took God's advice in the early days of his reign but then turned to the wretched habit of worshiping idols later on. Foolish, foolish man! Didn't he see what had happened to his father Joash when he turned away from God? And his grandfather?

So, what went right for him, and what went wrong? Well, for starters he decided to fight the Edomites to the south and hired a hundred thousand mercenaries from Israel to help him. He paid one hundred talents of silver for their services, but a man of God told him not to bring the Israelite warriors along. "They aren't godly men, and the Lord can't protect them in battle," the man said. So Amaziah went to battle without the hired mercenaries and soundly defeated the Edomites, but he brought back their pagan idols as trophies of war. Big mistake! He put the idols in Jerusalem, offered sacrifices and incense to them, and worshiped them! A prophet of God came by to chastise Amaziah for this, but the king threatened to kill him for it. Then Amaziah got it into his head that he needed to have a war with Israel too. He was badly defeated when he tried to pull it off. And it gets worse. After the battle, King Jehoash of Israel came to Jerusalem to steal all the treasures, take some hostages, and break a big hole in the city wall.

So, what could King Amaziah have done differently? Well, we know of at least two times God gave him advice. He should have humbly taken that advice, but when he threatened the Lord's messenger, things went from bad to worse. It's no wonder Amaziah's own people conspired against him later and assassinated him for all the trouble he brought them.

Rehoboam

He spoke to them according to the advice of the young men, saying, "My father made your yoke heavy, but I will add to your yoke; my father chastised you with whips, but I will chastise you with scourges!" 1 Kings 12:14

Rehoboam was a foolish young man. His father's advisors told him not to do it, but he ignored them. Instead, he listened to the advice of his young friends in the palace. "I'm raising the taxes!" he said to the tribal elders who gathered at Shechem for his inauguration as king. "I know you don't like the idea, but I'm going to do it anyway. If you think your yoke was heavy under my father, I'll make his policies look like Sesame Street."

That was the last straw, and what came next totally surprised Rehoboam, although it shouldn't have. The tribal elders shook their fists at him. "What share have we in the house of David?" they shouted. "We have no inheritance with the son of Jesse. You can have your throne, King Rehoboam, and we'll have ours! We're out of here!"

King Rehoboam knew he had really ticked them off now, and he sent a tax representative to try and smooth things out, but it was too late. It didn't work. The elders were so upset that they stoned the tax rep, and he died. The king knew things were getting out of hand fast, and he hopped onto his chariot to make a quick getaway. Off he raced to Jerusalem, and that was the end of the united kingdom of Israel. From that day forward, there were two kingdoms: Judah in the south, and Israel in the north.

What if Rehoboam hadn't been so unreasonable? What if he had listened to his father's seasoned advisors instead of his young cronies? Then he would have avoided a kingdom breakup. He would have kept twelve tribes instead of two. He would have collected way more taxes in the long run. That's a no-brainer. Too bad he didn't think that one through.

MAY 24

Solomon's Wives

> But King Solomon loved many foreign women, as well as the daughter of Pharaoh: women of the Moabites, Ammonites, Edomites, Sidonians, and Hittites. . . . And he had seven hundred wives, princesses, and three hundred concubines; and his wives turned away his heart. 1 Kings 11:1, 3

One of the best things that can happen to a man is to find a good wife. And a bad wife? Solomon would know all about that, because he had too many of them. According to the Bible he had nine hundred and ninety-nine too many. That's a lot of wives, and it must have been some kind of a record in his day!

Many of them he married to build good political relations with foreign governments. Many he married for their beauty, no doubt. And we can be sure that sometimes he married them simply because he always got what he wanted. He was king and in the habit of collecting wives.

But the prognosis for Solomon wasn't good. Unfortunately, when he was old, many of those wives turned his heart away from God. They had been worshipers of pagan gods, and now they influenced Solomon to worship them too. He built special places of worship where they could burn incense to Ashtoreth, the goddess of the Sidonians, and Chemosh, god of the Moabites. But Molech, god of the Ammonites, was maybe the worst pagan god of all, because worshipers of this god were sometimes required to offer their children as sacrifices.

Too bad Solomon didn't get married just once and be done with it. We don't really know who his first wife was, but if she was the Shulamite girl mentioned in his book Song of Solomon, he really messed up! The question remains. What if he hadn't married multiple wives? He would have been much happier, and, of course, so would they. He would have remained true to God and not led Israel to worship all their idols. And his first wife? She would have remained the one-and-only, best-loved wife of the wisest, richest, most famous king in Israel's history. Now that's romantic!

Two Mothers and Solomon

Then the woman whose son was living spoke to the king, for she yearned with compassion for her son; and she said, "O my lord, give her the living child, and by no means kill him!" But the other said, "Let him be neither mine nor yours, but divide him." 1 Kings 3:26

Can you believe this story? Two women who were living in the same house both had babies. Both were in the habit of sleeping in the same bed with their babies. One of the mothers accidently smothered her child during the night, and she tried to switch her dead baby with her friend's live one. Naturally, both claimed the live child.

The case was considered impossible to solve. Both women were prostitutes with questionable character, and the authorities felt the word of neither could be trusted. In the end, the case was brought to King Solomon, and to everyone's surprise he came through with flying colors. How? By making a decision that revealed the real emotions of each woman on trial. Today we would do a DNA test, but Solomon didn't have access to such technology in those days. He used good, old-fashioned logic and clever observations, and he totally blew the lid off the case. Granted, he wouldn't be considered the most ethical in his methods today, and people would be up in arms over the way he used the live baby as a pawn to help reveal who the real mother was. "Bring me a sword," he said as he reached for the baby. "Divide the living child in two, then give half to one, and half to the other."

Fortunately, the story has a good ending. The real mother protested and offered to give her baby to the other woman. Why? Because she loved the child and wished him every chance for survival. And the counterfeit mother? She said, "Nah! Go ahead and divide the baby!" What a callous, uncouth woman! What if she hadn't said, "Divide the baby"? Would it have mattered? No! Solomon had already analyzed the two women. He already knew who the real mother was. His charade was for everyone else in the court, so they would also know the truth.

Woman of Bahurim

Then the woman took and spread a covering over the well's mouth,
and spread ground grain on it; and the thing was not known. And when Absalom's
servants came to the woman at the house, they said,
"Where are Ahimaaz and Jonathan?" So the woman said to them,
"They have gone over the water brook." 2 Samuel 17:19, 20

A woman in the small town of Bahurim is remembered for the help she gave two boys who went on a secret mission for King David. The Bible doesn't identify her family name, but because of her quick thinking she saved the day for her king. Prince Absalom had revolted against the throne and successfully invaded Jerusalem without even shooting an arrow. Two boys named Jonathan and Ahimaaz were on the run with a message, making fast tracks for the Jordan River, where King David and his supporters were camping out.

Unfortunately, Jonathan and Ahimaaz were spotted by a spy, and that's when the real danger started. But evidently the boys knew the woman in Bahurim, or else God led them to her miraculously. Absalom's patrols were hot on their trail, and in the nick of time she hid the boys in a well. To further disguise their hideout, she threw a tarpaulin over the opening to the well and spread grain on it to dry. And it's a good thing she did, because the soldiers arrived just then and asked where the boys were. Fortunately, the woman was able to send the patrols on their way, giving the boys a chance to escape on another route.

What if the woman hadn't helped the boys? What if she had said, "I can't afford to take the risk"? Then the boys would have had to find another place to hide. Maybe they would have been late getting the info to David about Absalom's war strategies. In that case, the king would have been in danger. Sometimes we can control such factors, but sometimes we can't, and that's where faith in God enters the picture.

Woman of Tekoa

And Joab sent to Tekoa and brought from there a wise woman,
and said to her, "Please pretend to be a mourner, and put on mourning apparel; do
not anoint yourself with oil, but act like a woman
who has been mourning a long time for the dead." 2 Samuel 14:2

We don't even know her name. She lived in the town of Tekoa, south of Bethlehem, and was famous especially for her wisdom. But we know her best for the part she played in helping Joab bring Prince Absalom home to Jerusalem. Joab could see that David wasn't the same with Absalom in exile, and he decided he was going to bring the young man home at all costs.

He arranged to have the woman from Tekoa come see King David to make a petition, and it worked. David felt sorry for her. She came dressed in mourner's clothes, claimed to be a widow, and told a fabricated story. One of her sons had killed the other, and now the whole family wanted to have the murderer executed. "Please spare him!" she begged the king as she bowed her face to the floor. "Don't let them take my only son! My husband's name will die out without an heir!"

David assured her that no such thing would happen, and then, to his surprise, she turned the story on him. Why was he not bringing his own heir home, she asked. Of course, David could see now that he had been tricked, and he suspected his nephew General Joab was in on the caper. And so he allowed Absalom to return to Jerusalem, and we all know how that turned out.

The question remains, What if the woman of Tekoa had not helped Joab bring Absalom home to Jerusalem? Would Absalom have been able to sit in the gates and lie to the people about King David? Probably not. Would he have gotten a foothold in the hearts of all Israel? Not likely, and that means he would have never been able to stage his coup. Most important, thousands of men would have lived instead of dying in battle to help this selfish son of David.

Zadok

Then Zadok the priest took a horn of oil from the tabernacle
and anointed Solomon. And they blew the horn, and all the people said,
"Long live King Solomon!" 1 Kings 1:39

To be a priest in the nation of Israel was a big deal in the old days, and not just anyone could do it. Only men from the tribe of Levi were allowed to serve in that office, and only one could be the high priest. Well, Zadok qualified for the job on two counts. He was a Levite and next in line to be the high priest. But it didn't come about by accident.

When Prince Absalom tried to steal the throne from his father, many people remained loyal supporters of David, and Zadok was one of them. They fled Jerusalem with David to avoid bloodshed, and all the priests went too. But King David advised Zadok to stay in Jerusalem so he could take care of the sanctuary services as usual. While he was there he could keep an eye on Absalom and send his son Ahimaaz to David with messages about what exactly was happening in Jerusalem. That's exactly what Zadok did, and it saved David's life.

And then a few years later, when Prince Adonijah also tried to steal the throne, Zadok proved to be a loyal friend again. Many were supporting Adonijah in his attempt to become king, including Abiathar, the high priest, but not Zadok. When Adonijah invited everyone to a feast to proclaim himself king, Zadok and Nathan the prophet sprang into action. They advised David to crown Solomon king before the day was done, and that's exactly what he did.

What if Zadok hadn't remained loyal to David? Twice he could have supported the sons of David, but he did the right thing. He remained loyal to the Lord's anointed and helped put Solomon on the throne instead. And God blessed him for it, because that day David made him high priest of Israel instead of Abiathar, who was not loyal to the crown. Zadok had proved himself to be faithful, brave, and loyal to the Lord's anointed, and God blessed him for it.

Ziba

*So the king said to Ziba, "Here, all that belongs to Mephibosheth is yours."
And Ziba said, "I humbly bow before you, that I may find favor in your sight,
my lord, O king!" 2 Samuel 16:4*

Ziba was a steward of King Saul's property for years, and after Saul's death, he served Mephibosheth, Jonathan's crippled son. This was by order of King David in honor of Jonathan, his best friend who had also died in battle against the Philistines. In the long run, Ziba served no one but himself. Whatever he could do to get ahead, he did. That's the kind of man he was. Sneaky, underhanded, and greedy, he soon revealed his true colors. When David was fleeing Jerusalem at the time of Absalom's coup, Ziba met him on the road outside the city to show his support. He had with him two saddled donkeys loaded with lots of food for David. But the story now takes a strange twist. David asked where Mephibosheth was, and Ziba told him a big fat lie. "He's in Jerusalem, hoping the kingdom of Israel will be restored to him as the only surviving heir of Jonathan," Ziba said. That was a ludicrous idea! Absalom wanted the throne for himself. Why would he give it to Mephibosheth?

David was afraid for his life. He was under a lot of stress and probably not thinking clearly. "OK then," he said to Ziba, "I'll give you all Mephibosheth's property." That must have made Ziba happy. Things were turning out much better than he could have hoped. But he got a shock a few weeks later when David came back to Jerusalem and met both Ziba and Mephibosheth. The truth then came out, but David had given his word as king and decided to split the property evenly between them.

What if Ziba had been kind to Mephibosheth and hadn't lied to the king? Then he would have had a clear conscience the rest of his life, instead of being a thief. As it was, Mephibosheth continued to live in the royal palace. And Ziba? We hear nothing more about him, but we always remember him as a conniving, sniveling man who had to steal to be happy.

Two Cannibal Mothers

Then the king said to her, "What is troubling you?" And she answered,
"This woman said to me, 'Give your son, that we may eat him today,
and we will eat my son tomorrow.' So we boiled my son, and ate him.
And I said to her on the next day, 'Give your son, that we may eat him';
but she has hidden her son." 2 Kings 6:28, 29

Can you imagine two women having a conversation like this any day of the week? "Let's flip a coin. Heads, we eat your son today. Tails, we eat mine." Then it gets worse—when the conversation was over, they actually went through with the wager. These people were desperate. The Syrians had laid siege to Samaria and had been at it for so long now, there was nothing more to eat in the city. They had eaten all the sheep and goats, cattle and oxen, donkeys and camels, and even the cats and rats (yuck!). And when there was nothing more to eat, they turned on each other. Unfortunately, they picked the defenseless ones to eat first, like babies, and this is where our story line picks up. The king was out making his daily rounds on the city wall, when the woman in our Scripture verse begged him for help. Not surprisingly, he was horrified to hear her story. *How could a mother eat her own son,* we can imagine him thinking! But the problem wasn't just with the two women, or even the king! It was everyone's problem in Samaria! They had all rejected God, and He was the only One who could have saved them.

What would have happened if they had called on Jehovah instead of their foolish idols of wood and stone? Then God would have helped them, and they wouldn't have thought about eating their kids. How do we know that? Exhibit A: Elisha the miracle worker was right there among them in the city of Samaria. Exhibit B: A few days later, God graciously came through for them. The siege and famine actually ended when the Syrians flew the coop and headed for home. Too bad the women didn't call on God sooner.

Four Lepers at Samaria

Then they said to one another, "We are not doing right.
This day is a day of good news, and we remain silent. If we wait until morning light,
some punishment will come upon us. Now therefore, come, let us go and tell the
king's household." 2 Kings 7:9

Once upon a time, four lepers lived outside the walls of Samaria. Usually they begged for food from people who passed through the city gates, but things had changed now. Times were desperate! The Syrians had surrounded Samaria and laid siege to it, and now a famine was raging inside the city. There was no food for anyone to eat, not even the lepers.

"We're all going to starve," the lepers told each other. "We might as well go to the Syrian camp and beg for food. The worst they can do is kill us, and we're going to starve out here anyway." The sun had just set as they ventured near the camp, and to their shock they found it empty. Not a soldier was in sight. The Syrians had completely disappeared. Soon the lepers were eating good food around the camp-fire and collecting all kinds of treasures for themselves. It's not surprising that they soon began to feel guilty. "How can we enjoy all this food when we know our fellow Israelites are starving inside the city?" they asked one another. And so they went back to the gates of Samaria to tell the sentries of their amazing discovery. The people inside the city didn't believe them at first, but by morning light they realized it was true. Evidently God had spooked the Syrians by sending the sound of rumbling chariot armies on the evening air, and the enemy soldiers had fled. Behind them they left a trail of weapons and treasure and food.

And what if the lepers hadn't shared such good news with the city of Samaria? Clearly the people would have gone hungry, and it's likely many would have died before they discovered the truth. That's the way it is with the good news of salvation. To not share such news is a crime for the ages.

JUNE 1

Jehosheba

But Jehosheba, the daughter of King Joram, sister of Ahaziah,
took Joash the son of Ahaziah, and stole him away from among the king's sons
who were being murdered; and they hid him and his nurse in the bedroom, from
Athaliah, so that he was not killed. 2 Kings 11:2

She was a brave woman who did something no one else thought of at the time. Word arrived that King Ahaziah had been assassinated, and the wicked Queen Athaliah was in charge now. What would happen next? No one knew, but Jehosheba had a pretty good idea. She had seen it all before when Athaliah's husband, King Jehoram, came to the throne and executed all her uncles and cousins. Let's try to keep this straight. Jehosheba was the daughter of King Jehoram and sister to King Ahaziah, who had just died. That would make Queen Athaliah the wicked stepmother. It sounds like something you'd see in a fairy tale—or a nightmare.

Total pandemonium broke loose that morning when Athaliah and her bodyguard crashed the royal nursery. The mission? To kill all the grandsons and nephews. Everyone went to pieces with all the children screaming and running around. Everyone, that is, except Jehosheba. She couldn't save all the children, but she could save little Joash, her nephew, who was just a baby at the time. Quick as a wink, she ran away with him and hid. How she managed to escape, we don't know, but she ended up in the temple, where her husband, Jehoiada, was the high priest. And that's where little Joash lived for the next six years, hiding out—the secret heir to the throne. For a while Jehosheba probably didn't even let him go outside and play for fear someone might recognize him.

What if she hadn't rescued this little boy of destiny? What would have been the outcome of our story? We don't know, but God would have probably found another way to save him. He has a thousand ways to defeat Satan, you know. As it was, she lived to see the little boy grow and finally take the throne at the ripe old age of seven. Good work, Jehosheba.

Jehu

So the watchman reported, saying, "He went up to them and is not coming back;
and the driving is like the driving of Jehu the son of Nimshi, for he drives furiously!"
2 Kings 9:20

Jehu had quite a reputation as a crazy charioteer. We don't know a lot about his background, but his mission was to get rid of Baal worship in Israel—and everybody who had anything to do with it. For starters, he hopped in his chariot and headed for Jezreel, where Queen Jezebel lived—the biggest fan of Baal worship in Israel. "Who is on my side?" he asked as he drove up to the royal palace. Surprisingly, Jezebel's chamberlains threw her out the window and she fell three stories to the ground. The fall killed her, of course, and the wild dogs ate her for supper. Next, Jehu went to find Joram, the king of Israel, and Ahaziah, king of Judah, both Baal worshipers. He chased them in his chariot and killed them, then he made a circuit through all the cities of Israel in search of the other seventy sons of Ahab and killed them too. And finally, he called all the priests and prophets of Baal and invited them to a big feast in the temple of Baal. While they were there, he and his men went in and killed every last one of them. What a day of judgment for the worshipers of Baal! It was justice for all the babies that had been killed in the fertility rites of Baal worship. And it was a day of reckoning for everyone who had been duped by the priests of Baal. Amazingly, these judgments had all been predicted years before by Elijah the prophet.

What if Jehu had not executed these pagan worshipers of Baal? What if he had allowed them to continue their evil fertility rites in the name of religion with female and male prostitutes? Then the culture in Israel would have deteriorated much faster, and Israel would have been destroyed by enemy nations much sooner. As it was, Jehu's actions postponed judgment day for a few years and gave Israel a chance to learn about the God of heaven under the ministry of the prophet Elisha.

JUNE 3

Joash of Judah

Joash became king, and he reigned in Jerusalem forty years. . . .
Joash did what was right in the eyes of the LORD all the years
Jehoiada the priest instructed him. 2 Kings 12:1, 2, NIV

Joash was just seven years old when he was put on the throne of Judah. Now, why did people do things like that in the old days? I mean, how much good can a young boy do even if he is king? Most seven-year-old kids just want to ride bikes, play games, and eat.

In those days being king was very important, even if you were just a boy. And it could be very dangerous, especially if your grandmother was Athaliah the queen. It seems she really hated kids, because one day she went on a killing spree and killed all her grandkids—except Joash, who was a baby at the time. He was whisked away by Jehosheba and hidden in one of the secret chambers of the temple in Jerusalem. Six years later, the high priest Jehoiada put him on the throne. Joash loved God during those early years and even repaired the temple. As long as Jehoiada was alive, things went well for Joash. But when the old priest died, that was the end of it. For some reason Joash stopped worshiping God and bowed to pagan idols instead. And when Jehoiada's son Zachariah criticized him for it, Joash ordered him to be stoned to death. Wow! That's quite a switch. But evil always comes with a price. When Joash was not yet fifty, he was assassinated by two of his courtiers while he was in bed.

What if he had remained faithful to God? It would have been a nice way to show gratitude to Jehoiada and Jehosheba for all the help they had given him. He could have changed the course of history and possibly ruled longer than any king before or after. As it was, he led many people down the road to idol worship and all the nasty stuff that goes with it. He escaped death from his enemies when he was just a baby, only to die at their hands as a grown-up. Why? Because he forgot how much he owed to God, and when he did that, it left him no better than a sitting duck.

Micaiah

Jehoshaphat said, "Is there not still a prophet of the LORD here, that we may inquire of Him?" So the king of Israel said to Jehoshaphat, "There is still one man, Micaiah the son of Imlah, by whom we may inquire of the LORD; but I hate him, because he does not prophesy good concerning me." 1 Kings 22:7, 8

Have you ever felt all alone in a crowd, with no one on your side? The prophet Micaiah knew that feeling, and it wasn't much fun. King Ahab was planning to make war against the Syrians and wanted King Jehoshaphat from Judah to join with him in battle. Jehoshaphat was willing, but he wanted to hear God's advice on the plan. And so King Ahab called out several prophets, and they all said, "Go, for God will give you victory!" One of them, named Zedekiah, had a helmet with horns on it, and he was especially dramatic. "With these horns God will defeat the enemy and drive them out of Israel!" he shouted. For some reason, Jehoshaphat was a bit suspicious of these prophets and their predictions. Maybe he already knew their reputation, or maybe God impressed him that they were not godly men. "That's nice," we can hear him saying politely, "but is there at least one other prophet of the Lord that we might inquire of him?"

"There is one other, but I don't like him," King Ahab said. "He never makes nice predictions about me." Jehoshaphat wanted to hear what he had to say anyway. And Ahab was right. Micaiah did make a bad prediction about him and the coming battle. "I saw all Israel scattered like sheep on the hills!" he said, and Zedekiah, the false prophet, slapped him on the face for it. Micaiah was thrown in prison for his unpopular prediction, but the prophecy came true. When they went to fight the next day, the army was scattered and they lost the battle. Wow! That's really sad!

What if the two kings had listened to Micaiah? Wouldn't it have saved them a whole lot of trouble? Absolutely! You see, Ahab ended up dying in the battle, and Jehoshaphat almost died too. That's what you get when you don't listen to God's counsel.

The Rabshakeh

"Make peace with me and come out to me. Then each of you will eat fruit from your
own vine and fig tree and drink water from your own cistern,
until I come and take you to a land like your own—a land of grain and new wine, a
land of bread and vineyards, a land of olive trees and honey.
Choose life and not death!" 2 Kings 18:31, 32, NIV

This sounds like an offer you wouldn't want to refuse, doesn't it? But when someone tells you something that seems too good to be true, it probably is. That's what Sennacherib's field officer (the Rabshakeh) told the people of Jerusalem when the Assyrian army laid siege to their city. The Assyrians had conquered forty-six cities of Judah, and Jerusalem was the only remaining one in Palestine that hadn't surrendered or fallen.

The Rabshakeh stood at the city gates and called for Hezekiah to come talk to him, but the king refused. Instead, he sent out three of his own officers to do the honors: his palace administrator, field secretary, and scribe. They said very little to the Rabshakeh but took a message back to Hezekiah. "Surrender or die!" That was pretty much it, and it scared Hezekiah to pieces. But still he wouldn't answer the Rabshakeh, because Isaiah the prophet had advised him against it. After several days of this kind of thing going on, the Assyrian Rabshakeh tried one of the oldest tricks in the book. He began speaking to the common people in Hebrew, the language of Judah. What they were doing on the wall looking down at the Rabshakeh, we don't know, but they shouldn't have been there because he tried to tempt them with all kinds of things. Would he have delivered all the goodies he had promised? Not likely. It was just an old trick.

What if the Rabshakeh had left Jerusalem alone? What if he had decided that forty-six cities was enough, and left for home? Well, then, God's people would have been free again. And, the Rabshakeh? He probably died when God destroyed 185,000 Assyrian soldiers a few nights later. It didn't have to be.

Sennacherib

"Thus says Sennacherib king of Assyria: 'In what do you trust, that you remain under siege in Jerusalem? Does not Hezekiah persuade you to give yourselves over to die by famine and by thirst, saying, "The LORD our God will deliver us from the hand of the king of Assyria"?' " 2 Chronicles 32:10, 11

Sennacherib is a cool-sounding name, one that you might use for your pet horse, or dog, or maybe even an iguana. But the Sennacherib that Bible readers know about was an Assyrian king long, long ago. He was famous for many things, among them the building of a thirty-mile aqueduct, the construction of a thousand-foot stone bridge across the Gomer River, and his total destruction of Babylon by flooding the city using the Euphrates River.

Then there's the story about when he laid siege to Jerusalem, and said he had Hezekiah locked up like a bird in a cage. "Don't kid yourselves!" his messengers told the people standing along the walls of Jerusalem. "You belong to Sennacherib now, and no God of yours is going to deliver you from his hand!" But, of course, that is exactly what happened. Because Hezekiah and the people of Jerusalem prayed and believed God's promises, the Lord sent an angel to administer justice. The next morning, 185,000 Assyrian soldiers lay dead across the landscape around Jerusalem. How did that happen? One version of the story says they may have died from bubonic plague.

What if Sennacherib had decided he wanted to be nice and not be the bully of the Middle East? Well, then, he would have been blessed by God and lived a long and prosperous life. But, of course, that's not what happened at all. Because he was such a scoundrel and cared for nothing but his own legacy, his two sons, Adrammelech and Sharezer, assassinated him. And so in the end, the king of Assyria became like everyone else. He had power over everything in his kingdom except those who wanted to see him dead. And his own sons at that.

JUNE 7

Shishak

In the fifth year of King Rehoboam . . . Shishak king of Egypt came up against Jerusalem. And he took away the treasures of the house of the LORD and the treasures of the king's house; he took away everything. He also took away all the gold shields which Solomon had made. 1 Kings 14:25, 26

King Solomon was the most famous king in Palestine's history, but within five years of his death his son, Rehoboam, was already losing face in the international community. Shishak, who was pharaoh of Egypt at the time, was one of the first to take advantage of the situation. He came up to Jerusalem and made Rehoboam pay tribute to avoid war. This was a direct fulfillment of prophecy against King Solomon for all the temples and shrines he had built to satisfy his wives in their worship of pagan idols. Jeroboam, one of Solomon's government officers, had been in political exile in Egypt and, while there, had probably told Shishak about all the treasures in Jerusalem. The Bible says when Pharaoh showed up, he took everything of value: five hundred golden shields on the walls of the king's armory and palace; all the gold and silver in the royal treasury; and many of the sacred treasures in Solomon's magnificent temple. Probably the only thing left behind was the ark of God's covenant. That must have been hard for the people in Jerusalem! They had followed Solomon's example in worshiping pagan idols, and now God's protecting hand had been removed.

But what if Shishak had arrived in Jerusalem to find Rehoboam and his court praying for help in this time of crisis? In that case God might have allowed Shishak to take the shields of gold but perhaps asked him to spare the temple treasures. Or maybe Shishak would have taken nothing at all. But it's all a moot point. Shishak found no one calling on God, and as he marched out of Jerusalem it was clear the glory days of David and Solomon were in the rearview mirror.

Baruch

And the king commanded Jerahmeel the king's son, Seraiah the son of Azriel, and Shelemiah the son of Abdeel, to seize Baruch the scribe and Jeremiah the prophet, but the LORD hid them. Jeremiah 36:26

Baruch was Jeremiah's official scribe. When the prophet needed to dictate messages he had received from God, who helped him by writing it all out on parchment scrolls? Baruch. When King Jehoiakim cut up Jeremiah's scroll, threw it into the fire, and went looking for the prophet, who had to go into hiding? Jeremiah and Baruch. When it seemed there was no one Jeremiah could depend on, Baruch was there, no doubt the prophet's most faithful friend. When Jeremiah bought a piece of property in the town of Anathoth during the siege of Jerusalem, he let Baruch keep the deed for him. And together they did several writing projects. Experts tell us the two of them probably wrote the books of First and Second Kings.

But who was Baruch exactly? He was a man called by God to be a helper of one of Judah's last prophets, a man who had very few friends. Jewish tradition tells us Baruch came from an important family but was willing to throw in his lot with Jeremiah. After Jerusalem fell and rebels murdered Gedaliah, the governor of Judah, Jeremiah was forced to go to Egypt—and Baruch went with him. The man's life story ends in Egypt, because from that point forward we read no more about him.

What if Baruch had decided to abandon Jeremiah as everyone else did? He would have been safe from the king, no doubt, and wouldn't have had to go into hiding. And he could have probably avoided Egypt too. However, Jeremiah would have had to stand alone when his messages were rejected and when he was finally put in prison. Thanks to his devotion to God and the prophet, Baruch did the right thing. Today we remember him as the faithful scribe who stayed with the famous prophet to the bitter end.

JUNE 9

Ebed-Melech

Then Ebed-Melech the Ethiopian said to Jeremiah,
"Please put these old clothes and rags under your armpits, under the ropes." . . .
So they pulled Jeremiah up with ropes and lifted him out of the dungeon. And
Jeremiah remained in the court of the prison. Jeremiah 38:12, 13

Who was this man who seemed to come out of nowhere? And how was it that he managed to get Jeremiah some help when everyone else was scared to death of the king? It happened like this. Jeremiah had been thrown into prison by the king's courtiers for the second time. King Zedekiah was weaker than his princes and advisors, and he was afraid to do the right thing.

However, Ebed-Melech, who worked in the king's house, was not afraid to do the right thing. When he heard Jeremiah had been thrown in a dungeon full of mud, he went to the king. "We've got to get him out of there!" Ebed-Melech begged. "He'll die from hunger in that place."

The king was afraid to stand up to his princes, but he was glad someone had the courage to do what he should have done all along. So the king gave Ebed-Melech permission to get Jeremiah up out of the dungeon. However, Ebed-Melech knew it would be painful for the prophet if he pulled him out of the pit with ropes. So he took some old rags and told Jeremiah to put them on the ropes under his armpits. It was a thoughtful act of kindness, and we can be sure Jeremiah appreciated it.

What if Ebed-Melech hadn't been so thoughtful? What if he had been too afraid to help and said, "Let someone else do it"? Then Jeremiah would have suffered for days and weeks, and maybe even died. God might have provided another way for Jeremiah to be rescued, but Ebed-Melech would not have received the blessing of helping the famous prophet himself. What an example of kindness for all of us!

Hilkiah

Then Hilkiah the high priest said to Shaphan the scribe, "I have found the
Book of the Law in the house of the LORD."
And Hilkiah gave the book to Shaphan, and he read it. 2 Kings 22:8

Wow! What a surprise! Finding an ancient copy of the Scriptures that had been lost for decades would really be exciting. The copy Hilkiah discovered was very old, maybe one of only a few in existence. No one had seen it in years, and many must have thought it no longer existed.

King Josiah was on pace to rid Judah of evil, and giving Solomon's temple a makeover was part of it. That's why he sent Hilkiah the high priest and his crew into the temple—to clean and repair it in preparation for celebrating the up-coming Passover feast. All kinds of repairmen were hired: carpenters, builders, metalsmiths, and stonemasons. While the men were at work, someone discovered scrolls in one of the storerooms among the dust and clutter. Amazingly, God had preserved the scrolls that were hidden all those years, and it's a good thing He did. If Josiah's grandfather, Manasseh, had known they were there he would have destroyed them.

Hilkiah and his priests read the scrolls, and what they found shocked them. In great fear they showed the scrolls to Shaphan the royal scribe, and he in turn showed them to King Josiah. Unfortunately, the scrolls did not have good news for the king. When Shaphan read the passage in Deuteronomy 28 that lists the curses for disobedience to God's Law, King Josiah was horrified and ashamed. It was clear to him that judgment would come in punishment for Judah's great wickedness.

And what if Hilkiah and the priests had not done a good cleanup job? What if Hilkiah had decided not to read through the scrolls, and what if he hadn't taken them to Shaphan the scribe? Then, of course, Josiah would not have known about the bad days that were coming to Judah, and he wouldn't have been able to lead a revival to rebuild the nation. Good job, Hilkiah.

Jedidah

She speaks with wisdom, and faithful instruction is on her tongue. She watches over the affairs of her household and does not eat the bread of idleness. Her children arise and call her blessed. Proverbs 31:26–28, NIV

Jedidah was the coolest of moms—not only because she was living in the royal household of Judah, but also because she did a good job of raising her son to love God. Josiah became one of the most famous kings in Hebrew history, a direct ancestor of Jesus Himself, who came fifteen generations later, and it all started when he was a boy, just eight years old. What would it be like to have your son be crowned king at that age? Pretty scary, and yet pretty neat. Imagine it! The most powerful person in the country, and he's your son!

In those days kings usually got the job because of who their father was. Josiah's father was Amon, Jedidah's husband, and as a king he was a dud, lasting only two years. How so? Well, there was a palace revolution and his own servants assassinated him. That's where Jedidah and Josiah came in. We can be sure she became an advisor for the boy king, helping him behave like every king should; and she did a good job. The Bible says he didn't turn to the right hand or to the left. In other words, he did what was right in the eyes of the Lord and walked in all the ways of his father David. That's a pretty strong testimony for Jedidah and her son! God was glorified because she taught her son to put Him first, and He honored her and Josiah for it.

But what if Jedidah had said, "I can never make a difference for my son in the royal palace. There are too many negative influences. His father was a horrible jerk, and his grandfather even worse! I can't possibly make a dent in the evil I see everywhere!" Then, of course, little Josiah wouldn't have gotten such a good start. He wouldn't have helped fix God's temple, discovered the Law of God buried in temple rubble, or brought religious revival to Judah.

Jehoiachin

And he carried Jehoiachin captive to Babylon. The king's mother,
the king's wives, his officers, and the mighty of the land he carried into captivity
from Jerusalem to Babylon. 2 Kings 24:15

In 598 B.C. King Nebuchadnezzar came back to Jerusalem a second time. King Jehoiakim's reign had been a mess, so Nebuchadnezzar took him off the throne and replaced him with his son. Jehoiachin was only eighteen years old when he became king, and he reigned in Jerusalem for just three months. Why? We don't know the details, but it sounds as if kings were hopping on and off the throne of Judah like kids on a merry-go-round. Clearly he was evil like his father and uncle had been, and he must have done something to make King Nebuchadnezzar mad.

Then King Nebuchadnezzar showed up again. He hadn't returned to Babylon yet, and for some reason he now took Jehoiachin captive, along with his mother and wives. He also took ten thousand captives of Judah with him, including all the royal advisors, all the army officers, and all the skilled workers. He cleaned out the royal treasuries too, and took more stuff from Solomon's temple. Then he marched everybody off to Babylon. Was that the end of Jehoiachin? Not exactly. We read that some thirty-seven years later, Evil-Merodach, King Nebuchadnezzar's son, released Jehoaichin from prison and treated him better than any of the other captive kings living in Babylon. Surprisingly, he gave Jehoiachin and his five sons royal garments to wear and allowed them to eat regularly with the king of Babylon.

Wow! That's more of a fantastic finish than one might expect! All this shows what might have happened if Jehoiachin had behaved himself while on the throne of Judah. God would have blessed him if he had tried to be more like his grandfather, Josiah. If he had worshiped God instead of the pagan idols of Palestine, Jerusalem might not have been destroyed.

JUNE 13

Jehoiakim

Now the king was sitting in the winter house in the ninth month, with a fire burning on the hearth before him. And it happened, when Jehudi had read three or four columns, that the king cut it with the scribe's knife and cast it into the fire that was on the hearth, until all the scroll was consumed in the fire that was on the hearth.
Jeremiah 36:22, 23

Jehoiakim was twenty-five years old when Pharaoh Necho made him king of Judah in place of his younger brother Jehoahaz, who had lasted only three months on the throne. But Jehoiakim had his problems too. He was an evil king and went back to the pagan idols his father Josiah had worked so hard to destroy.

And then three years later, along came Nebuchadnezzar from Babylon. He conquered Jerusalem in 605 B.C., forced Jehoiakim to pay heavy taxes, and then allowed him to reign for eight more evil years. The prophet Jeremiah warned Jehoiakim that disaster was coming if he didn't turn from his wicked ways, but the king paid him no mind. When Jeremiah sent him a scroll containing a message of judgment, he cut it up piece by piece and threw it into the fire. And then he foolishly rebelled against Babylon. This made Nebuchadnezzar so angry that he finally came up to Jerusalem a second time (598 B.C.). Not surprisingly, he took all the treasures from the temple and royal palace and made Jehoiakim his captive. He also captured many members of the royal family, among them Daniel, Hananiah, Mishael, and Azariah.

What if King Jehoiakim had continued to rid Judah of pagan idol worship like his father, Josiah? What if he hadn't rebelled against Nebuchadnezzar? Then his reign wouldn't have ended. He wouldn't have been captured, and he wouldn't have died before being taken away to Babylon. Instead, his body was thrown outside the gates of Jerusalem and buried in an unmarked grave. No one mourned for him. No one cared. What a way to be remembered!

Jeremiah

"Before I formed you in the womb I knew you; before you were born I sanctified you; I ordained you a prophet to the nations." Jeremiah 1:5

Among the greatest prophets in the history of Judah stands Jeremiah. He was an amazing man, always ready to give any message God asked him to deliver. He was first called to prophesy against Judah when King Josiah was leading a revival. God asked Jeremiah to do all kinds of seemingly crazy things to get everyone's attention, such as playing war games, shaving his head, and walking around with a yoke around his neck. Bravely he warned everyone that their sins against God would bring the destruction of Jerusalem if they didn't repent. Once when he sent a scroll with a message of doom to King Jehoiakim, the king laughed at it. Then the king cut off pieces of the scroll, threw them in the fire, and went back to worshiping pagan idols, burning children as sacrificial offerings, and eating all kinds of hideous things like mice and bats.

However, Nebuchadnezzar finally put a stop to all this nonsense. In 605 B.C. he laid siege to Jerusalem and conquered it. Twice more in the next twenty years he marched against the holy city, emptying it of its treasures. Thousands were carried away into captivity. Jeremiah was there to witness it all until Jerusalem was the only city standing. King Zedekiah was the final king of Judah, and during his eleven years on the throne, Jeremiah was mocked, beaten, imprisoned, and nearly starved to death. But the prophet stood tall, remaining faithful to God.

What if Jeremiah had decided he wasn't going to do any of this? What if he had said, "I quit! I'm out of here"? Then, of course, God wouldn't have been too pleased. The accusation that Jeremiah was defecting to the Babylonians might have stuck, and he might have even been executed. However, in the end Jerusalem was completely destroyed, and Jeremiah had the last word because he was released from prison.

JUNE 15

Jonadab

But they said, "We will drink no wine, for Jonadab the son of Rechab, our father, commanded us, saying, 'You shall drink no wine, you nor your sons, forever.'"
Jeremiah 35:6

Jonadab was a descendant of Rechab, the leader of a clan in ancient Judah. Rechab had taken a vow that no one in his family would drink wine or any strong drink, and Jonadab now renewed that promise generations later. Like Abraham, Isaac, and Jacob, he also decided his family would not live in houses inside cities. Cities then, as now, were considered places of evil and great wickedness, where young people could be tempted by many things, especially wine and strong drink. Instead, Jonadab's family would live in tents. It was a good decision and paid off eventually, saving the lives of his whole family. Here's how it happened. When the Babylonians conquered Jerusalem, they took captive thousands of people in the city. Over the space of twenty years Nebuchadnezzar deported most of the people from the cities of Judah. However, the poor peasants and those who lived in tents were left behind to care for the land and keep it from growing up wild. Jonadab's family was among those caretakers, because they had not been a part of the rebellion in Jerusalem.

What if Jonadab had decided it was time to change some family values? What if he had decided to make that transition to the easy life of city dwellers? No more hard ground to sleep on. No more living with the sheep and goats. A little wine now and then to celebrate their new life. But then they would have marched off to Babylon with everyone else to live in a pagan land. They would have lost their freedom, died in exile, and maybe disappeared forever from the genealogies of the Jewish nation. But, of course, that was not the outcome for Jonadab and his clan. They stayed to live in the land of milk and honey, a reward for lives of simplicity.

Josiah

Thus Josiah removed all the abominations from all the country that belonged to the children of Israel, and made all who were present in Israel diligently serve the LORD their God. All his days they did not depart from following the LORD God of their fathers. 2 Chronicles 34:33

Josiah was a well-loved king. What was there not to like? As a godly ruler, he was a welcome relief after all the corruption and wild parties in Judah during the previous fifty years. Everyone admired the boy king for wanting to serve God faithfully. As a young man of twenty he got rid of all the shrines and altars where pagan idols were worshiped in the parks and gardens. Five years later, he began repairs on God's temple.

When the priests were cleaning the temple, they made the discovery of a lifetime that would change their world forever—an old copy of the Law of God. Quickly they took it to King Josiah and read it to him, and they got the reaction they were expecting. He tore his cloths and began to mourn as if he were at a funeral. Why? The scroll was a prophecy that Judah would be taken away into captivity if the people disobeyed the Law—if they didn't keep God's Sabbath, robbed the poor and took bribes in a corrupt system of justice, worshiped idols, and offered their children as sacrifices. And for generations that's exactly what had been happening. When Josiah asked Huldah the prophetess what they should expect, she said the people of Judah were indeed going to be taken away into captivity as punishment for all the corruption in the land.

What if the people of Judah had truly repented of their evil ways? What if Josiah had been able to convince them to get rid of wickedness in the land once and for all? Then maybe God would have delayed judgment day for a while or even indefinitely. He had done it before. He could do it again. It's too bad they didn't give it a try, because fifteen years after Josiah died, Nebuchadnezzar showed up.

JUNE 17

Ahab

Now Ahab the son of Omri did evil in the sight of the LORD,
more than all who were before him. 1 Kings 16:30

If we were to ask one hundred people which character in the Bible they most admire, Ahab probably wouldn't make the list. He had no faith in God, no backbone as king, and no scruples when it came to evil. He was one of the most wicked kings ever to rule the kingdom of Israel, and his decision to marry Jezebel didn't help any. From the day she came to the palace in Samaria she promoted the worship of Baal, a pagan fertility god who was considered to be the deity of storms and rain. Even worse, Ahab allowed his wife to kill many of the students at the schools of the prophets. Not surprisingly, when Elijah showed up with bad news about a time of "no rain," he became Ahab's number-one enemy. As the curse of famine settled on the land, Ahab became frantic and scoured the country to find the prophet and kill him. But that didn't stop Elijah from calling the nation to Mount Carmel to see a showdown between Baal and Jehovah. Years later, Ahab coveted the vineyard of a man near the palace, and again his wife Jezebel got him in trouble. She rigged a phony trial for the man who owned the vineyard and had him stoned to death, and then she gave the vineyard to Ahab.

In the end Elijah prophesied the death of Ahab and his entire family. Ahab died in battle against the Syrians, and the dogs licked the blood from his chariot by the pool of Samaria. That's a pretty morbid story to be telling, but it reminds us that those who live by the sword will die by the sword.

What if Ahab had decided he wanted to serve the God of heaven? What if he hadn't married Jezebel, or allowed Baal worship to become so entrenched in Israel, or killed so many innocent people in Israel? Then his seventy sons wouldn't have died at the hands of General Jehu, and his family flame wouldn't have been extinguished.

Boys and the Bears

He [Elisha] went up from there to Bethel, and as he was going up the road, some youths came from the city and mocked him, and said to him, "Go up, you baldhead! Go up, you baldhead!" So he turned around and looked at them, and pronounced a curse on them in the name of the Lord. And two female bears came out of the woods and mauled forty-two of the youths. 2 Kings 2:23, 24

This is a scary story! We've got to ask ourselves, did the boys see this coming or were they just plain clueless? Well, now, Bethel was a pretty bad place to live. For one thing, King Jeroboam launched his new kingdom in Bethel by setting up a golden calf for worship there. Not surprisingly, the city became a center for pagan worship ever after.

In this story, we see Elisha getting a rude welcome in Bethel. Young men came out of the city to curse and mock him as if he were some kind of criminal. Why? They didn't want prophets telling them what to do. Ungodly people have no sense of right or wrong, even if being kind could save their skin, so to speak. Elisha probably just shook his head in amazement at their antics, and then he suggested that God punish them for their impertinence. But God was way ahead of him, because it's here we see a rather unusual act of justice being played out. Two female bears came out of the woods and lit into that gang of boys like nobody's business. We don't really know what sparked the whole thing. Maybe the bears had cubs nearby and the boys were too rowdy to suit them.

The Bible says forty-two of them were injured, and maybe some even died later due to complications. Getting chewed on by bears can't be any fun. But what if they hadn't been so rude? What if they had treated Elisha with the respect he deserved? Then, of course, they would have been treated more kindly by the bears, and by God. That's the way it should be, and it shouldn't take a couple of bears to teach us that.

JUNE 19

Elders at Jericho

> Then he went out to the source of the water, and cast in the salt there,
> and said, "Thus says the LORD: 'I have healed this water; from it there shall be no
> more death or barrenness.'" 2 Kings 2:21

What would you do if your drinking water turned bad? Get a water purifier? Buy bottled water? Hook up a water softener or maybe a charcoal water filter to the water line coming into your house? None of those options were available in the days of Elisha, and that's why the elders of Jericho came looking for him. It was rumored that Elisha could do miracles, so they took him to their springs of water, which had turned very bitter. The water was almost impossible to drink and had poisoned the soil so that it was getting more and more difficult to grow anything there. "Will you help us?" they begged him.

Elisha was glad to help, but then he did something quite out of the ordinary. He asked for a new bowl, put salt in it, and poured the salt into the spring of water. Bingo! The water became pure and sweet to drink again, and the people of Jericho were happy.

Now, we have to ask ourselves, why would he use salt? What were the properties of salt that might make it be the best thing to use in that situation? Salt is a purifier, and it has also been used symbolically to represent the impact God's people can have on a society. Might it be good instead to admit that God doesn't really need anything to perform a miracle? He simply asks what we have in our hand and then uses whatever that might be to work wonders for us, as He did for the people in Jericho.

What if the elders hadn't come to Elisha for help? What if they had waited for him to come to them? What if they had said, we think the stories of Elisha's power are just rumors? Well, then they would have ended up like so many others, without hope, and without help from the God of heaven. And that would have been a shame, considering Elisha lived among them.

Elijah

And Elijah the Tishbite, of the inhabitants of Gilead, said to Ahab,
"As the Lord God of Israel lives, before whom I stand, there shall not be dew nor
rain these years, except at my word." 1 Kings 17:1

Elijah was an unusual man for an unusual time. Called by God in the days of Ahab and Jezebel, he stood alone, it seemed, against the most incredible odds. How do we remember him best? He prayed that God wouldn't send rain, to punish Israel for their sins, and then he entered Ahab's palace uninvited to make that announcement. The drought came as he predicted and was lifted again only when he prayed on Mount Carmel, but not before he had executed 850 prophets and priests of Baal. Then he ran seventeen miles to the city of Jezreel ahead of Ahab's chariot, went to sleep in the rain, and panicked when a messenger woke him up to tell him Jezebel was out to get him. He ran all the way to Mount Sinai to get away from Jezebel, only to find God waiting for him there to scold him. Why? For his lack of faith in God.

His remaining days were spent up in Israel, choosing a successor to carry on his work and dealing with the corruption in Ahab's palace. God directed him to choose Elisha to take his place as prophet and then went on to predict the downfall of Ahab's dynasty. Elijah predicted his death because Ahab had unjustly executed Naboth for refusing to sell his vineyard. A short time later, Elijah himself was taken to heaven in his famous chariot of fire. He disappears from history for almost nine hundred years, then reappears to comfort Jesus on the Mount of Transfiguration.

What if Elijah had not been a faithful prophet? What if he hadn't dared to do daring things for the God of all creation? Then he would have turned out to be an ordinary man, doing ordinary things that no one remembered. But because he was faithful, he is now in the heavenly courts helping prepare a place for you and me when Jesus comes again. That's right, he was translated, taken to heaven in a chariot of fire.

JUNE 21

Elisha

So the man of God said, "Where did it fall?" And he showed him the place.
So he cut off a stick, and threw it in there; and he made the iron float. 2 Kings 6:6

E lisha is one of the most amazing characters in the Bible. Unlike Elijah, who was seen as a man of great power, Elisha was considered a man of great peace. He was a man of the people, and through him God did more miracles than anyone else in the Bible except Jesus.

Let's take a look at some of those miracles. Following on the heels of Elijah's trip to heaven, Elisha parted the waters of the Jordan River. Then he purified the bitter waters at Jericho. When he went up to Bethel, young men mocked him about Elijah's chariot ride to heaven, and two bears came out of the woods to punish the boys. He brought a flood of water out of the desert hills in Edom to refresh the armies of Israel and Judah and then blessed them with victory over the Moabites. He helped a widow erase a debt by multiplying her oil. He gave a woman a long-awaited miracle child and then raised that boy to life after he died from heat stroke. He neutralized the poison gourds in a pot of stew, fed a hundred men miraculously with a few loaves of flat bread, healed Naaman of his leprosy, and then gave the disease to greedy Gehazi. He made an iron ax-head float on water, opened the eyes of his servant to see angels protecting them in Dothan, blinded the eyes of Syrian soldiers, and then opened their eyes again. Even after he died, a man was resurrected to life simply because his dead body touched Elisha's bones in his tomb.

Of course, it wasn't really Elisha doing any of these miracles—it was God. Elisha was only His servant and prophet. But what if he hadn't accepted Elijah's call to be his successor and serve in his footsteps? Then he would have missed out on all the blessings of helping people with his miracles and bringing them back to God. He would have missed out on being portrayed as one of the men in the Old Testament Scriptures who most resembled Jesus.

Gehazi

"Therefore the leprosy of Naaman shall cling to you and your descendants forever." And he went out from his presence leprous, as white as snow. 2 Kings 5:27

Who was this Gehazi guy? In many ways he was like Judas—always self-serving, always greedy, and always looking for a get-rich-quick shortcut to riches. How did he end up working for the prophet Elisha, who was one of the most unselfish, Christlike characters in all the Bible? Good question. We don't know that answer, but we do know the reward for Gehazi's life philosophy, and that's a sad story indeed.

When Naaman came to Elisha and asked to be healed of his leprosy, Gehazi got excited because he realized the payoff would be like winning the lottery. And that's exactly what happened. Naaman was cured in the Jordan and offered Elisha gifts worth millions of dollars in today's currency. Elisha refused the honorarium, much to Gehazi's horror, and Naaman headed for home, happy to learn that Jehovah is a God of grace. The Lord gives freely, delivers miraculously, and asks nothing in return but a grateful heart. But that wasn't enough for Gehazi. He chased Naaman down the road to tell him a tall tale and then brought home two talents of silver for his private stash. Elisha was ticked off that Gehazi would do such a thing and sent him packing, but not before giving him the curse of Naaman—leprosy. Wow! What a way to go!

What if Gehazi hadn't been so greedy? What if he had realized this was the opportunity of a lifetime to share the light of God's goodness to a pagan man like Naaman? It's likely Naaman's king would have learned the truth about God's grace, making him much less likely to attack Israel. After all, how could he justify pillaging and robbing from a country whose God loved to give gifts? We will never know, because Gehazi disappeared into history, a broken man who carried the hated disease with him for the rest of his life.

Jezebel

Then Jezebel sent a messenger to Elijah, saying, "So let the gods do to me,
and more also, if I do not make your life as the life of one of them
by tomorrow about this time." 1 Kings 19:2

What a nasty woman! Jezebel was one of the most angry, self-centered, evil women in the entire Bible. She was probably the single greatest fan of Baal, god of rain clouds and agricultural fertility, and she made worshiping him the national religion of Israel. Her religion promoted wild parties to worship Baal, and God's prophets condemned her for it. Not surprisingly, she was nothing but trouble for God's people in Israel and hunted them down like an animal possessed by Satan. And then there was Elijah. She hated him too. Here was a man empowered by God to bring fire down out of heaven, part the waters of the Jordan River, and raise the dead. And yet when Jezebel threatened to have him executed, he freaked out and ran for the hills! Now that's a woman with a lot of power!

Elijah predicted her death, and Jehu, general of the army, carried out the sentence. It happened like this. Jehu knew Baal worship was rotting the nation of Israel from the inside out, and Jezebel was the cause of it, so he called for her death. Not surprisingly, no one stood in his way. She was older now, and they all knew her reign with Ahab had been filled with corruption and vice. When Jehu drove up to the Jezreel palace in his chariot, she was waiting for him, all decked out in makeup and fancy clothes, sitting in a third-story window. He called for her servants to throw her out the window, and they didn't argue. Ouch! That had to hurt!

What if Jezebel had decided to serve the God of heaven instead of Baal? What if she had said, "I don't want to be wicked anymore"? In that case she would be remembered today as a woman of class, a godly queen who put God first. Instead, the stray dogs of Jezreel came along and ate up her body before it could even be buried. What a way to go!

Manasseh

Manasseh was twelve years old when he became king,
and he reigned fifty-five years in Jerusalem. But he did evil in the sight of the LORD,
according to the abominations of the nations whom the LORD
had cast out before the children of Israel. 2 Chronicles 33:1, 2

Fifty-five years? That's a long time! Unfortunately, most of those years were a disaster for Judah. Manasseh came to the throne as a mere boy, and his ideas about how a country should be run were nothing like his father Hezekiah's. The thing he seemed to hate most was the religious reformation his father had started in Judah, and he set out to change all that. The Bible says he became more wicked than any of the kings before him. How'd he do that? He started by rebuilding the high places with their shrines for worshiping strange gods. He worshiped many pagan idols right in God's temple, and even offered one of his sons as a burnt sacrifice, probably to the god Molech. When Isaiah and other prophets warned him what would come if he didn't reverse his engines, he got angry and even executed some of them, shedding much innocent blood. Hebrew tradition tells us Manasseh executed the prophet Isaiah by sawing him in two.

Well, it all came to a head when God allowed the Assyrians to take King Manasseh captive and haul him away to prison. While in chains, he had a reality check and realized how horribly wicked he had been. He had ignored God's warnings for years, and look what it had cost him. However, the resulting curse on Judah was even worse. When the Assyrian emperor allowed him to go back to Jerusalem, Manasseh tried to undo all the evil he had done, but it was impossible.

What if Manasseh had listened to Isaiah and God's other prophets? What if he had counted the cost for a life of wickedness? Then he could have prevented thousands and thousands of people from being lost eternally by his example. He would have saved the life of his own son and, of course, avoided being taken captive by the Assyrians.

JUNE 25

Zedekiah

Moreover Jeremiah said to King Zedekiah, "What offense have I committed against you, against your servants, or against this people, that you have put me in prison?" Jeremiah 37:18

Jerusalem was a mess! By now Nebuchadnezzar had marched on Judah twice, and he was getting sick of all the fighting and rebellion. "I'll give y'all one more chance!" we can almost hear him saying. And so he set Zedekiah on the throne in Jerusalem. Zedekiah was twenty-one years old when he became king, and he reigned eleven years. Unfortunately, he was a bad king like Jehoahaz, Jehoiakim, and Jehoiachin before him.

But God had compassion on Zedekiah and kept sending him messages through the prophet Jeremiah. The king was warned that he must repent of all the evil he was doing. He must pay his taxes to King Nebuchadnezzar as he had promised, or Jerusalem would be destroyed. Unfortunately, Zedekiah was a poor choice for king because he was weak and listened to the princes in his palace, who were always grumbling. They told him to ignore Jeremiah's warnings and even put the prophet in a deep pit to keep him quiet.

Finally God decided He could do nothing more to save the nation of Judah, and He allowed Nebuchadnezzar to march up against Jerusalem one last time. Zedekiah realized his number was up and tried to flee the coop. Under cover of darkness, he and his wives and sons fled east toward the Jordan River, but Nebuchadnezzar's sentries caught up with them and brought them back.

It didn't have to turn out like that. None of this would have happened if King Zedekiah had just listened to Jeremiah and done as God asked. In the end it wasn't a very pretty picture. Zedekiah was blinded and hauled away in chains, after he saw his sons killed. Then the soldiers of Babylon burned down the house of God and all the palaces, and even broke down the wall of Jerusalem. What a waste!

King Mesha of Moab

And when the king of Moab saw that the battle was too fierce for him, . . . he took
his eldest son who would have reigned in his place,
and offered him as a burnt offering upon the wall. 2 Kings 3:26, 27

This is a very unusual story! It's a bit brutal, but it tells us what can happen when people reject the God of heaven for idols of wood and stone. King Mesha from Moab was at war with Israel and Judah. The desert heat was so great that everybody ran out of water, but the prophet Elisha performed a miracle for Israel and Judah. God sent water out of the mountains to fill the desert ravines and provide water for the horses and mules to drink.

Surprisingly, on the morning of battle, King Mesha mistook the waters for blood in the red sandy ditches and rushed to battle, only to find himself outmatched and unprepared. The battle went badly for King Mesha, and there was a great slaughter, but he escaped with seven hundred of his best warriors. They fled to their capital city, and the Israelites laid siege to it, threatening the Moabites with starvation. In desperation King Mesha decided to make the ultimate sacrifice to Chemosh, the chief god of the Moabites. Such a sacrifice required the life of a child, usually a son, and that's exactly what Mesha did. He took his son up on the city wall and offered him as a sacrifice to his bloodthirsty god. The Bible says the Israelites were so disgusted that they stopped the siege, packed up their gear, and went home.

What a despicable thing for King Mesha to do! What if King Mesha had learned from King Jehoshaphat's example in Judah? He could have known about the wonderful blessings of serving Jehovah, the God of Israel, who had done many miracles for His people. The fate of his son and his kingdom could have been so different if he had been a worshiper of the one true God.

Little Maid

The Syrians had gone out on raids, and had brought back captive a young girl from the land of Israel. She waited on Naaman's wife. Then she said to her mistress, "If only my master were with the prophet who is in Samaria! For he would heal him of his leprosy." 2 Kings 5:2, 3

How would you feel if you were captured and taken hostage by enemy soldiers? What would you do if you couldn't get back home and they made you a slave? Would you freak out? Would you feel God had abandoned you? There's a story in the Bible about that very thing, and the hero of the story was an Israelite girl who had been taken captive by Syrian raiders. We don't know her name, but she was an amazing young girl, and braver than brave. Even though she was a slave in the home of Captain Naaman, she wanted to help him. Here's how it happened.

One day, Captain Naaman came home from the doctor with bad news. He had leprosy, the most dreaded disease in those days, and there was no hope that he would ever recover. When the slave girl heard the news, she immediately thought of Elisha back home in Israel. "If Captain Naaman would go to Samaria, the prophet would be able to heal him for sure," she said. Naaman must have been impressed with her recommendation because he decided to find Elisha immediately. Down to the capital city of Israel he went with his bodyguard and a camel train of gifts. And sure enough, he finally found Elisha, the miracle worker the slave girl had told him about. The story ends well, with Naaman being healed when he took a bath in the Jordan River, just as Elisha had instructed.

What if the little servant girl hadn't told Naaman about Elisha? What if she had kept all his miracles a secret? She didn't have to share that info, especially since his people and her people were mortal enemies! If she hadn't, Naaman would not have been healed. He would have died prematurely from one of the most dreaded diseases in history! What a kind thing for her to do!

The Fool at Samaria's Gate

Now the king had appointed the officer on whose hand he leaned
to have charge of the gate. But the people trampled him in the gate,
and he died, just as the man of God had said. 2 Kings 7:17

This is a tragic tale, and the officer who died in this story was a victim of his own lack of faith. A famine was raging in the city of Samaria. The Syrians had laid siege to the city to starve the people into submission. Food was nonexistent for the most part. The scant food supplies available were being sold by the rich at astronomical prices. The people were willing to eat anything by now. They had already eaten all the bats and cats and long-tailed rats, and now they were eating things like pigeon droppings and even their own children. King Joram was desperate and went searching for Elisha, because the prophet had predicted the famine.

He wanted to arrest Elisha so he could kill him, but the prophet made a strange prediction. "The Lord is going to have mercy on you, O king," he said. "About this time tomorrow in Samaria, a seah of fine flour will be sold for a shekel, and two seahs of barley for a shekel."

The king's personal attendant laughed when he heard this. "Even if the Lord would open windows in heaven, this could never happen!" he snorted. "It will happen," Elisha told the king's attendant, "and you will see it with your eyes, but you shall not eat of it." Amazingly, the prophecy came true in every detail just as Elisha said it would. That very night, God caused the enemy soldiers outside the city to be frightened, and they ran off. This ended the siege and allowed the people to leave the city the next morning. Not surprisingly, in the enemy camp they found food by the ton.

And the officer who laughed at Elisha? Would it have helped if he had believed the prophet's prediction? Probably. Unfortunately, he never got to enjoy any of the food, because he died in the mob that stampeded through the city gates that morning. What a way to die!

JUNE 29

Naaman

And he [Naaman] returned to the man of God, he and all his aides,
and came and stood before him; and he said, "Indeed,
now I know that there is no God in all the earth, except in Israel;
now therefore, please take a gift from your servant." 2 Kings 5:15

Naaman was a proud man, almost too proud for his own good. It's fortunate he had advisers, or charioteers, or bodyguards (whatever they were), who would give him straight talk. And it's even more fortunate that he listened to them. Here's how it happened.

He had the most dreaded and incurable disease of his day—leprosy. A little Israelite slave girl in his home told him there was hope and sent him on a wild-goose chase to Israel for healing. It wasn't intended to be a goose chase, but, no thanks to King Joram of Israel and Naaman himself, that's exactly what it turned out to be.

When the general arrived in Israel's capital city of Samaria, King Joram thought Naaman was trying to pick a fight to start a war. "No one can heal such a disease!" we can hear him shout. The general eventually found his way to Elisha's house but was miffed at the prophet when he didn't come out to greet him in person. "Where's the magic in this?" we can hear him demanding. "Don't I deserve some respect?" Of course, he didn't understand that Elisha was merely testing his sincerity and his worthiness to receive the blessing of such a miracle. Thankfully, he listened to his advisors and took their advice. He washed in the dirty Jordan River seven times, and, wonder of wonders, he was cured! He wanted to pay Elisha a handsome reward for his service, but, as the story goes, Elisha told him to keep his gifts. The grace of God is free for the taking.

What if Naaman hadn't listened to his bodyguards? What if he had gone home without taking the simple cure? Then, quite simply, he would have died a leper. As it was, his obedient faith in God was what made him whole. Now that's cool! Good move, Naaman!

Naboth

So Ahab spoke to Naboth, saying, "Give me your vineyard,
that I may have it for a vegetable garden, because it is near, next to my house;
and for it I will give you a vineyard better than it. Or, if it seems good to you,
I will give you its worth in money." But Naboth said to Ahab,
"The Lord forbid that I should give the inheritance
of my fathers to you!" 1 Kings 21:2, 3

What a bad deal for Naboth! There's no way he was going to come out on top in this case! We don't know much about him except that King Ahab wanted to buy his vineyard. Naboth said no. It was his family inheritance, and he wasn't allowed to sell it. The king went off to his bed to pout, and that's where Queen Jezebel found him.

"This is ridiculous!" she shrieked. "No king acts like this! If you want the vineyard, I'll help you get it. Piece of cake." And the evil woman set out to do just that.

She sent letters to the elders and nobles of Naboth's town, telling them to rig a trial. What would be the charges? Naboth was guilty of treason against the king and blasphemy against God. As if she really cared about God!

Her scheme worked. Naboth was sentenced to death in the fake trial, and King Ahab took his land. But Elijah knew the story, and God sent him to take action. He appeared in the vineyard one day to pronounce judgment against Ahab and the royal family for shedding innocent blood.

What if Naboth had said, "I'll sell! I don't want any trouble!" Such a decision might sound safe, but it wouldn't have been fair. We have to admire Naboth for sticking to his decision. To live in fear is no way to live at all. As it turned out, the king and queen paid a heavy price for their violence and injustice in the land. We remember Naboth for being an honorable man, but Ahab and Jezebel are only seen as murderers and thieves.

Obadiah—Ahab's Servant

For so it was, while Jezebel massacred the prophets of the LORD,
that Obadiah had taken one hundred prophets and hidden them,
fifty to a cave, and had fed them with bread and water. 1 Kings 18:4

Obadiah was one of the good guys. He loved God and cared more about others than about himself. As governor of King Ahab's palace, he saw all the evil going on in the kingdom, but what could he do? He was only one man. He knew, of course, that Queen Jezebel was the biggest problem! When she was establishing Baal as the chief god of Israel, she set up his images all over Israel. She built temples in his honor and shrines for his worship. To make things worse, she started killing God's prophets, including all the students at the schools of the prophets. Obadiah knew this was wrong and took action. Risking his own life, he secretly hid one hundred of these students and prophets in two caves. Bread and water was all he could manage to give them at the time, but it saved their lives. Praise God for men like Obadiah down through the ages!

During a major drought in Israel, Obadiah was sent to find pasture for the royal herds of horses and mules. Imagine his surprise one day to find Elijah waiting along the road after being hidden by God for three years! "Tell Ahab to come see me! I'm ready to talk," Elijah told him.

But Obadiah was suspicious and fearful. "When we get back, you'll be gone," he said, "and then the king will have my head!" But Elijah promised Obadiah he wasn't going anywhere.

That's the kind of man Obadiah was—kind, loving, and brave. God blessed him for being a good servant of Ahab and at the same time a protector of God's people. What if Obadiah had decided he wasn't going to go against the system to protect "enemies of the state," as Queen Jezebel called them. Then the lives of one hundred prophets would have likely ended, and, of course, as a godly man, Obadiah wouldn't have been able to sleep nights. Thank God for men like Obadiah, who always seem to do the right thing at the right time!

Priests and Prophets of Baal

"Now therefore, send and gather all Israel to me on Mount Carmel,
the four hundred and fifty prophets of Baal, and the four hundred prophets of
Asherah, who eat at Jezebel's table." 1 Kings 18:19

Who were the priests and prophets in this story, and how many were there? Well, the Bible says Jezebel had hired 850 of them to run her temples and worship services, and they were all bad guys. How's that? Here are the details of the story. God had sent a drought and famine in the land to teach Israel some lessons about who it was that sends the rain. God was the answer, and not Baal or Ashtoreth, as Jezebel wanted everyone to believe. But how to prove it was the question. So, Elijah called all the people of Israel to the mountaintop at Carmel for a grand showdown. Was Baal stronger than Jehovah, or was it the other way around? The god that burned up the sacrifice they offered would be considered the god of choice.

The prophets and priests of Baal then built an altar to honor Baal on top of Mount Carmel, and that began their charade. They danced and screamed and whooped it up all day, begging Baal to burn up their sacrifice. But Baal didn't respond. Noon passed, and the afternoon came. By now they were getting frantic and began to cut themselves with sharp knives to make Baal feel sorry for them! Ouch! I'd say they knew there was a lot at stake. They had made extreme claims about the power of Baal, but all day he had remained silent. What a fiasco!

When Elijah rebuilt the altar of God and offered a sacrifice to the Lord, everyone got the surprise of their lives. With a simple prayer lasting a few seconds, he called fire down out of heaven to consume the sacrifice. Wow! What a lesson! Of course, we all know these imposters were executed. What if the prophets and priests of Baal had decided they didn't want to worship their heathen idols anymore? Then clearly their lives would have been spared, and they could have helped Elijah start a great reformation in Israel.

JULY 3

Elisha's Servant at Dothan

And Elisha prayed, and said, "LORD, I pray, open his eyes that he may see."
Then the LORD opened the eyes of the young man, and he saw. And behold, the
mountain was full of horses and chariots of fire all around Elisha. 2 Kings 6:17

What would you do if you woke up one morning to find that the hotel you were staying in was surrounded by enemy soldiers? That's what happened to the prophet Elisha and his servant while they were staying in the city of Dothan. The servant was the first one to make the discovery that fateful morning, and he was frantic with fear. "What are we going to do?" we can hear him shouting in desperation. "They've got us surrounded!"

Of course, there was no fear in Elisha's heart. He had been in danger before, and God always delivered him out of his troubles. "Don't worry," he told his servant. "Those that are with us are more than those that are with them." But he knew the young man would have no real idea what he was talking about. He couldn't see the angels of God whose job description was to protect the servants of the Lord day and night. They were hidden behind the veil that stood between them and the supernatural world. Then Elisha prayed and asked God to perform a miracle for the young servant at his side, who was staring at the Syrian army surrounding the city. "Lord, please open his eyes that he may see," said Elisha, and the Lord heard that prayer. Suddenly the panoramic view of the mountains came to life, revealing an army of supernatural horses and chariots of fire. Not surprisingly, the young servant was speechless.

And we might ask the question, What if the servant hadn't been a godly young man? What if he hadn't believed God could protect him and the prophet? Then the chariots of fire might well have stayed under cover, and he would have missed out on the splendor of God's heavenly wonders. What a glorious once-in-a-lifetime experience that must have been!

Shunamite Woman

Now it happened one day that Elisha went to Shunem, where there was a notable woman, and she persuaded him to eat some food. So it was, as often as he passed by, he would turn in there to eat some food. 2 Kings 4:8

From the story line we get the impression that this woman was important in that part of Israel, and wealthy as well. The prophet Elisha had to go on the road a lot, and she offered him a chance to stop in from time to time to get a bite to eat. Then she went a step further. She built a private room for Elisha to stay in whenever he came by. Elisha was very impressed and asked the woman what he could do for her. Did she want any favors from the king or maybe extra protection from the army? But the woman said she needed nothing. She was content to live a simple life in Shunem.

Then Elisha's servant, Gehazi, hit on something. "She has no son," he said. "Why not ask God to give her a son?" That's exactly what they did, and a year later she gave birth to a baby boy, and everybody loved him. As he grew, he often went to work in the fields with the servants and his father. One day, however, he got too much sun and developed heatstroke. His mother carried him home, but the little boy didn't make it. By noon he was dead. She was desperate and rode off to find Elisha because she felt he was the only one who could help. Did she think Elisha would raise him from the dead? We don't know, but that's exactly what happened.

What if the Shunamite woman hadn't been so kind to Elisha? She could have put him up at a local inn each time he came to town, but she went above and beyond the call of duty, and for her kindness she received the gift of a child. Later, when her child got sick and died, Elisha was there to raise that little boy to life. What a blessing she was to Elisha! What a blessing Elisha was to the little boy, and what a blessing God was to them all!

JULY 5

Sons of the Prophets

Then they said to him, "Look now, there are fifty strong men with your servants.
Please let them go and search for your master,
lest perhaps the Spirit of the LORD has taken him up
and cast him upon some mountain or into some valley." 2 Kings 2:16

Can you believe it? Elijah, one of the greatest miracle workers in the Bible, had just gone to heaven in a chariot of fire. He had parted the waters of the Jordan earlier that day, and so had Elisha when he returned to Jericho. Lots of miracles all squeezed into one day, and the young men from the schools of the prophets had seen it all. There were about fifty of them, so there was no shortage of witnesses on which to base their faith. And yet they still came up with a ridiculous conclusion! Elijah must be stranded somewhere! He must have fallen out of the sky and landed somewhere on a mountain or in a desert valley! "Let's go look for him!" they shouted.

Elisha was embarrassed. Not for himself, but for them. These young men were students in the schools of the prophets! They were supposed to be men of faith, men who trusted God, men who had seen Elijah in action and should have recognized miracles when they saw them! "It won't do any good," Elisha told them. "He's gone to heaven in a chariot of angels!" But they went anyway and spent three days combing the Jordan valley in search of a man who wasn't there. And, of course, they came back at the end of the hunt disappointed and disillusioned.

But what if these young men had believed that Elijah had indeed gone away that day to heaven? Then they would have saved themselves a lot of walking and a lot of grief over the loss of their mentor, Elijah. They would have been praising God that their master had gone to heaven, something very few people in the history of the world have done. What a privilege would have been theirs!

Ahasuerus

In those days when King Ahasuerus sat on the throne of his kingdom, which was in Shushan the citadel, . . . in the third year of his reign he made a feast for all his officials and servants—the powers of Persia and Media, the nobles, and the princes of the provinces. Esther 1:2, 3

His name was Ahasuerus, otherwise known as Xerxes. He was the most powerful man in the world at that time, and one of the richest men who ever sat on a throne. But he had his liabilities. He was a vain man. He was shallow in his relationships and probably the worst military strategist of his century. In one battle, as many as 150,000 of his Persians soldiers fought three hundred valiant Spartans and almost lost. In a battle at sea, his armada of up to twelve hundred boats fought a fleet of 371 Greek ships and lost. He started a military campaign in the west with as many as half a million soldiers and came home with only a few thousand. He should have been devastated at these losses but instead called for a beauty contest. This is when Esther enters the picture, and from here on out the story really gets interesting.

When a plot unfolded to assassinate Xerxes, Mordecai intercepted the plans, and Esther relayed a message in time to save the king's life. He then signed a decree for the death of all Jews in the kingdom, which included Mordecai and Esther. Now things really got crazy around the palace. With great courage, the two of them worked together to approach the king and ask him to help spare their people. And although the Medo-Persian law could not be overturned, it could be amended, and that is exactly what King Xerxes did—he made a new law that allowed Jews to defend themselves against their executioners.

What if Xerxes hadn't been such a vain, reckless egomaniac? Well, for one thing he would have saved millions of Persian soldiers from death. He would have realized early on just how valuable Mordecai was in his court. He wouldn't have signed that ridiculous death decree; and he would have had time to learn about the God of heaven from his beautiful wife Esther.

JULY 7

Belshazzar

"You have lifted yourself up against the Lord of heaven. They have brought the vessels of His house before you, and you and your lords, your wives and your concubines, have drunk wine from them. And you have praised the gods of silver and gold, bronze and iron, wood and stone, which do not see or hear or know; and the God who holds your breath in His hand and owns all your ways, you have not glorified." Daniel 5:23

Belshazzar was a weak ruler and ultimately a failure as a king. He squandered the empire built by his grandfather Nebuchadnezzar and wasted his final days in feasting and dancing. Even on the eve of Babylon's collapse as a superpower, King Belshazzar was having a party. He knew the Medo-Persian army had surrounded Babylon and laid siege to the city, but Babylon was well prepared for such an assault. There was enough food in the city to last twenty years, so Belshazzar had no worries. Or did he? If his informants had done their job, they would have known King Cyrus had diverted the river Euphrates to another channel, leaving the river channel dry under the walls. And that's exactly how Cyrus conquered Babylon: He marched into the city through the riverbed. But not before God sent King Belshazzar a message telling him the kingdom of Babylon was finished. "You have cursed the God of heaven and blasphemed His name!" Daniel told the king as a supernatural hand wrote a cryptic message on the palace wall. "You are weighed in the balances and found wanting!"

That night, Belshazzar died, but not for lack of knowledge—he simply ignored the warning signs. What if Belshazzar had listened? What if he had confessed his sin of drinking from the holy vessels of gold and silver brought from the temple in Jerusalem? Then God might have had mercy on him and provided a way of escape for him like his father, Nabonidus. Instead, the young king died without hope on the night of Babylon's invasion.

Belshazzar's Queen Mother

The queen, because of the words of the king and his lords,
came to the banquet hall. The queen spoke, saying, "O king, live forever!
Do not let your thoughts trouble you, nor let your countenance change.
There is a man in your kingdom in whom is the Spirit of the Holy God.
And in the days of your father, light and understanding and wisdom,
like the wisdom of the gods, were found in him." Daniel 5:10, 11

Who was this woman? The saga in Daniel 5 tells us she was the queen mother. So she was possibly the daughter of King Nebuchadnezzar, and Belshazzar's mother. It's not likely she was even at the banquet that night, and yet sometime during that evening she must have shown up because of all the commotion there. Here's what happened.

When the queen mother arrived in the banquet hall, she noted that a deathly silence had settled over the room, broken only now and then by a faint scream and the sobs of a drunken guest. There in full view on the wall were glowing letters, and she was told a mysterious hand had written them.

King Belshazzar was a mess by now. He was so nervous his knees were knocking together. The queen mother was sure he would have a nervous breakdown, so she told him about Daniel, a Jewish man who had served under her father, King Nebuchadnezzar. "There is a man in your kingdom in whom is the Spirit of the Holy God," she said. "And in the days of your father, light and understanding and wisdom, like wisdom from the gods was given to him."

That was quite a testimony for the queen mother! Daniel deciphered the writing, which predicted the end of Babylon, but too late the queen's son realized his kingdom was at an end. And what would have happened if the queen mother hadn't called Daniel in? What if she had just let her son sweat it out? Then it's likely no one would have known the message of warning God had written on the wall, and today we wouldn't have one of the most exciting stories in all the Bible.

JULY 9

Bigthana and Teresh

That night the king could not sleep. So one was commanded to bring the book of the records of the chronicles; and they were read before the king. And it was found written that Mordecai had told of Bigthana and Teresh, two of the king's eunuchs, the doorkeepers who had sought to lay hands on King Ahasuerus. Esther 6:1, 2

In the book of Esther, we find the story of two bad guys named Bigthana and Teresh. Unfortunately, we don't know much about them. Were they old or young, educated, or from a peasant background? Did they know each other before they came into the service of the king? Did they like cheese sandwiches or cold cereal or smoothies? The one thing we do know about them is that they were bodyguards of King Ahasuerus in the days of Esther.

Assassinations were common even in the palaces of emperors. Security needs were high. The best of bodyguards were hired, and personal attendants were even appointed to stand outside the royal bedchamber doors when the king was sleeping. And that was the job of Bigthana and Teresh, until one fine day when they plotted to assassinate the king. The Bible doesn't tell us exactly how they planned to carry it out. Maybe they were going to smother him with a pillow or stab him with a dagger. Whatever it was, Esther's cousin, Mordecai, who worked in the court, overheard them talking. He foiled their plot by sending a message to Esther, who reported the matter to the king. That was the end of Bigthana and Teresh. They were killed the same day. Much later, Mordecai was rewarded with a royal reception and parade.

Now, what if Bigthana and Teresh hadn't plotted to kill the king? What if they had been content to serve their king as bodyguards? They could've been rewarded for being good servants, and even helped uncover future assassination plots against their king. Instead, they were executed for treason.

Cyrus

Thus says Cyrus king of Persia: All the kingdoms of the earth
the LORD God of heaven has given me. And He has commanded me
to build Him a house at Jerusalem which is in Judah. Ezra 1:2

Cyrus was quite a king! He conquered the Medes by 550 B.C., defeated Lydia in 547 B.C., and overran Babylon in 539 B.C. To overthrow Babylon, he had his soldiers divert the Euphrates River out of its channel (it ran under the city wall and through Babylon), so the water level in the riverbed would be low enough to allow them to march into Babylon. Sounds like the Persians were an unstoppable war machine, doesn't it? Actually, King Cyrus was one of the most well-liked rulers of that era. Historians tell us the Babylonians were so tired of King Belshazzer's frivolous parties and wasteful spending that they welcomed Cyrus the conqueror with cheers when he marched through the gates of Babylon.

Shortly thereafter, Cyrus was shown the prophecies of Isaiah, predicting he would free the Jews and let them go back to rebuild Jerusalem. He was impressed that a prophet had mentioned him by name 150 years before his birth and eventually decided to issue that decree. But not without a struggle. The book of Daniel tells us a real battle took place between Jesus and Satan over the decree that Cyrus would eventually write. For three weeks the angel Gabriel worked day and night, and Jesus Himself finally had to take charge. The forces of good eventually won, and the Jews were allowed to go home.

What if Cyrus hadn't listened to Isaiah's prophecy? What if he had refused to write that decree? Then God would have had to free the Jews through some other means. The bottom line is that Isaiah predicted it, because God showed him it would happen—and Cyrus got to be part of that wonderful fulfillment. How truly blessed he was!

Daniel

But Daniel purposed in his heart that he would not defile himself with the portion of the king's delicacies, nor with the wine which he drank. Daniel 1:8

Take a look at this story found in Daniel 1. Daniel had just arrived in Babylon as King Nebuchadnezzar's prisoner of war. After several months on the road from Judah, he was being given the chance of a lifetime. The prize? An education in the royal academy of arts and sciences on a fully funded scholarship. He would attend classes in math and astronomy, language and literature, religion and philosophy. If he did well he would be given a government job with really good benefits, including a penthouse suite of apartments in the royal palace. What an opportunity to advance, don't you think, considering he was a captive and should by all rights have ended up being a slave! Considering all these factors, if you had been an average captive from Judah, would you have traded places with Daniel? Most people would.

There was a catch hidden beneath all these opportunities and privileges. The king had a menu for his students, and on it were all kinds of foods, especially wine and meats, that had been dedicated to pagan gods. And Daniel was supposed to eat them and drink them if he wanted to stay in the program.

Now here's the question of the day: If you were there in Daniel's shoes, would you have drunk the king's wine and eaten the king's meats? The pig on the platter, the lobster salads, the shark meat, or whatever kinds of taboo food he was being offered? If Daniel had caved on this decision, we probably wouldn't be reading his story, because he would have failed the test. But he didn't. Because he chose to honor God, he passed with flying colors and ended up being the most powerful officer in two consecutive kingdoms. Very, very cool, Daniel.

Daniel's Accusers

So the governors and satraps sought to find some charge against Daniel concerning the kingdom; but they could find no charge or fault, because he was faithful; nor was there any error or fault found in him. Daniel 6:4

In the new kingdom of Medo-Persia, Daniel was promoted beyond his fellow governors and satraps. They didn't like it, of course, and decided to stop him. They left no stone unturned in their efforts to expose him by some scandal, or maybe frame him in some misdeed. But Daniel was untouchable. He was a man of integrity and honest as the day is long.

They resorted to the only thing they could think of. "We won't find any charge against Daniel unless it has to do with his allegiance to his God," they said, and that's what they set out to do. But it wasn't easy. Finally they hatched a plan to write a decree, have King Darius sign it, and then enforce it as a law of the Medes and Persians, which couldn't be changed.

It worked—at first. The king fell for the flattering terms of the decree, which said that no one should worship any god but Darius, or suffer death in a lion's den. Getting the king to sign was the hard part; watching Daniel's every move was easy. When their spies caught him praying to God three times daily, they reported to the king what they had witnessed, the King was horrified at his mistake, but Daniel was sentenced to a night with the lions anyway.

What if the advisors hadn't been so jealous? What if they had admired Daniel for his integrity instead of trying to kill him? They thought it was a smart plan, but they didn't take into account that Daniel's God could save him from the lions. That one little mistake cost them everything. The next morning, Daniel came out of the lions' grotto alive, and his accusers were thrown in for the lions' brunch.

JULY 13

Three Army Captains

Again, he sent a third captain of fifty with his fifty men. And the third captain of fifty went up, and came and fell on his knees before Elijah, and pleaded with him, and said to him: "Man of God, please let my life and the life of these fifty servants of yours be precious in your sight." 2 Kings 1:13

What's this story all about? Why did this military captain feel the need to get down on his knees and beg Elijah to spare his life and the life of his soldiers? Well, now, that would be the rest of the story, wouldn't it? King Ahaziah had fallen and hurt himself pretty badly. That's why he sent messengers to sorcerers in Ekron to ask Beelzebub, god of flies, if he was going to recover. But Elijah intercepted the messengers on the road to Ekron and told them the king wouldn't recover. He would die.

Amazingly, the messengers didn't recognize who Elijah was, but from his description, King Ahaziah did. So, the king got mad and sent an officer with fifty soldiers to arrest Elijah, but, of course, it didn't work that way. No one should be giving orders to a man whose prayer can call fire down from heaven! At least, that's what we would think, right? Elijah was quite surprised too. "You can't talk to a man of God like that," he said, and wouldn't you know it, fire came down out of the sky and burned up the fifty soldiers. Wow! Even more shocking was the fact that another captain then came out with another fifty soldiers and made the same demand! And they got incinerated too. OK, this is bizarre!

Now a third captain arrives, but this one is wiser than the first two. He doesn't get rude with the prophet but begs for mercy, and it saved him and his men. What if he hadn't been so polite? Well, we know how that would have turned out. We might rather ask ourselves, what if the first two captains had been polite? Clearly they didn't feel the need to show respect to a prophet, but they should have. Not long after this he got a chariot ride to heaven.

Widow of Zarephath

Then the word of the LORD came to [Elijah], saying, "Arise, go to Zarephath,
which belongs to Sidon, and dwell there. See, I have commanded a widow there to
provide for you." 1 Kings 17:8, 9

God always takes care of His people, even when all seems lost. That's exactly what happened to Elijah, prophet of God during the reign of Ahab and Jezebel. When a drought and famine hit the nation of Israel, God sent Elijah north to the town of Zarephath to get help from a poor widow. Here's the story. The woman and her son only had enough food for one last meal, and they were out gathering sticks to prepare the food when Elijah showed up. All that was left was a little oil in a jar and a handful of flour. Imagine a stranger coming to your house and asking you to give him the last of your food. That's exactly what happened to her! Elijah knew that God wanted to perform an amazing miracle for the widow and her son if they would trust Him. After the woman had used up the last of the oil and flour to make some bread for Elijah, God rewarded her kindness and faith. There was more oil in the jar and more flour in the bin—every day for more than two years!

Then something even more amazing happened to the woman and her son. The boy got sick and died, and again Elijah came to the rescue. He raised her son to life! Wow! That's amazing! Only a man or woman of God could do such a thing!

What if the woman hadn't agreed to feed Elijah first? What if she had said, "My son eats first"? Then it's very likely the two of them would have died from starvation. And even if they had survived the famine, when her son died later, without Elijah around, who would have raised the boy to life? What a disaster this whole story might have turned out to be! Think about it. The fate of this woman's son was dependent on her kindness to a complete stranger.

JULY 15

The Widow's Oil

Then [Elisha] said, "Go, borrow vessels from everywhere,
from all your neighbors—empty vessels; do not gather just a few.
And when you have come in, you shall shut the door behind you and your sons; then
pour it into all those vessels, and set aside the full ones." 2 Kings 4:3, 4

What an exciting time it must have been to live in the days of Elisha! Everywhere he went, things happened. Big things! Surprising things! Miraculous things! Like the time he helped a woman whose husband had died. Times were tough! She had maxed out all her credit cards and couldn't pay them off. OK, they didn't have credit cards in those days, but the creditor was coming to take her two sons and sell them as slaves. Ouch! That couldn't have been much fun! Anyway, she went to Elisha and cried her eyes out over this nightmare of a dilemma, and wouldn't you know it, he did a very strange thing! He asked what she had in her house. When she told him, "Only a small jar of oil," he told her to go collect jars and pots from all over town. "Put them in your house," he said, "then shut the door and begin filling the jars with oil."

Whew! I'd like to have been a fly on the wall that day to see what happened next! Something big was coming! It was in the air! She did as she was told, and then with the help of her sons she began pouring. And pouring. And pouring. No matter how much she poured, there was always more oil to pour. Until she ran out of jars and pots, that is. Only then did the supply of oil stop. We can imagine the mixed feeling she must have had when the oil stopped flowing.

What if she hadn't acted in faith? What if she had deviated in the slightest from following Elisha's directions? We can guess that her blessings would have been fewer indeed, if any at all. Surely her huge increase in oil and the payment of the debt in full topped her wildest dreams to answered prayer. But that's the way it is when we serve God. Amen!

Agabus

And as we stayed many days, a certain prophet named Agabus
came down from Judea. When he had come to us, he took Paul's belt,
bound his own hands and feet, and said, "Thus says the Holy Spirit,
'So shall the Jews at Jerusalem bind the man who owns this belt,
and deliver him into the hands of the Gentiles.' " Acts 21:10, 11

A gabus was a prophet of the Lord in the days of Paul. We first catch sight of him when Paul traveled through Tyre, a Roman city along the coast of the Mediterranean. Agabus was a rather dramatic sort of fellow, and when Paul announced he was going up to Jerusalem, the prophet advised him against it. "It's not safe in Jerusalem," he insisted. "The Jews will stone you for sure." But Paul was persistent. He didn't usually let people talk him out of what he wanted to do. He knew he would be traveling to Rome soon, and before going, he wanted to visit Jerusalem one more time. In this case he was counting on the Lord to keep him safe.

Agabus could see Paul was headed for trouble, so he used an object lesson to warn him one last time. Reaching for the belt around Paul's waist, he tied his own hands and feet with it. "The Holy Spirit has told me the Jewish leaders in Jerusalem are going to turn you over to the Romans," he said. Paul nodded his head, thanked Agabus for the warning, and went up to Jerusalem. And what happened? He got into trouble just as Agabus said he would. And he ended up on trial before the Jewish Sanhedrin. He got caught in a mob of angry people. He did end up in prison under a Roman guard.

What if Agabus hadn't bothered to warn Paul? He didn't have to, since he knew Paul wouldn't listen anyway. But others at that meeting heard his warning and would have had their faith strengthened when they saw the fulfillment of that prophecy. Though things don't always turn out the way we want, God always sends His people help when they need it most.

Baby Jesus

So it was, that while they were there, the days were completed for her
to be delivered. And she brought forth her firstborn Son,
and wrapped Him in swaddling cloths, and laid Him in a manger,
because there was no room for them in the inn. Luke 2:6, 7

This is the story of the ages. It's the story in which God came down to humankind as a baby in order to bring humans up to God. He came at a time in history when humans' inhumanity to each other was near a breaking point. Slavery, disease, and corruptness were a part of human existence everywhere. Only God could turn this old world around, and He did it through the birth of His dear Son. Jesus was born to a peasant couple in the little village of Bethlehem. Not in a hospital bed or a nice hotel, but in a stable where cows and donkeys had bedded down for the night. There were no doctors present to make sure everything turned out all right. No medicines or sanitary conditions to make the delivery safe. Joseph wrapped Him in a special cloth they had brought for His birth and then laid Him in a feedbox with straw where livestock usually ate. What a story! What a beginning for the Savior of the world! If the innkeeper who turned Mary and Joseph away could have known who this baby was, he would have been horrified at the treatment he gave the poor family. Could it be that this was all part of God's master plan, that Jesus should not be born in a palace or the mansions of the rich? He was to be born in the most unlikely place, where the humblest of the humble could be born.

For sure, the story of Jesus' birth has been a very special one down through the centuries. Even today we talk about the stable where the Son of God was born, and we celebrate that event every Christmas. What if He had decided He wouldn't come to this wretched world filled with poverty and rejection and sin? Then we would not have a Savior to save us. Thanks to the Father, Son, and Holy Spirit, He did come, and now we are brothers and sisters to this baby.

Mordecai

So Haman took the robe and the horse, arrayed Mordecai
and led him on horseback through the city square, and proclaimed before him, "Thus
shall it be done to the man whom the king delights to honor!" Esther 6:11

Mordecai was quite a guy! He was one of the most opportunistic men in the Bible, and a hero several times over. For one thing, he raised Esther, his young cousin, to become one of the great women of the Bible. He also uncovered a plot to assassinate the king and thought nothing of it when he got no credit for it. Then when a decree was passed to have all the Jews in the Persian Empire destroyed, Mordecai urged Esther to do something about it. "Go see your husband, the king, and get us some help!" he told her. His greatest enemy in the empire was Haman, the prime minister of Persia, and the two were continually at odds. Haman hated Mordecai because the Jew wouldn't bow to him, and it was for this reason that he suggested the decree to kill all Jews. Later, Haman mistakenly thought the king wished to honor him, and he suggested a song and parade in celebration. Ahasuerus liked the idea and told Haman to give all these honors to Mordecai. In the end, Mordecai and his people were vindicated, Esther got her rewritten decree, and Mordecai was made prime minister in place of Haman. Mordecai was quite a national hero, don't you think?

What if he hadn't refused to bow the knee to Haman? What if he hadn't risked his life to save the king? What if he hadn't demanded that Esther go see the king? None of these was the easy way out, but they were all the right thing to do. Mordecai took all these risks, so he must have been a very brave man. God was honored by Mordecai's bravery, the king's life was saved, and all the Jews in the kingdom were spared. Oh, and one more thing. Without Mordecai's stand-up kind of courage, the king would have never noticed him and made him prime minister.

Nebuchadnezzar

"And at the end of the time I, Nebuchadnezzar, lifted my eyes to heaven, and my understanding returned to me; and I blessed the Most High and praised and honored Him who lives forever: for His dominion is an everlasting dominion, and His kingdom is from generation to generation." Daniel 4:34

Nebuchadnezzar was one of the smartest, boldest, fiercest rulers of his day. He conquered the eastern Mediterranean world and then gave Babylon a make-over. The outer city walls were made of yellow bricks, the gates of blue, the palaces of red, and the temples white. Even more impressive were the brightly decorated pictures of bulls, dragons, and lions he built right into the walls. The capital city was at least eleven miles in circumference, and his famous hanging gardens have long been considered one of the seven wonders of the ancient world.

God wanted Nebuchadnezzar to know there was more to life than conquering and building kingdoms. Twice he spoke to the king in dreams (about a metallic man and a gigantic tree). Four times the Lord demonstrated Himself through miracles so Nebuchadnezzar would know the God of heaven (Daniel's test scores; a forgotten dream; three young fire walkers; and a king gone crazy). The king finally accepted Jehovah as his God, but not before he spent seven years crawling around in the fields like a wild beast. His hair grew tangled and matted, his teeth turned yellow-green, and his nails got long and grotesque, like the claws of a bird. His clothes became tattered and eventually fell off, but it didn't matter. His hairy body collected all the filth of the fields and woods where he lived, making him barely distinguishable from the wild donkeys.

What if King Nebuchadnezzar hadn't accepted Jehovah as his God? Likely, then, he would have remained a wild beast for the rest of his life. He would have roamed the fields looking like a baboon, growling like a lion, and smelling like a warthog. But the Holy Spirit finally brought him to his senses, and because of this we will one day meet him in heaven.

Nehemiah

And I said to the king, "If it pleases the king, and if your servant
has found favor in your sight, I ask that you send me to Judah, to the city of my
fathers' tombs, that I may rebuild it." Nehemiah 2:5

Nehemiah was one of the great heroes in Hebrew history. He first comes to our attention while working as a cupbearer for King Artaxerxes in the Persian palace at Shushan. Many Jews had returned to Judah nearly a hundred years before, but they were not doing well—the walls of Jerusalem were still broken down. This caused Nehemiah to be very upset. When the king saw how unhappy he was, he sent his cupbearer home to Judah to take care of business. And that's exactly what Nehemiah did when he arrived in Jerusalem a few months later.

At first, he didn't tell anyone why he had come. Instead, he went out at night to survey the city. The place was a disaster, all overgrown with thorns and brambles, and Nehemiah's donkey couldn't even pick its way through the stones and rubble. But the next day he lowered the boom. "We're going to rebuild the city walls," he told the leaders and the people, and then he set out to organize the work crews by clans and families. Construction materials had to be gathered, and special tools had to be built to handle the heavy work. Stones had to be cut, dragged to the work site, and fitted in place. Work progressed quickly, but there was opposition on every hand. Leaders from the surrounding nations tried to stop the work on the walls, so Nehemiah posted guards and ordered everyone to keep their weapons near them as they worked. It was a marathon building project, but finally, after just fifty-two days, the walls and gates were finished.

What if Nehemiah hadn't gone to Jerusalem to help build the walls? And what if he hadn't put his faith in God to help him do it? Then the job wouldn't have gotten done. The devil and his allies surrounding Judah would have been victorious, and God's people would have suffered even more. We can thank God for leaders like Nehemiah.

JULY 21

Shadrach, Meshach, and Abed-Nego

"O Nebuchadnezzar, we have no need to answer you in this matter. . . .
Our God whom we serve is able to deliver us from the burning fiery furnace,
and He will deliver us from your hand, O king. But if not, let it be known to you,
O king, that we do not serve your gods, nor will we worship the gold image
which you have set up." Daniel 3:16–18

What would it be like to be threatened with death in a blast furnace if you didn't bow to an idol? That would be a heavy price to pay, but Shadrach, Meshach, and Abed-Nego faced it with courage.

Why all the hubbub? King Nebuchadnezzar had built a ninety-foot image on the plains of Dura for everyone to worship. History tells us there was an attempted coup on the throne, and this exercise was an effort to scare everyone into submission. And the three Hebrews? They refused to bow because their loyalties were with the God of heaven. He alone was deserving of their worship. They wished to honor Him and His commandments that called for their allegiance.

When the king realized their love for God exceeded their fear of him, he was hopping mad. "Heat those blast furnaces hotter than hot!" we can hear him shouting in a rage. The young men were thrown in, but the outcome wasn't what Nebuchadnezzar expected. Amazingly, they were not even touched by the flames! And then the king saw someone else with them. "Who's that fourth man in the fire?" he demanded incredulously, quite forgetting that no one should have survived the heat at all. "He looks like the Son of God!"

What a story! What an honor it must have been to walk and talk with Jesus in the flames! But what if the young men hadn't remained true in their convictions? What if they had bowed to the idol like everyone else? Then the political representatives on the plains of Dura wouldn't have had such a grand introduction to the God of heaven. And, of course, the boys wouldn't have met the Son of God personally. Good choice, Shadrach, Meshach, and Abed-Nego.

Vashti

> But Queen Vashti refused to come at the king's command brought by his eunuchs;
> therefore the king was furious, and his anger burned within him. Esther 1:12

Vashti was a woman of extraordinary beauty and certainly one with great dignity and class. She lived in a lavish palace. History describes it as having magnificent gardens, extensive banquet halls with marble pillars, and couches made of silver and gold.

She is remembered as the queen of Persia who bravely dared to disobey her drunken husband. He had thrown a party for all his government officials that lasted 180 days, and during the final week he called for Vashti to dance for him and his guests. Vashti was entertaining the wives of all the government officials and refused to come. Maybe she knew they were all drunk, but maybe she just didn't want to parade herself around like one of the king's exotic dancers. Did she know what might happen if she refused? Absolutely.

And, indeed, it didn't go well for her. Acting on the advice of his court counselors, Xerxes (also known as Ahasuerus) decided to banish Vashti from the palace and replaced her with a new queen. This was a very interesting outcome. Why didn't Xerxes have Vashti executed when she refused to answer his summons? He was the king! If a queen could be killed for coming to see him without being invited, we have to ask ourselves why he wouldn't kill a queen who outright disobeyed him.

Clearly she was a courageous woman, and it's too bad things turned out for her the way they did. Or is it? What if she had danced for the king? What if she hadn't been thrown out of the palace? Well, all things work together for God's people, that's for sure. We don't know where Vashti ended up, but we do know that God helped Esther, the new queen, save her people from extermination. That's a pretty big accomplishment and a happy ending of sorts for everyone. Maybe even Vashti.

JULY 23

Zeresh

Then his wife Zeresh and all his friends said to him, "Let a gallows be made, fifty cubits high, and in the morning suggest to the king that Mordecai be hanged on it; then go merrily with the king to the banquet." And the thing pleased Haman; so he had the gallows made. Esther 5:14

We know what a beast Haman was, but what about his wife, Zeresh? We don't really know much about her—what she looked like, what day of the week she had her hair done, her favorite foods, how many children she had, or if she had any real friends. She must have been truly flattered when her husband was appointed prime minister of Persia. Think of all the perks that came with government jobs in those days—parties at the palace, deeds to cities and lands, access to the royal treasury, and hobnobbing with all the snobby elite of Sushan.

But every night when Haman came home, she had to listen to his complaints about Mordecai. She had to listen to his rage at all Jews and his plans to kill them. She knew he had written a decree and offered to pay ten thousand talents (about 377 tons) of silver into the royal treasury to see that it was enforced. She saw how flattered Haman was to be invited as a special guest to Esther's banquet, but also how embarrassed he was to have to lead the Mordecai parade.

And, like any loyal wife, she supported her husband in all these outrageous plans. She advised him to build a gallows to hang Mordecai. She cheered him on when he got to go to Queen Esther's second special banquet. Did she know what would happen if her husband hated everyone who disagreed with him? Did she know that those who kill by the sword will die by the sword? Maybe not, but she should have been smart enough to figure it out. What if she had? What if she had told her husband Haman, "Enough is enough! Stop being so greedy!" Then she wouldn't have lost him. He would have lived. His property would not have been confiscated, and she wouldn't have ended up a poor woman. In the end, that's what comes from greed and hate.

Sanballat and Tobiah

But it so happened, when Sanballat heard that we were rebuilding the wall, that he was furious and very indignant, and mocked the Jews. . . . Now Tobiah the Ammonite was beside him, and he said, "Whatever they build, if even a fox goes up on it, he will break down their stone wall." Nehemiah 4:1, 3

Coming home from Babylonian captivity was very exciting for the Jews, but the enemies surrounding Judah were not happy at all. They were afraid Judah would become a powerful nation again.

Sanballat the Samaritan and Tobiah the Ammonite were especially upset and planned how they might sabotage the work going on at Jerusalem. They offered to help rebuild the city, but Nehemiah turned them down. He knew these guys were idol worshipers who only wanted to make trouble. Over and over again they tried to get him to come dine with them, or have a conference with them, or make a treaty with them, but he always refused. "Why should I take time off and leave my important work here in Jerusalem?" he said.

This made Sanballat and Tobiah even angrier. They thought they could attack the city and stop the work, but Nehemiah had the workers keep a sword or spear beside them all day as they worked. And it worked. By the end of fifty-two days the wall of Jerusalem was complete, and the danger was past. It must have been a relief for Nehemiah, but Sanballat and Tobiah knew they had lost the war.

What if Sanballat and Tobiah had been kind to Nehemiah? What if they had joined the Jews and said, "We want to worship Jehovah like you"? Then the Samaritans and Ammonites would have been truly blessed by the example of their leaders, and maybe even their hearts could have changed too. Maybe by the time Jesus came centuries later, the Jews and Samaritans could have been friends instead of enemies. Too bad! So sad.

Andrew

One of the two who heard John speak, and followed Him,
was Andrew, Simon Peter's brother. John 1:40

Andrew grew up in Bethsaida and made a living by fishing on the lake of Galilee with his brother Peter. He was an uncomplicated man, simple in faith, and ready to trust Jesus in all things. We don't find him being the bad guy in any of the stories during Jesus' ministry. He didn't have serious character issues like Judas, or a bad temper like James and John, or a suspicious past like Simon the Zealot.

When he heard John the Baptist at the Jordan River telling everyone that Jesus was "the Lamb of God who takes away the sins of the world," Andrew believed it was true. Not surprisingly, he discovered Jesus was indeed the Messiah everyone had been waiting for, and then he brought his brother Peter to Jesus. Together, they left their fishing boat to become full-time disciples of Jesus.

Andrew was a key figure in many of the stories that followed during the ministry of Jesus. He was at the wedding feast in Cana when Jesus turned water into wine. He was the disciple who brought a little boy's lunch of loaves and fishes to help Jesus feed five thousand hungry people. During Passion Week, he and Philip brought some Greek visitors to see Jesus in the outer court of the temple. A few hours later, he was one of four disciples on the Mount of Olives when Jesus gave specifics about the signs of His second coming.

What if he hadn't followed Jesus to become one of His disciples? What if he had stayed in the fishing business? Clearly he would have missed out on three wonderful years with Jesus as the Savior performed miracles, comforted the poor, and preached the gospel. And, of course, he would have missed out on other adventures. Christian tradition tells us he went to Scotland as a missionary and later died a martyr in Greece. But praise God, like the other disciples, he now awaits the resurrection morning when Jesus will raise him to everlasting life.

John

When Jesus therefore saw His mother, and the disciple whom He loved standing by, He said to His mother, "Woman, behold your son!" John 19:26

John the beloved was quite young when he first met Jesus. He was born in Galilee, a fisherman by trade, and he became interested in Jesus the Messiah when he heard John the Baptist preaching about "the Lamb of God that takes away the sins of the world." For more than three years he walked the roads of Galilee and Judea, witnessing Jesus' ministry. He was one of the few who stayed with Jesus at His trial and crucifixion; and he was the one Jesus asked to take care of His mother Mary.

Throughout his lifetime John endured much for the sake of the gospel. As a Christian in the early church he suffered cruel beatings and imprisonment, and even escaped from prison with the help of angels. According to church historians, he witnessed the destruction of Jerusalem and later was arrested and brought to Rome during the reign of the emperor Domitian. The cruel emperor ordered John executed by being thrown into a vat of boiling oil, but miraculously the faithful disciple was preserved unharmed. He was then banished to the Greek island of Patmos to keep him from spreading the gospel. However, while on the island he received visions from God and many visits from angels to encourage him to be faithful. Finally, John was the only one of the original twelve disciples to die a natural death.

What if John hadn't decided to follow Jesus and become His disciple? Well, he would have missed the three best years of his life with the Son of God. He would have also missed out on all that persecution and mistreatment in the early church. But then, maybe even more important, he wouldn't have written five books in the Bible: the Gospel of John, three epistles to the early church, and, of course, the book of Revelation. What a legacy he left behind!

Matthew

After these things He went out and saw a tax collector named Levi,
sitting at the tax office. And He said to him, "Follow Me." Luke 5:27

Matthew was a tax collector, or what was commonly called a publican. In Jesus' day his job was considered the bottom of the barrel in society, as professions went. It wasn't surprising that everyone hated Matthew for being a tax collector. What shocked them most was what Jesus said to him: "Follow Me." It was a simple invitation, but it must have been the words Matthew was hoping to hear, because he didn't hesitate for a second. Immediately he got up, handed his money box to the Roman soldier standing guard at the tax booth, and walked away down the street with Jesus. The transformation that came over Matthew at that moment was amazing! It was the most startling decision of his life, but one he would never regret. From that day forward he became one of Jesus' most faithful disciples.

Jesus had often said, "Whoever wants to follow Me must leave everything behind: mother and father, the things of this world, and, of course, the love of money." And for Matthew this all made sense. Now he was unselfish and kind, and very happy for the change Jesus had brought to his life. He was so excited that he decided to hold a big reception with Jesus as the guest of honor. Town drunks, woman friends, and fellow tax collectors were invited, and Jesus made them all feel at home.

What if Matthew hadn't become a disciple of Jesus? What if he had felt too unworthy and kept on being a hated tax collector? Then he wouldn't have gone on to do great things for God. He wouldn't have had the chance to go as a missionary to faraway countries. He wouldn't have died as a martyr while preaching the gospel, and he wouldn't be our example today of what it means to give up everything in this world to follow Jesus.

Priests and Scribes

And when he had gathered all the chief priests and scribes of the people together, he inquired of them where the Christ was to be born. So they said to him, "In Bethlehem of Judea, for thus it is written by the prophet." Matthew 2:4, 5

The priests and scribes were part of the political establishment that rejected Jesus as the Savior of the world, starting back in 4 B.C. when He was born. How could it be that the religious leaders of the day did not recognize this baby boy as the Messiah? For one thing, He wasn't born in a palace or the home of rich aristocrats. For another, the priests and scribes hadn't been notified personally of His coming. Instead, shepherds were spreading a story that angels had told them the Savior of the world had been born in Bethlehem of Judea, under the very noses of the temple priests in Jerusalem. Next, the Magi came from the East in search of the King of the Jews. Their arrival was startling and posed a threat to everyone. The priests and scribes were expecting a Messiah to come any day now, as predicted by the prophets, but no one knew who He might be.

King Herod brought everything to a head. First, he heard the news from the Magi, and then he called in the priests and scribes. "Where is this Messiah to be born?" he asked. The priests and scribes didn't seem too interested in the conversation, and that made Herod suspicious. "In Bethlehem of Judea," they finally said. Herod sent the Magi on their way to complete their search, but that's as close as the priests would come to meeting the Savior of the world. He disappeared a few hours later into the land of Egypt. Not until the Feast of Passover twelve years later would they have a chance to meet Jesus again.

What if the priests had accepted Jesus? What if they hadn't rejected Him as the coming King? Then they would have had a front-row seat along with the shepherds, Magi, and angels that this Baby Jesus was indeed the Messiah, the Savior of the world.

Shepherds

Now there were in the same country shepherds living out in the fields,
keeping watch over their flock by night. Luke 2:8

What was it like to be a shepherd in Jesus' day? What was it like to live out in the fields with sheep, keeping watch over flocks by night? What was it like to go through sleepless nights to protect the lambs from predators and bandits, to be smelly and have people look down their noses at you for having that job? It was a thankless, lonely job. A humble job. We can imagine the shepherds sitting close to their fire to keep warm the night Jesus was born. We are told they were talking about the promises found in the Scriptures that a Messiah would be coming any day now. As they talked, an angel unexpectedly stood among them, his face shining like a hundred suns. "Don't be afraid," he said. "I've got good news. Tonight, right here in Bethlehem, in the City of David, a Savior has been born. He is your Messiah who will die for the sins of the world." The shepherds were shocked. Could this be true? Almost in answer to their thoughts, the hills surrounding Bethlehem were suddenly lit up with a choir of angels in the sky. "Glory to God in the highest, and His blessings of peace to people everywhere!" they sang.

And then they were gone. The sweet strains of music died away in the night, and soon the hills of Bethlehem were dark and silent once again. But the shepherds were very excited. "God has spoken to us from heaven," they told each other. "We are so blessed! Let's go now and look for the baby! He's right here in Bethlehem!" And off they raced to find him.

What if the shepherds hadn't been so humble? What if they had not been studying the Scriptures in search of the Messiah? Then God might have passed them by. He might not have sent the angels to sing in excitement about Jesus' birth. In that case they wouldn't have been the first ones to see the Baby Jesus who had come to take away the sins of the world.

Simeon and Anna

And behold, there was a man in Jerusalem whose name was Simeon,
and this man was just and devout, waiting for the Consolation of Israel,
and the Holy Spirit was upon him. Luke 2:25

Now there was one, Anna, a prophetess. . . . And coming in that instant
she gave thanks to the Lord, and spoke of Him to all those
who looked for redemption in Jerusalem. Luke 2:36, 38

We don't know very much about Simeon or Anna. They were both old and very religious. Both spent a lot of time in the temple, and both appeared to be prophets.

We catch a brief glimpse of them as Mary and Joseph brought the Baby Jesus to the temple for His dedication when He was eight days old. Simeon was the first to notice Jesus and walked over to see the baby. Evidently the Holy Spirit had revealed to Simeon that he wouldn't die until he had seen the Savior of the world. "Lord, now let me die in peace," he prayed as he lifted Jesus up in his hands. "My eyes have seen this little baby who will bring salvation to the world." Those were nice words for Mary and Joseph to hear, but Simeon also had words of sadness for Mary. "Hard days are coming for you," he told her. "A time is coming when you will feel like a sword has pierced through your soul." He was predicting Jesus' death on the cross, but, of course, Mary could not see the future.

Then it was Anna's turn. She lived in one of the rooms at the temple and had spent all her time there fasting, praying, and praising God. And when she saw Jesus she got excited. "Thanks be to God," she told everyone standing nearby. "This little child will be the One to redeem us all from this world of sin!"

Now, what if Simeon and Anna hadn't come to the temple that day? What if they had decided to sleep in or stay at home all day? Then they wouldn't have met Jesus. And they wouldn't have had the blessing of holding the Savior of the world in their arms.

Wise Men

Now after Jesus was born in Bethlehem of Judea in the days of Herod the king,
behold, wise men from the East came to Jerusalem, saying,
"Where is He who has been born King of the Jews? For we have seen
His star in the East and have come to worship Him." Matthew 2:1, 2

We call them wise men today, though they have traditionally been called the Magi. They were men of influence, wealth, and education. It's not clear where they came from, or how far they traveled to worship the Baby Jesus. History tells us it was probably from the ancient land of Persia in the East—a journey that would require months of travel. The star they saw led them to Jerusalem first, where it rested above the temple. This was the first of several opportunities for Jewish leaders to see that Jesus had indeed been sent from heaven as the world's Messiah. But the wise men found no one watching and longing for Jesus. They saw indifference and fear that such a One might steal the limelight of power.

King Herod was even worse. He feared his own position might be taken from him should this "Messiah" actually come to be. This is why he asked the wise men to locate Jesus and then tell him where He was, so that he might "worship Him also" (Matthew 2:8).

They found Jesus all right, but not in the palaces of the affluent, as they had expected. They gave their gifts in worship of Him, sensing that they were in the presence of God. And then, as they came, so they returned, without notifying King Herod, because God gave them a dream unmasking Herod's real intentions.

And what if the wise men hadn't studied the Scriptures? What if they hadn't followed the star? What if they hadn't been listening to the Holy Spirit to tell them Jesus was in danger? Then they would have missed out on the chance to honor the One who called the universe into existence. What a blessing they received, and what a story they left behind!

Zacharias

Now his father Zacharias was filled with the Holy Spirit, and prophesied, saying:
"Blessed is the Lord God of Israel, for He has visited and redeemed His people."
Luke 1:67, 68

This is a pretty bizarre story. Zacharias thought he was too old to become a father. He was excited about the idea of it all right, but he doubted that it would actually happen.

Here's the story line. He was a Levite priest who served in the temple at Jerusalem once a year for about two weeks. One day he was at the altar of incense, offering up prayers for the people, when suddenly an angel appeared on the right side of the altar. An angel standing on the right like that usually meant good news for God's people. But Zacharias was afraid, as we can imagine he would be. It's not every day that one gets to see an angel from heaven, let alone one who has come to give you a message personally.

The message? Zacharias and his wife were going to have a son. He would be a miracle baby due to their age but also because he would grow up to do a special job for God. Zacharias's reaction? "No way, we're too old," he told the angel. Wow! First, he was afraid of the angel, and next thing we know, he was challenging the angel about the promise of a son to come! That was pretty brazen, and the angel took him to task for it, promising him he would be a mute until the baby boy was born! Amazing!

So, what's the takeaway from this story? Men like Zacharias need to keep in mind that God says what He means and means what He says. In other words, He always has the last word. What if Zacharias had believed the angel? In that case, he probably would have been commended by the angel instead of being scolded. Yikes! And, of course, he wouldn't have lost his voice.

AUGUST 2

Judas

Then Satan entered Judas. . . . So he went his way and conferred with the chief priests and captains, how he might betray Him to them. And they were glad, and agreed to give him money. Luke 22:3–5

The story of Judas is one for the history books. He was a gifted man and a born leader, but he had real character issues. He was by nature dishonest and self-serving, and though the other disciples weren't aware of it, he sometimes used his sticky fingers to help himself to the money in the money bag. In addition, Judas had questions about why Jesus was waiting so long to set Himself up as Israel's prophetic King. Over time, he hatched a plan to settle the issue once and for all. He would arrange a confrontation between Jesus and the big shots at the temple, Jesus would show His true colors, and Judas would get all the credit. Peculiar thought, that the God of the universe would need help in marketing Himself to a world He had created and now came to save.

Jesus never gave up on Judas. On the night of the Last Supper, Judas felt the Spirit of God calling him to repentance for the corrupt deed he was about to commit. He ignored the warning and went out into the night to finalize his plans with the chief priests. The real irony of the story is that a few hours later he had the nerve to show up at the Garden with the temple mafia and betray His Master with a kiss. What a sham! The infamous act made Judas one of the most notorious characters in history. For more than three years He had walked and talked with the Son of God, and now he was selling Him for the price of a slave! Thirty measly pieces of silver!

What if Judas hadn't been so greedy? What if he had decided to trust Jesus to set up His kingdom when He was ready? Then he wouldn't have had to watch as Jesus was dragged away to trial. He wouldn't have had to repent with bitter tears at having helped shed innocent blood. He wouldn't have hung himself later that day in an act of desperation. It's a shame! Today we only remember Judas Iscariot as the one who betrayed the Son of God with a kiss.

Peter

Jesus said to Simon Peter, "Simon, son of Jonah, do you love Me more than these?" He said to Him, "Yes, Lord; You know that I love You." He said to him, "Feed My lambs." John 21:15

Peter was a good man, though a tough character; he was uneducated, unsophisticated, and brash and impatient too much of the time. When mothers brought their children to see Jesus, Peter turned them away rudely. When temple authorities asked if Jesus was a temple taxpayer, Peter said yes indignantly, not stopping to think. When he saw Jesus talking with glorified heavenly messengers on the mount of transfiguration, he could think of nothing better to say than, "Come on! Let's set up monuments for everybody here on the mountain!"

He was the first disciple to testify that Jesus was the Christ, the Son of the living God, and promised he would be loyal to Jesus and faithful to his dying breath. That was a great plan, but on the night of Jesus' trial he caved and swore he had never even met "the Man." And when Peter caught sight of Jesus looking at him across the courtyard, it humbled him inside and out. In shame he ran from the palace, overwhelmed at what he had done.

Little wonder, then, that he was grieved when, a few weeks later, Jesus asked him three times, "Do you love me, Peter?"

"Yes, Lord," was all Peter could say. "You know I love You!" And then Jesus did something very unusual. He opened the doors to the future to give Peter a glimpse of what was coming—what this devotion would cost him.

What if Peter had never joined up with Jesus? Then he wouldn't have denied Jesus, but he also wouldn't have had the chance to repent and promise to follow Jesus forever. And, of course, he wouldn't have had to hang on a cross as a martyr for the gospel of Jesus. But then again, his example wouldn't be there for all of us who want a crown of life like the one he will receive.

Thomas

Jesus said to him, "Thomas, because you have seen Me, you have believed.
Blessed are those who have not seen and yet have believed." John 20:29

Are you one who tends to see a glass of water as being half empty rather than half full? Do you tend to demand evidence for the power of God in your life before you believe? Then you can probably relate to "doubting Thomas," as we like to call him.

In spite of this, he was very devoted to Jesus. When the Lord told the disciples He was going up to Judea to see Martha and Lazarus, Thomas was worried. He had seen the religious leaders in Jerusalem get so mad that they wanted to stone Jesus. But he hung right in there. "Let's go to Judea too, so we can die with Jesus," he told the other disciples bravely.

Unfortunately, Thomas had his moments when faith went out the window. The first evening after Jesus' resurrection, Thomas wasn't among the group of disciples as they gathered in the upper room. He didn't see Jesus come in through the closed door of the chamber. He didn't hear Jesus tell the disciples, "Peace be to you." He didn't see the nail marks in Jesus' hands or the scar in his side. That didn't happen until eight days later, when Jesus again appeared to the disciples. Then it was that Jesus told Thomas, "Blessed are those who have not seen and yet believe."

What became of him after Jesus went back to heaven? Christian tradition tells us Thomas went as a missionary to India, where he died as a martyr for his faith. Was it worth it? You bet! Today in India, the legends are still told of Thomas and his work there as a Christian. What if he hadn't followed Jesus as one of His disciples? Then he wouldn't have been blessed to walk and talk every day for three years with the Savior of the world. What if he hadn't been so doubtful when everyone told him Jesus had risen? Then Jesus would have commended him for his faith instead of scolding him for lack of it.

Crowd at the Triumphal Entry

And a very great multitude spread their clothes on the road; others cut down branches from the trees and spread them on the road. Then the multitudes who went before and those who followed cried out, saying: "Hosanna to the Son of David! 'Blessed is He who comes in the name of the LORD!' " Matthew 21:8, 9

Who were these people? They were farmers, shepherds, carpenters, stonemasons, weavers, potters, bakers, bankers, merchants, and peasants. They were so excited because it was clear to them that Jesus was finally going to make the announcement they had all been waiting to hear: He was the Messiah! He was finally going to give the Romans a good thumping! He was finally going to set up His everlasting kingdom! Can you imagine the excitement? Can you imagine the electricity in the air that warm Sunday afternoon? The custom of the day demanded that everyone lay their coats and cloaks on the road for His donkey to walk over. Hundreds waved fresh-cut palm branches. Thousands sang their hosanna songs. Men shouted, women danced, and children ran excitedly along the swarming crowd.

In addition to the crowd, the disciples were also ecstatic, thinking that the big day had come. They had been counting on it for more than three years, and now they were sure Jesus would become their King. There were others in the crowd who weren't so happy—the bigoted Pharisees and Sadducees, the indignant scribes, and the self-righteous priests. "Tell the people to stop singing so loud!" they told Him angrily. "They're disturbing the peace!" Can you believe that?

What if all these people hadn't sung praises to Jesus at His triumphal entry into Jerusalem? According to Jesus, the rocks would have cried out. But, honestly, many of the folks in that crowd were fickle. How do we know? Because just five days later they were shouting, "Crucify Him! Crucify Him!" Really? Really. It's a fact!

Joanna, Salome, and Susanna

Joanna the wife of Chuza, Herod's steward, and Susanna, and many others . . .
provided for Him from their substance. Luke 8:3

We always hear about the men who followed Jesus and helped Him in His ministry, but we sometimes forget there were women disciples too. The twelve disciples traveled with Him to preach, heal, and baptize, but who cooked for them? Who did their laundry? Where did they get the money they needed for traveling? Well, the Bible gives us a few clues about that.

As Jesus' ministry grew in Judea, and especially Galilee, many women began traveling with Jesus from place to place. We know of several. A woman by the name of Susanna was one of His followers, and a faithful supporter. Salome, the wife of Zebedee, and mother of James and John, ministered for Jesus when He was in Galilee. She also traveled with Him and His disciples on their final trip to Jerusalem, where she was an eyewitness of His crucifixion, and she accompanied several women to Jesus' tomb on the Resurrection morning to anoint His body with spices. Joanna, another follower of Jesus, was the wife of Chuza, steward in King Herod's palace. It's clear some of these women had money, and they were willing to help support His ministry with it.

What if these women had said, "We're not interested in following Jesus"? Or, "It's too hard traveling around from place to place, cooking over a campfire, sleeping on the ground, and doing our wash in the river. We want the comforts of home, where we can eat undisturbed without having to swat flies and mosquitoes. We don't want people staring at us or gossiping about us when we walk through town."

Then they would have missed out on the best three years of their lives. They would have missed encouraging Jesus, especially in the last week of His life, and wouldn't have been privileged to be the first ones at Jesus' tomb on that Resurrection morning.

John the Baptist

"He must increase, but I must decrease." John 3:30

John the Baptist was a different sort of character. He wore clothes made of camel skin and ate locust beans and honey. But he had a message that was really catching on. "Repent, for the kingdom of God is at hand!" he said. "The Messiah is on His way, and when He shows up He will change the world forever."

For a time, John lived in the wilderness, studied the Scriptures, and prepared himself for the task before him. But now his time had come to turn the world upside down. People were coming out from Jerusalem, all Judea, and even Galilee to hear his message and be baptized in the Jordan River. Right now, he was the most popular attraction since the days of Elijah the prophet. But he knew that would all change soon.

No one really knew much about him, including the scribes and Pharisees. Like everyone else, they came to see Him because it was the popular thing to do, but John called them a nest of snakes—evil and phony! Common folks came to see him as well as Roman soldiers and tax collectors. "Share what you have, be kind, and don't steal," John advised them all.

And when Jesus showed up, John got eloquent. "Behold, the Lamb of God who takes away the sins of the world," he said. From that day forward, as predicted, Jesus took the stage, and the road got rocky for John. Sadly, he ended up in prison and was eventually executed by King Herod.

What if John hadn't been a humble preacher who put Jesus first? What if he hadn't been willing to lay down his life for God? Then someone else would have had to do it. Someone else would have gotten the privilege of baptizing Jesus in the Jordan. Someone else would have become the most honored of prophets in the history of mankind. No kidding.

Lazarus

Now when He had said these things, He cried with a loud voice,
"Lazarus, come forth!" John 11:43

This is the story of a good man who died twice. It was never God's plan that death should reign supreme in this world, and Lazarus was one of those who paid the price. Not once, but two times.

Jesus and Lazarus were best of friends. Since the day Lazarus first met Jesus, his faith in Christ had been strong. There was no doubt in his mind that Jesus was the Messiah and the Savior of the world. One day, he got very sick, and his sisters were worried about him. They sent someone to find Jesus, but He didn't come right away. His disciples were quite surprised, but Jesus knew that if He waited, many would see the power of God and come to fully accept Him as the Savior of the world.

After two days, Jesus and His disciples went up to Bethany, and when they got there it seemed the whole village was in mourning. Martha and Mary were heart-broken and wondered why Jesus hadn't come in time to heal Lazarus. But Jesus told them not to worry. "I am the resurrection and the life," He said confidently (John 11:25). "Roll away the stone!"

Martha protested, since Lazarus had been dead four days, but strong men rolled the stone from the door of the tomb. "Lazarus, come out!" Jesus called, and that's exactly what the dead man did! He walked out, bound up like a mummy.

What if Jesus had come to Bethany to heal Lazarus in the first place? That would have been wonderful, but then we wouldn't have the miracle of Lazarus' resurrection. Jesus knew best. Truly, all things work together for good to those who love and serve God. Jesus waited with good reason, and we can be grateful He did. The resurrection of Lazarus is one of the most dramatic stories in all the Bible. It teaches us that God can heal us, but sometimes He doesn't right away because He has something much better in mind.

Martha

> But Martha was distracted with much serving, and she approached Him and said,
> "Lord, do You not care that my sister has left me to serve alone?
> Therefore tell her to help me." Luke 10:40

She was a good cook, but she was often very bossy. You couldn't live with her, but you couldn't live without her either. She watched out for Lazarus as any big sister would, but she felt her younger sister wasn't much help around the house. How do we know? Because of a story told in the Gospels. One day, Jesus and His disciples made the trip from Jericho up to Bethany. As usual, Martha was a gracious hostess and invited Jesus to stay with them at her house.

While the meal was being prepared, Jesus sat with His disciples, and, not surprisingly, Mary was with Him listening to all His stories. Meanwhile, Martha was preparing a tasty meal for everyone and getting ready to serve it. We don't know if Mary even gave her sister a thought, or if she felt she should have been helping Martha get things ready. Anyway, at one point Martha came into the room and told Jesus that Mary was being lazy. "Lord, don't You care that my sister isn't helping me?" she fussed. "Tell her to come do her part!" Jesus knew Martha needed help, but He also knew Mary was grateful that He had delivered her from a life of sin, and He wasn't about to chew her out. "Martha, you work too hard, and you need to worry less," He said. "Mary, on the other hand, has her priorities straight and shouldn't be punished for that."

We can be sure Jesus was grateful for the wonderful meal Martha made for Him, but what if she had a been a bit more like Mary? What if she had just made simple food and took more time to be with Jesus? He would soon be taken away from her and crucified on the cross. When that happened, we can be sure of one thing: She wasn't thinking so much about the lentil stew or flatbread or honey cakes she was making for Him. Now that's a lesson for us.

Mary Magdalene

Then Mary took a pound of very costly oil of spikenard,
anointed the feet of Jesus, and wiped His feet with her hair.
And the house was filled with the fragrance of the oil. John 12:3

Mary came from a good home and a loving family. Unfortunately, she ended up living as a prostitute in the town of Magdala. We don't know anything about her parents, but her new lifestyle must have devastated her brother Lazarus and sister Martha.

And then she met Jesus. Seven times He cast the demons out of her heart that were torturing her, and it changed her life forever. She was grateful for this miracle but wondered what could she do to thank Him for saving her from a life of sin. She had heard Jesus say He was going to die shortly, so she bought Him an alabaster jar of very expensive perfume that cost her a year's wages. Then she sneaked into the house of Simon the Pharisee, where he was throwing a party for Jesus. Kneeling at Jesus' feet, she broke the jar and poured the perfume on His feet. Soon the fragrance filled the room.

Then she began to cry as her heart overflowed with love for Jesus. With her long hair she tried to soak up the perfume that was dripping off His feet. Some frowned that a woman with her reputation was in the room. Judas complained that the perfume could have been sold and the money given to the poor. But Jesus defended her. "Why are you criticizing her?" He asked. "She has poured this perfume on me to prepare my body for burial."

Wow! What a touching story, which wouldn't have happened if she hadn't repented of her evil ways and surrendered her life to Jesus. Because of her gratefulness, and the jar of perfume, her story has been told over and over throughout the world. Her extravagant gift was accepted by Jesus, and today we're still talking about it.

Matthias

And they cast their lots, and the lot fell on Matthias.
And he was numbered with the eleven apostles. Acts 1:26

W ho was this guy? We know almost nothing about him before the book of Acts. He had followed Jesus since His baptism at the Jordan. He witnessed Jesus' amazing miracles and captivating preaching. Although not one of Jesus' original twelve disciples, church historians tells us he was one of the seventy disciples sent out on missionary journeys throughout Samaria. Most important, he became one of Jesus' most faithful disciples.

But it was his selection as one of the twelve that brought Matthias into the picture. When Judas betrayed Jesus into the hands of the priests and then went out and hanged himself because of the guilt, there was a hole left among the disciples.

We don't know exactly how the group came to select Matthias, but it was probably a typical method of the day. The details probably don't matter. God Himself directed the whole thing to bring about His purposes for the early church. Two men were chosen as semifinalists to fill the vacuum Judas left behind: Matthias and Joseph, also known as Barsabas—and the lot fell on Matthias.

What an honor for Matthias to be chosen as an apostle to lead the early Christian church in Jerusalem! But what if he hadn't followed the Holy Spirit's call to join up with Jesus? What if he hadn't traveled with the seventy disciples on their missionary journey through Samaria? Then he would have missed the opportunity of a lifetime to become a representative of Jesus in the early church. We don't know what his eventual fate was, but it's likely he traveled widely, and he may even have been martyred as a witness for Jesus. What matters most was his willingness to serve, and the fact that a mansion, harp, and crown await him on the resurrection morning.

AUGUST 12

Simon the Zealot

And when He had called His twelve disciples to Him,
He gave them power over unclean spirits, to cast them out,
and to heal all kinds of sickness and all kinds of disease. Matthew 10:1

We know him only as Simon the Zealot. It's probable that he was a member of a political gang that hated the Romans and fought for Jewish independence. In Jesus' day, Zealots were followers of a dynamic leader named Judas of Gamala, who had started a revolution some twenty years before.

When Simon met Jesus, he was hoping, like the other disciples, that Jesus would set up His earthly kingdom. He could see the talents and gifts Jesus possessed, but it wasn't long before he realized Jesus had other plans. And then when Jesus allowed Himself to be tried and crucified, Simon's hopes died. Jesus was not going to become the King of the Jews. He was not going to smash the power of the Romans and put the Jewish nation back in business as leader of the free world. And so the disciples laid Jesus in the grave and went into hiding for the longest Sabbath of their lives.

And then Sunday morning came, and rumors erupted that Jesus had risen from the dead. No one could believe it, but on Sunday evening Jesus appeared to the disciples in the upper room. What an epiphany! Ancient Christian tradition tells us Simon went on to become a missionary in northern Africa. What if he hadn't become a follower of Jesus? What if he had held out for a messiah who would overthrow Rome and set up an earthly kingdom? Then, of course, he wouldn't have become a missionary to spread the gospel. He wouldn't have died a martyr's death in Palestine during the reign of the Roman emperor Domitian. And he would likely be a forgotten man, missing even from the pages of the Bible.

Herod Antipas

Now when Herod saw Jesus, he was exceedingly glad; for he had desired for a
long time to see Him, because he had heard many things about Him, and he hoped
to see some miracle done by Him. Luke 23:8

Herod Antipas was a bad dude. He came from one of the most infamous families in the Bible. As one of at least seven Herods during the days of Jesus and the early church, he developed quite a reputation for himself. He was a son of Herod the Great—the Herod who killed all the babies in Bethlehem—and he left his own trail of outrageous behavior and cruel deeds.

He married Herodias, his brother Philip's wife—while his brother was still alive. That was the point on which John the Baptist hammered Herod. It cost John because Herod threw him into prison in order to please his wife Herodias and the Jewish leaders. That would have been bad enough, but then he executed the prophet.

It all started at his birthday party. His wife's daughter danced for him, and in his drunken state of mind he offered to give her anything she wanted. Coached by her mother, she asked for John's head on a platter, and Herod was spineless enough to grant it. After that he was never the same. When Jesus' fame as a healer and preacher propelled Him to greatness, Herod got spooked. He even thought that Jesus might be John the Baptist resurrected from the dead. When he met Jesus in person on the day of His trial, Herod refused to set Him free because Jesus would not perform a miracle for him.

What if he hadn't allowed Herodias to trick him into killing John? What if he had advised Pilate to let Jesus go? Without a doubt he would have gone to his grave minus the stain of these atrocities on his record. As it was, he later displeased Caesar, lost his throne in Galilee, and was sent into exile. That's what happens when we think only of ourselves.

AUGUST 14

Herodias and Her Daughter

And when Herodias' daughter herself came in and danced,
and pleased Herod and those who sat with him, the king said to the girl,
"Ask me whatever you want, and I will give it to you." Mark 6:22

Herodias must have been a very beautiful woman, but few would trade places with her. She had such a bad rep that today no one would think of naming a child after her. Clearly her looks were overshadowed by her evil heart, and her daughter followed closely in her footsteps. The two of them together became a deadly duo to practice any evil they could imagine in their hearts. Herodias had very little power in the kingdom of her husband, Herod Antipas, but she definitely had her hooks in him. Today we remember her as one of the most notorious characters in history.

John the Baptist embarrassed her publicly about her marriage to Herod, and she determined to make him squirm. To do this, she urged her husband to arrest John and put him in prison to punish him for daring to speak out against them. She wanted her husband to execute John for treason, but Herod was afraid to do that.

At her husband's birthday party, she came up with a diabolical plan. She arranged for her daughter Salome to dance for Herod to enchant him, and he took the bait. At the height of the party, when he was drunker than drunk, he offered Salome half his kingdom, and Herodias took him up on his offer. Coached by her mother, Salome asked for John the Baptist's head, and the rest is history.

What a despicable thing to do, but not a surprising act for a woman with satanic desires. What if she had listened to the voice of the Holy Spirit through John the Baptist? Then God would have blessed her and her husband. Herod Antipas would have kept his throne and remained in favor with Rome. She would have kept her luxurious home in Galilee and not been exiled with her husband to the ends of the earth. Too bad, Herodias.

Mothers With Kids

Then little children were brought to Him that He might put His hands on them and pray, but the disciples rebuked them. But Jesus said, "Let the little children come to Me, and do not forbid them; for of such is the kingdom of heaven."
Matthew 19:13, 14

Children are a gift from the Lord, and they are dearly loved by their mothers. That's the way it's always been. But Jesus loved children too. No matter how busy He was, He made time for them. Wherever He went, He always had a smile for children and a gentle touch. The children were a welcome change from the crafty scribes and wily Pharisees who dogged His steps wherever He went. Unlike the adults, children accepted Him for who He was.

In the days of Jesus it was the custom for children to be brought to a rabbi to be blessed. And so it was that mothers began bringing their children to see Jesus. He was the kindest Man they had ever known, and when He put His hands on the children to bless them, He made them feel as if they really mattered. The disciples had no patience for such things. In their minds, Jesus should be investing His time on more important things like healing the sick, preaching, and improving His relationships with leaders at the synagogues and temple. But Jesus knew what was really important, and He reminded His disciples often. In fact, when it came to children, He made it pretty clear. "If you want to go to heaven, you must become more like children," He said. "Your faith needs to be as simple and deep, and totally trusting in the Father."

What if the mothers of all those children hadn't really believed that Jesus cared? What if they hadn't brought their children to Jesus for a blessing? Then the children would have never seen how loving Jesus really was. They would have never become disciples of Jesus and Christians in the early church. They would have never become missionaries for Him to help spread the gospel. That's how it goes with kind deeds to children. They always pay forward.

People of Nazareth

Then He said, "Assuredly, I say to you,
no prophet is accepted in His own country." Luke 4:24

Nazareth was Jesus' hometown. His mother and father had grown up there, and He had worked in Joseph's carpenter shop. And now He was back, worshiping among them as He had when a boy. It wasn't a pretty town, but it was home. One Sabbath He was invited to stand and read from the Scriptures. An attendant handed Jesus a scroll of the prophet Isaiah. At first they were curious to see Him back in town. They had heard stories of His mysterious powers to heal and His ability to preach. But when they heard Him read from the book of Isaiah, they began to get angry. Why? Because He told them He was the Messiah described in the scripture passage. "The Spirit of the Lord is on Me, because He has anointed Me to proclaim good news to the poor. He has sent Me to comfort those who are heartbroken and bring healing to the blind, to set people free from Satan and proclaim a time for peace."

Didn't they want a Messiah? Maybe, but maybe they just wanted to see a king come riding in on a flashy horse. What they were getting instead was a poor, uneducated man born into a working-class family. As far as they were concerned, Jesus was an imposter at best, and a blasphemer at worst. Blasphemy called for the death sentence, and they quickly became a mob serving as judge, jury, and executioner. Out of the synagogue they pushed Him, toward a nearby cliff to throw Him down. But as the story goes, He miraculously escaped.

Wow! That's quite a reaction! Quite a temper tantrum for them all. And for what? Why get angry because He wasn't what they were expecting? The Scriptures said that One such as Jesus would fulfill the prophecies. If the people of Nazareth had accepted Him as their Messiah, the pages of history would be quite different. Nazareth would have been celebrated as the place that gave the world a Messiah. What a shame they missed their chance.

Rich Young Ruler

Now as He was going out on the road, one came running,
knelt before Him, and asked Him, "Good Teacher,
what shall I do that I may inherit eternal life?" Mark 10:17

How much money would you need to be happy? A million dollars? Ten million dollars? A billion dollars? Now, how would it feel if you had to give all that up? If you can imagine such a thing, you would know how the rich young ruler must have felt who came for that special interview with Jesus. The Bible doesn't really tell us that much about him. We don't know his name, and we don't really know who he was, or even what exactly he did for a living. We just know he had a lot of money and owned a lot of things.

When he met Jesus, he dropped to his knees in the dirt of the street and said, "Good Teacher, what shall I do that I may have eternal life?" That was a hard thing for a wealthy Jew to say, since everybody thought rich people who served God automatically had a place in the kingdom of heaven.

Jesus told him to keep the commandments, and the young man agreed, but it was obvious he felt he needed to do more. "There's only one thing you lack," Jesus added. "Sell everything you have—your houses, your lands, your shops, your flocks and herds. Give everything you have to the poor. Then take up your cross to follow me, and you'll have treasure in heaven."

Were the disciples surprised to hear Jesus say such a thing? Absolutely! For a rich man to give up all his money and possessions to follow Jesus seemed like a really difficult thing to do. Most people don't want to give up all the things they've worked so hard to get.

What if the rich young ruler had done that? What if he had given up everything and followed Jesus? Then he would have probably become one of the most famous disciples of all. Not because of all the money he had, but because of all the money he gave up.

Simon the Pharisee

Then one of the Pharisees asked Him to eat with him.
And He went to the Pharisee's house, and sat down to eat. Luke 7:36

Simon was a very important man in Israel, but he was not a very nice person before he met Jesus. As a Pharisee, he would walk down the street in fancy clothes, praying loud prayers. He would send trumpeters to announce that he was going to give money to the poor. He liked to show off his tithes and offerings by bringing bags of coins to pour clattering in the metal offering boxes at the temple. And there was the secret side of his life where he sometimes drank and partied with lady friends all night.

All that ended when he became a leper. This was the worst thing that could happen to a person in Jesus' day. Now he would have to leave his home and live in a leper colony somewhere. But then he met Jesus. We don't know when it happened, but Jesus changed his life forever by healing him of his leprosy. The Bible says Simon was so grateful that he became a disciple of Jesus, and he then showed his appreciation by inviting Jesus to a banquet in his home. Mary Magdalene sneaked into that feast too, and Simon was very upset about that. Not only was Mary a former prostitute, but he had also had an affair with her himself—and he was afraid everyone would find out. Jesus read Simon's mind but didn't embarrass him, and He told him a story about forgiveness instead.

We don't know what became of Simon after Jesus went back to heaven, but it's likely he finally became a Christian. Hundreds of Pharisees and priests did just that. But what if Simon hadn't accepted Jesus as the Messiah? What if he had rejected him as the rest of the Jewish Sanhedrin did? Then the miracle of life Jesus had given him in place of leprosy would have been in vain. Why? Because in the end he would have lost out on eternal life.

Widow's Mites

So He said, "Truly I say to you that this poor widow has put in more than all;
for all these out of their abundance have put in offerings for God,
but she out of her poverty put in all the livelihood that she had." Luke 21:3, 4

She was a poor woman and a widow without a son to care for her. She came to the temple in Jerusalem to worship and give an offering to the Lord. Anyone watching would have doubted she had anything to give at all. And considering the two mites she ended up giving, it would seem there was little point. A mite was worth less than one tenth of a penny.

The average folks brought their average offerings, and the rich merchants and Pharisees came with plenty. The offering boxes were made of metal and shaped like trumpets so when coins of gold, silver, and copper were dropped in, they would clatter. Naturally, if a whole sack of coins was poured in it made quite a racket. Of course, that was exactly what the self-righteous Pharisees wanted, because then everyone would know how much they had given.

The widow didn't need to worry much about that. Her two tiny coins would hardly make a *clink* when they hit the box. Jesus saw this and commented on it. "See that woman there?" He asked His disciples. "In God's eyes she's given more than all the others combined. They gave with much to spare, but she sacrificed to give all she had."

It was obvious she had little in this world, but it was also clear she had God's blessing for giving her all. What if she hadn't given those two tiny coins? No one would have cared or thought badly of her. She was destitute. After giving the mites, there was nothing left to buy even a bit of food. But God has ways of helping those who willingly share what they have, and we can be sure He did that for the widow. Then, too, the story of this woman's generosity went far and wide, even to the ends of the earth, wherever the story of salvation is told. How do we know this? Well, you and I are talking about it now, aren't we? That's very cool!

Woman at the Well

"Come, see a Man who told me all things that I ever did.
Could this be the Christ?" John 4:29

In the days of Jesus, many groups were treated as if they didn't matter—Gentiles, slaves, women, and Samaritans. This was clearly demonstrated in a story about a visit Jesus and His disciples had in the city of Sychar in the region of Samaria. The Samaritans were not at all friendly toward the Jews, and the Jews hated the Samaritans.

It was about noon the day Jesus came to town, and it was a hot one. Jesus' disciples went into town to buy some food, but He stayed behind to rest at the village well. While He was sitting there, a Samaritan woman came out to draw water from the well. She didn't talk to Jesus or even say hello, because women in those days didn't speak to men in public places. Even more important, she was a Samaritan, and Samaritans didn't speak to Jews.

He asked her for a drink of water, and in turn offered her the Water of Life. She was living a lonely life, desperate for love and acceptance, and when Jesus miraculously showed that He knew all about her, she was amazed. Minutes later, she rushed back to the city to tell everyone she had found the Messiah. The whole village came out to see Jesus. They were curious about the changes they saw in the woman, and when they heard Jesus speak words of life, they invited Him to stay a while. For two days He and His disciples taught the people about God's plan of salvation. What a wonderful change had come over the city, and all because one woman shared her testimony about what Jesus had done for her!

What if she hadn't shared her testimony? What if she had failed to lay down her pride and listen to the Man from Nazareth? She would have lived out her hopeless life of despair in Sychar and died a lost woman. Instead, she opened her heart to Jesus and shared her testimony of what He had done for her. And because of this, many Samaritans were introduced to the Savior of the world.

Women Weeping on the Via Dolorosa

And a great multitude of the people followed Him, and women who also mourned and lamented Him. But Jesus, turning to them, said, "Daughters of Jerusalem, do not weep for Me, but weep for yourselves and for your children." Luke 23:27, 28

It was the worst day in Jerusalem's history, though few people realized it. Jesus of Nazareth, the most amazing Miracle Man to walk the face of the earth, was in the streets of Jerusalem walking to Calvary. This God-man had come across the galaxies to stand up against the forces of darkness. He carried a cross upon His shoulders for you and me, bearing the sins of the world that would ultimately break His heart. The cruel soldiers stood guard. The demons of darkness watched in scorn. The taunting crowds were there—many in that mob had sung His praises the day He rode into Jerusalem like a king.

The Savior's body was wracked with pain, but in those moments He only had thoughts for the women who were weeping. They couldn't see the days ahead, but He could. Just thirty-seven years in the future, Jerusalem was going to be surrounded by the Roman armies. They would lay siege to the city, crucify Jewish revolutionaries on the hills surrounding Jerusalem, and storm the walls to overthrow the city. Jews within the city would kill and eat one another during a time of desperate famine and starvation.

What if all those people in the streets had listened to His warning? What if they had turned that procession around? What if they had repented of their sins and their revolution of repentance had caught on at the temple? Then the Jewish leaders wouldn't have crucified the Son of God. Jesus would have had to die another way to pay for the sins of the world, but His own people wouldn't have been guilty of it. And Jerusalem might not have been destroyed. Small wonder that Jesus told these women to weep for themselves and their children.

Zacchaeus

Then Zacchaeus stood and said to the Lord,
"Look, Lord, I give half of my goods to the poor; and if I have taken
anything from anyone by false accusation, I restore fourfold." Luke 19:8

Zacchaeus was a wee little man; a wee little man was he. He climbed up in the sycamore tree, for the Lord he wanted to see." Many of us think immediately of this song when we think of Zacchaeus, the man who was very, very short, and very, very rich, and hated by everyone very, very much.

The year was A.D. 31. The city of Jericho was known for its tax collectors, and Zacchaeus was the most famous one of them all. He was a Jew, but he might as well have been a Gentile because he worked for the Romans collecting taxes. In those days, tax collectors were cheaters and thieves. They would tax you for anything and everything they could possibly get out of you. If you had to sell your home to pay a tax debt, your loss was their gain.

Because of the way Zacchaeus made a living, he was an outcast and wasn't allowed in the synagogue. It was a lonely life, and though he was very wealthy, he had few friends in Jericho. The only kinds of people who would come to his house for dinner or a party were other tax collectors and the other people no one else liked.

Then Jesus came to Jericho to see him. Zacchaeus didn't know that, which is why he climbed up in a tree to catch a glimpse of the Miracle Man from Nazareth. But Jesus told him to come down out of the tree because He wanted to go to Zacchaeus's house to eat dinner. That was a shocker for the little man. No respectable person had done that in a long, long time.

That was the turning point for Zacchaeus. He gave his heart and money to God. What if he hadn't opened his home to the Man of Galilee? What if he hadn't turned everything over to God? Then he would have grown old without the peace of God in his heart, and though very, very rich, he would have died a very lonely, broken man.

Ten Maidens

"Then the kingdom of heaven shall be likened to ten virgins
who took their lamps and went out to meet the bridegroom.
Now five of them were wise, and five were foolish." Matthew 25:1, 2

The story Jesus told about ten young maidens who prepared for a wedding feast is a classic. Five of the maidens got ready for the big event by bringing extra oil. That way, if they ran out of oil they could refill their lamps. The other five did not bring extra oil. Whoops!

Time passed. It got dark, and the young maidens all lit their oil lamps, thinking the groom would soon arrive. But he didn't. They waited and waited. And then finally at midnight, a messenger came running through the streets shouting, "The bridegroom is coming! Get up! Go out to meet him!" The maidens jumped up to join the wedding party and discovered their lamps had gone out. They all trimmed the wicks in their lamps, but since the oil had run out, the lamps couldn't be lit. The five "wise" maidens poured their extra oil into their lamps, but the five "foolish" maidens had none. "Please share some of your oil with us," they begged.

"Can't do it," said the five wise maidens. "If we do, we won't have enough for ourselves. You'd better go buy some." And so the foolish maidens ran off to find some oil, but while they were gone, the groom arrived to get his bride. The wedding procession then left the house, made its way to the groom's house where everyone was invited in, and the door was shut.

What if the wise maidens had shared their oil with the foolish ones? Then they would have all run out of oil on the way to the feast, and no one would have been able to see in the dark city streets. And without their lamps, the maidens wouldn't have been allowed into the reception—no light, no invite. That was their job. What if the five foolish maidens had brought an extra supply of oil? Then everyone would have lived happily ever after. That was a possible ending to this story, and Jesus would have liked that ending best of all.

Blind Man at Bethsaida

He took the blind man by the hand and led him outside the village. When he had spit on the man's eyes and put his hands on him, Jesus asked, "Do you see anything?" He looked up and said, "I see people; they look like trees walking around." Once more Jesus put his hands on the man's eyes. Then his eyes were opened, his sight was restored, and he saw everything clearly. Mark 8:23–25, NIV

Can you imagine what it would be like to be blind for much of your life and get a chance to see again? Jesus performed many such miracles during His ministry, but this is probably one of the most unusual. It happened in Bethsaida, the original hometown of Peter and Andrew, when a blind man's friends brought him to Jesus. What a blessing to have such good friends!

Jesus had taken a lot of heat from the Pharisees everywhere he went, and on this day He wanted to avoid negative publicity, so he took the blind man out of the city. Then he did a really strange thing. He put some spit on the man's eyes and asked him if he could see. "I see trees walking around like people," the blindman said. Wow! That must have been a bizarre experience!

This is the only recorded miracle of Jesus where He healed a man in two stages, and He must have done it for a reason. Maybe it was to test the man's faith. Maybe it was to test the faith of the disciples watching. Anyway, Jesus finally healed the blind man completely, and he went away praising God.

But we have to ask ourselves, What if the blind man's friends hadn't had faith that Jesus could heal their friend? What if they hadn't brought him to Jesus? What if the blind man had gotten mad at Jesus for healing him halfway? Then maybe Jesus wouldn't have finished the job. But the man did believe. He did play along with the "game," so to speak, and Jesus rewarded him for it. What a blessing Jesus was to the blind man and his friends, and His disciples!

Blind Man Healed at Temple

His parents answered them and said, "We know that this is our son,
and that he was born blind; but by what means he now sees we do not know, or
who opened his eyes we do not know. He is of age; ask him.
He will speak for himself." John 9:20, 21

One Sabbath Jesus was visiting the temple in Jerusalem when He noticed a blind man begging. "I am the light of the world," He said as He squatted on the ground and scooped up some clay dirt in His hand (John 9:5). Then He spit on the clay and rubbed some of it on the blind man's eyelids. "Go wash your eyes in the pool of Siloam," he said. The man did as Jesus asked, and wonder of wonders, he was healed! Everyone was amazed when they heard the news and wanted to know who had healed him, but all he could say was, "His name is Jesus."

The Pharisees were very upset when they heard about the miracle and called a private meeting to talk about it. Whoever did this cannot be a Man of God because He doesn't keep the Sabbath day holy, they said. They asked the man's parents about the episode, but his mother and father refused to answer because they were afraid of being expelled from the synagogue.

The Pharisees called the man in again to ask if he thought Jesus was a sinner. The man shrugged. "Maybe He's a sinner, and maybe He's not, but one thing I know. Once I was blind, but now I see. Why are you asking me all these questions? Do you want to become His disciples too?" This really made the Pharisees angry, and they kicked the man out on his ear.

What if the man hadn't had faith in Jesus? What if he hadn't gone to wash his eyes? Then, of course, he wouldn't have been healed. The Pharisees and all the people of Jerusalem wouldn't have had yet another proof that Jesus was the Son of God. Most importantly, the man wouldn't have been able to give the Pharisees an invitation to become disciples of Jesus.

AUGUST 26

Canaanite Woman and Her Daughter

A Canaanite woman from that vicinity came to him, crying out, "Lord, Son of David,
have mercy on me! My daughter is demon-possessed and suffering terribly." . . .
Then Jesus said to her, "Woman, you have great faith! Your request is granted."
And her daughter was healed at that moment. Matthew 15:22, 28, NIV

In Jesus' day the Jews thought God liked only them. They thought nobody else could have a place in heaven. They despised tax collectors, Gentiles in general, and especially Samaritans. But Jesus wanted to show His disciples that this was not the way God felt about these people. He doesn't snub anyone. Everyone is a potential child of God. To make His point, Jesus took His disciples on a road trip north of Galilee into the hill country of Phoenicia.

One day a Phoenician woman began following Jesus. "Have mercy on me, O Lord, Son of David!" she called. "My daughter is possessed by a devil and is suffering terribly!" She had heard about Jesus' miraculous healing powers and knew He was her only chance for her daughter to be normal again.

"It's not right to take the children's bread and toss it to the dogs," Jesus told her. It seems strange that Jesus would say such a thing, but He wanted to show His disciples how their exclusive attitude affected others. The woman never missed a beat, reminding Jesus that even the dogs eat the crumbs that fall from their master's table. Jesus was very impressed with her faith and told her to go home. Her prayer had been heard.

The woman realized she must come boldly before the throne of God to tell Him what she needed. But what if she hadn't? What if she hadn't been persistent in asking Jesus to heal her daughter? Then her daughter would have probably remained possessed. She wouldn't have been healed. Instead, the woman went home and found that the girl had been freed from the demon at the very moment Jesus gave the command. Incredible miracle! Amazing faith!

The Crippled Woman

And behold, there was a woman who had a spirit of infirmity eighteen years, and was bent over and could in no way raise herself up. . . . And He laid His hands on her, and immediately she was made straight, and glorified God. Luke 13:11, 13

We don't know how old she was, but she had been deformed with a hunchback for eighteen years. Today we think she may have had a severe case of rheumatoid arthritis or maybe scoliosis. What caused it? Perhaps diet. Maybe an infection. Maybe an injury or accident of some sort.

We don't know where she lived exactly, but she must have been a faithful member of the local synagogue, and when Jesus showed up, she was in the right place at the right time. Imagine how happy she must have been to have Jesus heal her! Imagine what it was like to have her health back and to walk upright again! Unfortunately, the ruler of the synagogue wasn't a bit happy about it. Jesus had healed the woman on the Sabbath day, and that was against the traditions of the Pharisees. "You can heal six days of the week," he growled. "Don't be doing it on the Sabbath."

But Jesus wasn't too happy about those rules, and He came right to the point. "You guys are just a bunch of hypocrites," he said. "You don't see anything wrong with watering an ox or donkey on the Sabbath. Why wouldn't you want to help this woman who has been held by Satan in chains of sickness for eighteen years?"

What if the woman hadn't gone to the synagogue that day? What if she had stayed home to rest? She was bent over and in lots of pain, so no one would have blamed her. Of course, in that case she would have missed her chance to be healed by the Miracle Man of Galilee. She was healed just a few months before Jesus was crucified, so she might not have had a second chance. What a blessing for her, and she must have thanked God every day of the rest of her life.

AUGUST 28

Demon-Possessed Man in the Synagogue

Now in the synagogue there was a man who had a spirit of an unclean demon. And he cried out with a loud voice, saying, "Let us alone! What have we to do with You, Jesus of Nazareth? Did You come to destroy us? I know who You are—the Holy One of God!" Luke 4:33, 34

What would it be like to see a demoniac in church? Scary? Terrifying? Disturbing? Yeah, well it has happened before, as I'm sure you know. Lots of times. Satan may not like going to church, but he doesn't want you and me to go either, so sometimes he brings a circus to disrupt our worship. That's what this story is all about.

It was the Sabbath day, and Jesus was visiting at the synagogue in Capernaum. Suddenly, the stillness of the morning service was shattered. "Why have you come here?" a man shouted with a crazy light in his eyes. "I know who you are! You're the Holy One of God! Have you come to destroy us, Jesus of Nazareth?" Suddenly he began running toward Jesus, screaming at the top of his lungs! His eyes bulged from their sockets, and he clawed at the air. But Jesus wasn't afraid. It was an awful sight! Then, just before he reached Jesus, the demoniac fell to the floor, writhing and twisting as if in pain.

Jesus frowned at the man. "Be quiet!" He said firmly, as if He were talking to an unseen power in the room. "Come out of him!" The man began to shake violently, gave one last bloodcurdling scream, and then became calm. Jesus had delivered the man from Satan's power, and everyone was excited to see such a thing.

What if the man hadn't wanted Jesus to help him? What if he hadn't come to the synagogue at all? Then he wouldn't have had a chance to meet Jesus. He wouldn't have been delivered from Satan's viselike grip. He wouldn't have been healed of demon possession. What a blessed man he was for sure, filled with the peace of God!

The High Priest's Servant

And one of them struck the servant of the high priest, cutting off his right ear. But
Jesus answered, "No more of this!" And he touched the man's ear and healed him.
Luke 22:50, 51, NIV

His name was Malchus, and he was a servant of Caiaphas, the high priest. We
know very little about him except that he was with the mob that came to the
Garden to arrest Jesus and that Jesus performed a miracle for him. "Do good to
those who hate you," Jesus had said many times, and there is no better story of
kindness towards one's enemies than this one.

When the mob of temple guards and priests surrounded Jesus to bind him
and lead Him away, the disciples must have realized this was a trap to catch Jesus.
"Lord, shall we fight?" they shouted. It was clear Peter was expecting some kind of
a skirmish, because his first reaction was to defend Jesus. Pulling out his sword, he
swung it with all his might at Malchus, who was standing too close. He probably
wanted to kill Malchus but only managed to cut off his ear, and this saved the man's
life.

It all happened so fast. Jesus was already being bound with ropes but immediately released His hands and did the most surprising thing. He picked up
Malchus's ear off the ground and replaced it on the side of the servant's head. What
a shocker! Malchus would have had to go the rest of his life without an ear on one
side of his head, but Jesus healed the ugly wound! Wow! What a turn of events!

What if Malchus had refused to be part of the mob that arrested Jesus? He
should have known better, even if his boss ordered him to do it. Every time he
touched his brand-new ear he would have been reminded that Jesus was an amazing Miracle Man sent from heaven. We don't know what became of Malchus after
this event, because he disappeared into history. Did he later become a Christian
like many Jews who witnessed the final events of Jesus' life on earth? Only in
heaven will we learn these details, and hopefully Malchus will be there to share
them with us.

AUGUST 30

Nobleman's Son at Capernaum

And there was a certain royal official whose son lay sick at Capernaum. When this man heard that Jesus had arrived in Galilee from Judea, he went to him and begged him to come and heal his son, who was close to death. John 4:46, 47, NIV

Jesus healed many people during His ministry, and they all had something in common. In every case, those who wanted healing needed to have at least a mustard seed's worth of faith to receive the gift. This story is no exception. In the city of Cana lived an official who worked for the household of Herod Antipas. One day at noon this royal official came looking for Jesus to beg for help in healing his son, who had a bad fever. Jesus knew the official wasn't sure he believed that He was the Messiah. However, he was sure Jesus would help him because he was an important official for the royal family.

Jesus knew the royal official would not believe unless he actually saw a miracle, and He told him so. The man was shocked that Jesus could read his heart. He became frightened as he realized his lack of faith might cost him the life of his son. "Please, sir!" he begged, "come down to Capernaum before my child dies."

"Go on home," Jesus kindly replied, "your son will live." A look of peace now settled on the official's face as he realized Jesus meant it. His prayer had been answered, and he left that very hour for Capernaum. The hour grew late, and he had to stop for the night. The next morning, he went on his way again and was met by his servants, who brought news that his son had been healed. The fever had left him. When? About noon the previous day. That was the turning point in the official's life! He and his family now knew that Jesus was the Son of God. But what if he had decided Jesus wasn't the Messiah? What if he had insisted, "I'll only believe if I see?" Then, quite logically, his son wouldn't have been healed. He wouldn't have been given back his life, and that would have been a pity.

Pharisees

"Woe to you, scribes and Pharisees, hypocrites! For you are like whitewashed
tombs which indeed appear beautiful outwardly, but inside are full of
dead men's bones and all uncleanness." Matthew 23:27

These guys were the melancholy political perfectionists of the Jewish world. Tradition was the name of the game, and the rules of tradition had to be followed to a T or they weren't happy. They believed in paying a faithful tithe down to the last leaf of mint and thyme, and washing their hands repeatedly, and fasting twice a week faithfully. These were good things, weren't they? Absolutely, unless you were just trying to score brownie points with God.

They believed in sending messengers through the streets announcing when they were going to give alms to the poor, but they told the poor they were sinners and could never be saved.

And the Sabbath? They had so many rules about how to keep it, no one understood what the Sabbath was for anymore. There was a rule against spitting on the Sabbath because that would be considered watering the lawn, which, of course, would be work. You could not carry a handkerchief on the Sabbath day because that would be work—unless you sewed it to your coat. Then it could be understood to be part of your clothing.

And when Jesus came along, He made it almost impossible for the Pharisees to continue on with their charades. He told them that God wanted people to be merciful, kind, and humble. They should be willing to turn the other cheek and walk an extra mile. They were to love their enemies and do good to those who treated them like dirt.

But what if they hadn't been so self-absorbed? What if they hadn't been so caught up in their traditions and religious rituals? Then they could have listened to Jesus' words of life and believed that His miracles were sent from God. They wouldn't have rejected Him as their Savior or betrayed Him to the Romans to be crucified. They would have accepted Him as the Son of God. Wow! That's a switch!

SEPTEMBER 1

Sadducees

Then the high priest rose up, and all those who were with him (which is the sect of the Sadducees), and they were filled with indignation, and laid their hands on the apostles and put them in the common prison. Acts 5:17, 18

The Sadducees were the power brokers of Jesus' day, ruling the Jewish nation with the help of the Romans. Many of them sat on the councils of the Sanhedrin, and at the time of Jesus' crucifixion, one of them was the high priest. Today we would probably consider them a bit strange. Although they were worshipers of God, they didn't believe in angels. They didn't believe in life after death. They didn't believe in most of the Scriptures. To them, only the five books of Moses were inspired by God.

The Sadducees were constantly at war with the Pharisees, much like political parties are today. The only time they seemed to get along was when they were fighting a common enemy. It happened when they were trying to get rid of John the Baptist. It happened as Jesus' ministry grew in popularity. And it happened when the early church was first getting a foothold in Palestine.

With the help of Herod, they managed to get John executed. With the help of the Romans, they crucified Jesus. With the help of the Pharisees, they scattered the early Christians. Why? Because they were afraid. If the new Christian movement won too many converts, the Sadducees might die out.

What if they hadn't been so mean? What if they had taken the whole Bible as the Word of God? Then the Holy Spirit could have shown them that Jesus of Nazareth was indeed the Messiah. He would have helped them preserve their nation. Unfortunately, they were too stubborn and stuck up to do that. And guess what? All their fears came true. All their cruel efforts to snuff out the followers of Jesus just multiplied the Christians even more. Finally, their nation perished, and their religious party disappeared into oblivion.

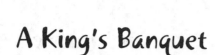

A King's Banquet

"Then he said to his servants, 'The wedding is ready, but those who were invited were not worthy. Therefore go into the highways, and as many as you find, invite to the wedding.' " Matthew 22:8, 9

We might call this the wedding of the century, because money was no object and the guest list was a mile long. Quite simply, no stone was left unturned to make this the ceremony to end all ceremonies. The king and his royal household had been planning this big day since forever, and now the big week had arrived.

The king sent his couriers out to tell the guests it was time for the wedding feast. "Come to the banquet," they said. "Everything is ready." However, the invitees turned them down with one excuse after another. The servants were shocked, and they threatened to report these insults to the king. The invitees got angry and beat the messengers, even killing some of them. When the news reached the king, he was furious at their ungrateful treatment of his messengers. That very night, he sent his army to execute the guilty guests and burn their cities.

Then he sent his servants out to invite others more deserving of the banquet. Into the streets and alleys they went until they found enough guests to refill the guest list. Everyone was invited, and all were given formal clothes to wear in the banquet hall.

The king came into the banquet hall to greet the guests himself but was surprised to see a man not dressed in the wedding suit he had been given. "Throw out the ungrateful wretch!" roared the king. "He doesn't deserve to be here." And they kicked him out.

What if the original guests had accepted the invitation by the king? Or what if the man thrown out had worn the gift of clothes provided by the king? I think the answer is obvious. The king would have been vindicated, and the guests would have received their gifts so generously given by the king.

SEPTEMBER 3

Treasure Hunter

"Again, the kingdom of heaven is like treasure hidden in a field, which a man found and hid; and for joy over it he goes and sells all that he has and buys that field."
Matthew 13:44

Have you ever imagined hunting for treasure in an old house, an abandoned silver mine, or a sunken treasure ship? The Bible tells us a story about a treasure and the man who found it. He was working in a field, plowing the soil or digging out rocks for a local farmer, when he uncovered the treasure. Most likely it was silver coins or pieces of gold, or maybe it was family jewelry hidden in a clay jar. The man's eyes must have grown wide at finding such a treasure, but the field didn't belong to him, so he couldn't keep it. However, if he could scrape enough money together, he could buy the field.

If he was married he probably went home and told his wife he wanted to buy the piece of land where he had been working. The problem? Now he must somehow raise the money to buy it. For starters, if he had any money or family jewelry, he set it aside to be used to buy the property. Then he started selling off all his possessions. If he owned land, that was the first thing to go, and then went the donkey, or the yoke of oxen he used to plow his fields. Next came his tools. By now his wife must have thought he was crazy, but he didn't care. He had a secret no one knew about. In the end he probably sold his furniture and any extra clothes, and maybe even his family waterpots.

And when he finally had enough money, he went and bought the land—knowing what it was really worth. But what if he hadn't been willing to sell off all his family's things? Well, quite logically, he wouldn't have been able to buy the land and keep the treasure. And the lesson for us in this story? God's kingdom is like treasure. It's worth more than anything else in this world, and we must be willing to give everything we have if we want to possess it.

Good Samaritan

"But a certain Samaritan, as he journeyed, came where he was.
And when he saw him, he had compassion. So he went to him and bandaged his
wounds, pouring on oil and wine; and he set him on his own animal, brought him to
an inn, and took care of him." Luke 10:33, 34

Everybody loves a good story, and this is one of the best. Once upon a time, a Jewish businessman left on a journey from Jerusalem to Jericho. The road was a dangerous one and not safe for travelers, but he decided to take the risk anyway. Sure enough, when the traveler had gone partway down an empty stretch of the road, he was attacked by bandits. They beat him, stripped him of his money and clothes, and left him to die.

Now, it just so happened a Jewish priest came along that way and saw the man lying there half dead. He knew he should help the poor man but was afraid when he saw the blood, and so he crossed to the other side of the road to go on his way. A short time later, a temple worker passed the spot on his way up to Jerusalem. He saw the unconscious, beaten victim along the road and went over to get a closer look. However, he was afraid the robbers might be waiting nearby, so he also went on his way, leaving the man all alone. Still later that day, a Samaritan came down the road on his donkey and was surprised to see the Jewish traveler all beaten and bruised. Like the other travelers before him, the Samaritan was afraid of the bandits, but he couldn't ignore the victim. He treated his wounds, put him on his donkey, and took him to the nearest inn.

What if the priest and temple worker had stopped to help the poor man? They were Jews, and religious leaders at that, so it would have been the obvious thing to do, since he was one of their countrymen. But they didn't stop to help him, and that showed the true nature of their character. And the Samaritan? He was the only decent one of the three. We might have expected him to be the one not to help, but he defied the odds, and for this he is remembered, respected, and revered.

SEPTEMBER 5

Merchant and His Pearl of Great Price

*"Again, the kingdom of heaven is like a merchant seeking beautiful pearls, who,
when he had found one pearl of great price,
went and sold all that he had and bought it." Matthew 13:45, 46*

This is the story of a man who knew exactly what he wanted. He was a successful merchant who traveled the world looking for choice pearls. One day he found the pearl of his dreams. It was bigger and brighter and more beautiful than any he had ever owned or seen before, and he knew he had to have it. But it was beyond his reach financially. He didn't have enough money on hand to buy it, or enough in savings with the money changers. However, that didn't stop him from putting the pearl on his wish list, and he set out to raise the money. The Bible says he sold everything he had to buy it, and we can only imagine what that might have cost him. For starters, he probably sold the other pearls he had in stock and any valuable jewels he owned. If he had a farm or villa, he sold that. If he had livestock, he traded them for ready money.

He might have had to barter a bit to get the owner to settle on a price, and when the seller realized how much the merchant wanted the pearl, he may have even raised the stakes. No matter, because the merchant had his heart set on the pearl and was determined to get it.

When he finally had the money, he sealed the deal and walked away with the prize. Today we call it the pearl of great price because it cost more money than anyone had ever paid for a pearl. It was gorgeous. It was magnificent. It was almost priceless.

But what if the pearl merchant hadn't been willing to pay the exorbitant price? What if he had been content to settle for smaller, less exquisite pearls? That's a no-brainer. He would have kept all his other possessions, and someone else would have owned the pearl. And what's the message for us here? If you want something badly enough, you won't stop until you get it. That's the way it is with things of real value, like family, and truth, and the Word of God.

Prodigal Son

"And not many days after, the younger son gathered all together, journeyed to a far country, and there wasted his possessions with prodigal living." Luke 15:13

In the tale of the prodigal son, we see a rebellious boy who thought only of himself. He couldn't see how good he had it at home and had to lose everything before he would admit it. He wanted out of the family and made that clear when he asked for his inheritance ahead of schedule. It must have been a lot of money, since his father was a wealthy landowner. That was a pretty serious thing to do in those days, never mind how much money it was. It would be like saying, "I'm not willing to wait for my money until you die. Can you give it to me now?" But he took the money and absconded with it to never-never land. Where he went and what exactly he did with it, we will never fully know, but we have a pretty good picture. The Bible says he went far away and wasted his wealth in wild living. That means he was probably going to parties, drinking alcohol, and spending his time with the wrong kind of friends.

A lifestyle like that can't last forever. Sooner or later, his money would run out, and when it did, his friends would fly the coop. And they did. After his friends had drained him of his last shekel, they deserted him. And it got worse. A famine hit the land, and he ended up living with pigs—hungry enough to eat their leftovers. Finally, when his heart and spirit were gone, he came to his senses and headed for home. He had his apologies all planned out when he arrived, but his father would have none of it and threw him a big welcomehome party.

What if the prodigal hadn't come home? He may have starved to death or died of disease or old age in some pigpen. What if he had never left home in the first place? Then he wouldn't have wasted his time and inheritance far away, wishing for the love of his father. That's what it's like when we leave our heavenly Father's side. We always have regrets.

SEPTEMBER 7

Prodigal's Brother

"Lo, these many years I have been serving you;
I never transgressed your commandment at any time;
and yet you never gave me a young goat,
that I might make merry with my friends." Luke 15:29

The parable of the prodigal son is probably one of the most famous stories of all time. The story focuses on the prodigal, but an important secondary character is his brother. We could call him "big brother." The Bible doesn't say anything about how big brother felt when his younger prodigal brother took one-third of the family estate and shipped off to a faraway country. We don't know everything he was doing at home while his prodigal brother was away, but we do know that he was a hard worker.

When the prodigal finally came home, big brother was the last to know. He had been out working in the field, and when he came near the house, he heard music and dancing. He called one of the servants to ask about it, and what a shock he got! "Your brother has come home," the servant said, "and your father has killed a fattened calf to celebrate."

When big brother heard this news, he was hoppin' mad and refused to join the party. Who can blame him? The father came out to reason with him but got an earful! "All these years I've been working on the farm for you like a slave!" big brother said. "I've always obeyed your orders, but you've never given me anything so I could celebrate with my friends! Not even a young goat! And yet when this worthless son of yours comes home, who has wasted your money on wine, women, and song, you kill the fattened calf for him!"

What a finish to a story that could have ended on a happy note! What if big brother had accepted and forgiven his brother? It would have been a difficult thing, but it would have helped heal the family. Likely, the father died with his two sons still being enemies. And remember, those who are blessed most from forgiveness are the ones who forgive others.

Prodigal's Father

"And he arose and came to his father.
But when he was still a great way off, his father saw him and had compassion, and
ran and fell on his neck and kissed him." Luke 15:20

Once upon a time, there was a prosperous landowner who had two sons. The older one was hardworking and devoted to the family. The younger son was restless and irresponsible—demonstrating these traits when he asked his father for his share of the inheritance early. It was as if he told his father, "I wish you were already dead!" In spite of how wrong it seemed for the son to do such a thing, amazingly, the father divided his property between his two sons as the younger boy had asked.

The younger son skipped the country and became known as "the prodigal." Time passed. He never wrote home or sent messages, and soon people in his village forgot he had ever been part of the family. But the father didn't forget his runaway son, and he always hoped the boy would someday come home. And one day he did. The father saw him coming and, while he was still a long way off, ran to meet him, threw his arms around him, and kissed him. The son tried to protest his father's kindness, but the father ignored his apologies and called for his servants. "Quick! Bring my best robe and put it on him. Put my official ring on his finger and royal sandals on his feet. Bring a fattened calf and prepare it for a feast. Let's eat and celebrate, because my son is finally home."

What if the father had never forgiven his son? What if he had not been waiting for the prodigal when he came home? Well, the son would have had no place to go, that's for sure. And what if the father had not given the prodigal his inheritance early? Well, it's likely the son would have left home anyway, and then maybe he would have never come back. Ever. These are the kinds of choices our heavenly Father gives us. His love never dies. His devotion never ends.

Rich Man, Poor Man

But he said to him, "If they do not hear Moses and the prophets,
neither will they be persuaded though one rise from the dead." Luke 16:31

This is one of the most interesting allegories in the Bible, and many have misunderstood what Jesus was trying to say when he told the story. He wasn't teaching a lesson on what happens when you die, or that the amount of money a person has necessarily makes him good or bad. He was talking about character—and that we have one life to get it right.

The rich man was a fat cat wallowing in his riches, so to speak. Daily he was dressed in purple and fine linen, and he enjoyed fine pastries and wines in his sumptuous villa. And then there was the poor beggar man who lived in the street outside the rich man's gate. He was dirty and unkempt, infected with parasites and covered with oozing ulcers. Sadly, he was malnourished, but the rich man ignored him.

Of course, living in the street can take its toll, and before very long the poor man died. When he reached heaven he got to sit next to Father Abraham at the banqueting table. The rich man also died and was taken to hell to receive the just punishment for the way he had treated the poor. He looked across the gulf between heaven and hell and asked if the poor man could bring him some water to quench his thirst, but Abraham denied him relief. The rich man then begged that messengers be sent to his brothers still on earth to warn them about the fires of hell. Again Abraham refused the request. "They have their chances now," he said, "and plenty of stories in the Bible about what kind of men they should be."

What if the rich man had been compassionate and cared for the poor man? Would it have made a difference in the destiny of his eternal soul? Absolutely. Jesus said He cares about the poor and destitute among us. Whatever we do to them, we do to Him. Better behave!

Lame Man at the Pool of Bethesda

One who was there had been an invalid for thirty-eight years. . . . Then Jesus said
to him, "Get up! Pick up your mat and walk." John 5:5, 8, NIV

In Jerusalem, a pool of water called Bethesda was surrounded by five porches. At this pool, lots of people who were sick came for healing. At certain times of the year the water in the pool would swirl and bubble. The legends of folklore said an angel might even be stirring the waters and that such waters were magical. Rumors said that the first person who stepped into the pool after the waters swirled like that would be healed of their disease. No matter that these stories were mere fairy tales. Such a thing was dangerous because the stronger ones among the sick would trample the weak.

And then Jesus came to town and saw a sick man lying there by the pool. The man had been sick for thirty-eight years and couldn't remember ever being a normal person. "Do you want to get well?" Jesus asked, and the man tried to explain that he had no one to put him in the water. Jesus didn't listen to the exuse. "Pick up your mat and walk," was Jesus' simple reply. The man didn't know what to think, but in faith he jumped to his feet, picked up his mat, and left the pool area. "Praise God!" we can hear him shouting. "I'm cured!"

You can imagine this caused quite a stir among the Pharisees. "Who gave you permission to carry your mat on the Sabbath?" they demanded. "It's against the law to do that!" But the man who had been healed didn't even know who Jesus was. When the scribes and Pharisees finally found out it was Jesus, they were very angry. Even though He could perform amazing miracles, they rejected Him as the Messiah, and Jesus had to leave Judea.

But what if the crippled man had refused help on the Sabbath? Then he wouldn't have been healed. And if the Pharisees hadn't rejected Jesus, they wouldn't have gone on to crucify Him. God wouldn't have rejected them as a nation and Jersualem wouldn't have been destroyed less than four decades later.

SEPTEMBER 11

Lost Sheep

"And when he comes home, he calls together his friends and neighbors, saying to them, 'Rejoice with me, for I have found my sheep which was lost!' " Luke 15:6

There once was a man who had a hundred sheep. One evening when he came home, he counted the sheep and discovered one was missing. Where it was, he had no idea. It could be anywhere. The hour was late, and he was tired and hungry, but if he was going to find it, he needed to do it quickly. Darkness was falling fast. Without a thought for himself, he left his ninety-nine sheep in the care of a servant and went out into the evening. As he retraced his steps, he looked for signs of the lost sheep along the way. He checked every grassy patch and watering hole where they had been, but found nothing. It was getting dark now as he picked his way down a narrow canyon, and he had to light a torch. Thorns cut through his sandals as he climbed a rocky pathway. It was colder now, and he heard wolves howling in the distance, so he hurried faster. Was he too late? Had the poor sheep already been killed?

And then, to his great excitement, he heard the cry of his sheep, faint and weak, somewhere in the darkness. Praise God, it was still alive! He finally found it caught in a thorny thicket, and he lifted it on his shoulders to carry it home. With great excitement he called in his friends to tell them the good news. "Let's have a feast!" he told them, "I've found my lost sheep."

That's a happy ending for a story that could have gone quite differently. What if the shepherd had decided going out into the cold, dark night wasn't worth the effort? After all, one sheep out of a hundred was a small loss. Well, then, the sheep would have likely died from exposure or else ended up on some wild beast's menu. Of course, the good shepherd is Jesus, and He could have said the same about you or me. Fortunately, He loves even one child of God an infinite amount, and we should thank Him a million times for it!

Caiaphas

Then the high priest tore his clothes, saying, "He has spoken blasphemy!
What further need do we have of witnesses? Look, now you have heard His
blasphemy! What do you think?" They answered and said,
"He is deserving of death." Matthew 26:65, 66

Caiaphas was the high priest in Jerusalem during Jesus' ministry, having been appointed by the Roman governor Valerius Gratus in A.D. 18. Actually, he bought his way into the position. In that time, the office of high priest at the temple in Jerusalem always went to the highest bidder, and in Caiaphas's case it was a no-brainer. His father-in-law, Annas, had been the high priest before him, so Caiaphas's appointment would keep the high position in the family.

As leader of the scribes and Pharisees at the temple, he was the instigator in bringing Jesus to the Sanhedrin for trial. Concerning Jesus, Caiaphas said to his colleagues, "He's stirring the whole country up, and that's going to make trouble for us with the Romans! He deserves to die. It's better that one man die than the whole nation perish!" And they fell for it. They tried Jesus, the Son of God, as a blasphemer and turned Him over to the Romans.

What if Caiaphas hadn't done it? What if He had listened to the Holy Spirit? What if he had admitted that One who could raise the dead must indeed be the Messiah sent from heaven? Then he would be honored today as the one who proclaimed Jesus as the Savior of the world, and not a murderer. Instead, he is remembered for the despicable deed of sentencing Jesus to death. For this he will be raised in the special resurrection to see Jesus come again. Along with Pilate and the cruel Romans soldiers who beat Jesus so badly at His trial, Caiaphas will see Jesus in all His glory. When that time comes, he will understand exactly Who and What Jesus is. I wouldn't want to be in his shoes.

Girls Who Accused Peter

And a certain servant girl, seeing him as he sat by the fire,
looked intently at him and said, "This man was also with Him." Luke 22:56

They probably had no idea they were causing so much trouble for Peter. Were they curious? Maybe they were teasing a bit. Or were they actually trying to get him arrested too? We'll never know. One thing's for sure, they scared Peter nearly to death and pushed him to do something he vowed he would never do. The story went something like this.

When Jesus was arrested, He was dragged off to the estate of Caiaphas the high priest, where members of the Sanhedrin began to interrogate Him. John followed the crowd into the courtyard because he knew the servants of the household. He also made arrangements for Peter, but although he came in readily enough, he felt like a fish out of water—and he was scared stiff.

That's when the trouble started. Peter was squatting near a fire, trying to stay warm in the cool evening air, when a servant girl first noticed him. "You were with Jesus, weren't you?" she asked, looking straight at Peter. He denied any such thing and nervously moved nearer the courtyard gate. Another servant girl saw him and insisted she had seen him with Jesus of Nazareth, but again he fiercely denied it, this time with an oath. And then a third time someone accused him of being a disciple of Jesus. This time Peter came totally unglued and began to curse and swear his denial of Jesus.

What if these servant girls hadn't harassed Peter so many times? What if they hadn't pushed him to the edge with their accusations? Then Peter might never have denied Jesus. On the other hand, what if Peter hadn't cared what they said? What if he had dared to admit he was indeed a follower of Jesus? In that case, he might even have helped convert the servant girls to become followers of Jesus too. Wouldn't that have been a story to tell!

Laborers in the Vineyard

"So the last will be first, and the first last.
For many are called, but few chosen." Matthew 20:16

Have you ever felt like someone else got the credit for the work you did? That you worked twice as hard as they did and then got paid half as much as them? If you have, then you can probably relate to the workers in this story.

One morning a landowner went to the marketplace to hire laborers to work in his vineyard. "I'll pay you one denarius a day," the landowner said. It was a fair wage for a day's work at that time, so lots of men signed on to his crew. They went to the vineyard and worked all morning, harvesting grapes in the hot sun. At noon, the landowner went to the market to hire more workers, and he agreed to pay them a fair wage. They joined the men working hard in the vineyard, but by midafternoon it was clear more workers were needed. At three o'clock the boss went to the market to hire even more workers, and then again an hour before sunset. Each time he promised to pay a fair wage.

At the end of the day, everyone lined up to get paid. The boss told his paymaster to give a day's wage to those who had come one hour before sunset. He also paid a day's wage to those who had come at three o'clock and noon. And last of all, he paid those who had been working all day. How much? A day's wage. "It's not fair!" they complained. "You paid the others more than you paid us."

"Didn't I pay you one denarius for a day's work just as we agreed?" the land owner replied.

Jesus told this story to remind us that God wants to give eternal life to everyone, no matter how long or short they've been serving Him. Even if you give Him your heart on your deathbed, you can still receive a crown of life.

What if those of us who have served God all our lives should selfishly resent this? Jesus died for everyone! If we're unhappy that others are being given eternal life, we may prove to be unfit for a crown of life.

A Master and His Talents

"For the kingdom of heaven is like a man traveling to a far country, who called his own servants and delivered his goods to them. And to one he gave five talents, to another two, and to another one, to each according to his own ability; and immediately he went on a journey." Matthew 25:14, 15

What specific talents or abilities do you have that make you unique? Can you beat all your friends as a wide receiver in football? Are you already a recording artist? Can you make money grow on trees? If you have these kinds of natural gifts, you are blessed by God.

In the Bible, a talent didn't mean gifts or abilities but an amount of money. Jesus told a story about the money-making abilities of three servants who were given talents by a businessman. He called his servants and divided his money among them to see what they would do with it while he was gone. He gave five talents to one servant, two talents to another, and one talent to a third. Each servant received what the businessman thought he could handle.

After the businessman left on his journey, the first servant started a business using his five talents and made another five. The servant who had received two talents also doubled his talents. But the servant who received one talent did nothing with his money. Maybe he was angry because the master had given him less money than the others, or maybe he was lazy and didn't like to work. Anyway, the Bible says he took the money, dug a hole in the ground, and buried his master's money. When the businessman came home, he called his servants in to see what they had done with his money. He found that the first two servants had doubled their money, and he promoted them to important positions on his estate. However, when he discovered the third servant had done nothing with his talent, he fired him.

Like the businessman, God invites us to develop and use the gifts He has given us. What if we don't? Then eventually these abilities will atrophy like an unused muscle, and we will lose them. This would be sad indeed.

Pharisee and Publican

"Two men went up to the temple to pray,
one a Pharisee and the other a tax collector." Luke 18:10

If you had a choice, which would you rather be, a proud Pharisee or an outcast publican? Pharisees were religious leaders in Jesus' day—rich, popular, and arrogant. Publicans were tax collectors, also rich but hated by everyone, and almost as despised as lepers. So, now, take your pick. A story Jesus once told might make it easier for you to decide.

Two men went up to the temple one morning to pray, one of them a Pharisee and the other a publican. Now, the Pharisee was a self-righteous man. He wore long sleeves and tassels on his fine temple robes, and he bragged all day about how good he was. "Dear God, I thank you that I'm not a sinner like the publican," he said. However, he cared little for the poor and sick around him, and he gave money to them only when it made him look good.

The publican's robes were the kind worn by rich and famous folks, but he had a bad reputation. He collected taxes for the hated Romans. Everyone knew him to be a thieving cheat because he charged taxpayers way too much money every chance he got. The publican knew he had done many bad things in his life, but he came to the temple anyway. "Please, God," he prayed, "be merciful to me, a good-for-nothing sinner!"

Now, everyone watching could see that the publican and Pharisee were very different from one another, standing there in the temple court. The Pharisee was proud and conceited, but the publican had tears running down his face. What if the Pharisee had been more humble like the publican? What if he had asked God to help him to be genuine and considerate of others? Then he would have gone home at the end of the day content and at peace with God. Unfortunately, he never made that leap to spiritual hyperspace. It's not surprising, then, that only the publican's name was written in heaven's book of life.

SEPTEMBER 17

Rich Fool

"But God said to him, 'Fool! This night your soul will be required of you; then whose will those things be which you have provided?' So is he who lays up treasure for himself, and is not rich toward God." Luke 12:20, 21

Would you rather be a poor genius or a rich fool? Better not answer that question until you've read this story. Once there was a rich man who had a large farm. One year, everything seemed to go just right for him on the farm, and God especially blessed him. Wonder of wonders, he had a bumper crop! In fact, he harvested so much grain that he had no place to put it all. What to do with the grain was the question. The rich farmer was not an especially kind man, so it never occurred to him that he could share his grain with others. And now he made the biggest mistake of his life. He said, "I'll tear down my barns and build bigger ones, and there I will store my extra grain. That way I can eat, drink, and be merry for as long as I like."

Uh-oh. That night God came for a visit. "You fool!" He said. "This is the day you will bite the bullet. Then who will get everything you've hoarded for yourself?" Wow! What a way to go!

What if he hadn't been so selfish? What if he had said, "I need to be less greedy"? With that attitude he could have thrown a big party and shared what he had with all the poor and homeless in town. He could have sold the extra grain and donated money to help the sick. He could have given some of the grain to be used as seed for other farmers in the area so they would have really good crops the next year. But he didn't do any of these things, and that's what made him a fool. He didn't understand that it was God who had given him a bumper crop from all the seed he had planted. He didn't stop to think that God had showered him with every blessing, like the rain that fell to water his crops and the sunshine to make them grow. What's our conclusion? There's nothing worse than being a fool, except maybe a rich fool.

Scribes and Priests at Jesus' Trial

When morning came, all the chief priests and elders of the people
plotted against Jesus to put Him to death. Matthew 27:1

These guys were the lowest of the low. Losers, that's what they were! All of them! They knew it was time for the Messiah to show up. They knew He would come out of Bethlehem. They knew He would heal the lame, the deaf, and the blind, and even raise the dead. They knew He would come riding into Jerusalem on a donkey and even cleanse His Father's house. It was all prophesied, and yet they rejected Him anyway.

To top it all off, they rigged His trial so they could execute Him like a common criminal. They collaborated with one of Jesus' own disciples to betray Him into their hands with a kiss. They kidnapped Him in the dead of night and staged a trial at the Sanhedrin, both of which were against Jewish law. They called for witnesses who had been paid to testify falsely against Him. They told Pilate all kinds of lies to get a conviction in a Roman court of law, and when that failed, they threatened to report him to Caesar if he didn't rule in their favor. And finally, they pushed for crucifixion, a crime reserved for the worst cutthroats and villainous thieves. All this for a fellow Israelite, a kindred Jew, a Son of Abraham—the Messiah.

Then they refused to have Him called the "King of the Jews" and asked instead that Caesar be their king, calling down His blood on them and their children. They even stood around the cross taunting Jesus to call on heaven for help and dared Him to come down off the cross.

What if He had? Would they have believed Him to be the Messiah for which they had waited so long? No, they would have found other ways to reject Him. Satan had filled their proud hearts with a desire for power and fortune, so they rejected forgiveness from sin and salvation from Jesus Christ. That's right. They loved this world more than they loved God.

SEPTEMBER 19

Two Houses

"Therefore whoever hears these sayings of Mine, and does them,
I will liken him to a wise man who built his house on the rock. . . .
But everyone who hears these sayings of Mine, and does not do them,
will be like a foolish man who built his house on the sand." Matthew 7:24, 26

This is the tale of two houses and the builders who made them famous. One builder focused more on the speed at which he could build his house. The other insisted on a firm foundation. You know where this story is going, of course. The first man put up his house in record time, disregarding the condition of the ground on which he built. The materials may have been nice, and the architectural design pleasing to the line of sight, but little time was spent on its foundation. A foundation on sand was good enough for him. The second builder would have liked a house with a high appraisal value, but he decided strength was more important than beauty. Digging deep was his game, because he knew building on solid rock would help him sleep well at night.

So it went with the builders as the weeks passed. Up went the first house in record time, and while the second builder was finishing up his foundation, the first was already putting on his roof. Did the building style make a difference in the long run? You bet it did, but only one had planned for it!

One night the winds were very strong, and a storm blew up from the sea. The rain came down in torrents, the streams rose, and raging winds beat against the two houses. The one on the rock stood tall because of its foundation on the rock, but the house on the sand toppled and collapsed because it was built on sand.

What if the first man had built on solid rock too? Well, it's safe to say his house would have weathered the storm, and we wouldn't be singing songs that end with, "The house on the sand went smash." Jesus advises us to build on the Rock of Ages. If we do, we'll have no regrets.

The Unforgiving Servant

"Then his master, after he had called him, said to him, 'You wicked servant! I forgave you all that debt because you begged me. Should you not also have had compassion on your fellow servant, just as I had pity on you?' " Matthew 18:32, 33

This story is about a ridiculously foolish man. Why? Because he wasn't smart enough to forgive others as he had been forgiven. Here's how it happened. Once there was a king who had a high-ranking official who owed him ten thousand talents—in today's dollars that would be millions—and he couldn't pay it. The king ordered all the property and assets of the official to be sold in order to pay the debt. This was still not enough, and, as was the custom of the day, the man, along with his wife and children, were to be sold into slavery. On the day of the sentencing, the official fell to his knees before the king and begged for mercy and time to pay the debt. To his surprise, the king agreed and then did something unexpected. He forgave the entire debt.

The official was so relieved that he left the king's presence rejoicing. But on his way out, he saw a man who owed him a hundred denarii, perhaps fifty dollars. The official told the man he needed to pay the debt, and the poor man fell to his knees, begging for time. To the surprise of the witnesses, the official grabbed him by the throat and sent him to prison for not paying the debt.

Soon, word got back to the king, and he ordered the official to appear before him again. "You wicked servant! I forgave you that large debt because you begged me. Shouldn't you also have had compassion on your fellow servant, just as I had pity on you?"

What a lesson on forgiveness for us all! What if the king hadn't had compassion on his official in the first place? The man owed a lot of money! But the king did have pity, which makes the guilt of the official even greater. Like the king, we need to have compassion for others because we know how forgiving our heavenly Father has been with us.

Woman and Lost Coin

"Or what woman, having ten silver coins, if she loses one coin, does not light a lamp, sweep the house, and search carefully until she finds it?" Luke 15:8

Who would spend a whole day searching for a lost coin? Is any coin going to be worth that much? How hard would it be to find a coin in the first place? Houses in those days were built quite small, and the average family didn't have that much furniture.

Actually, in our story the silver coin was probably part of a headpiece the woman had received at her wedding. It may have even been part of her marriage dowry, and in that case it would have had an additional sentimental value. Cleaning the house would have been harder than we think. Most floors in those days were made of dirt, so something like a coin could have easily stayed hidden in the dust of a corner or under a bed.

Jesus said the loss of such a coin would have caused any woman great anxiety. Housecleaning might have been her least favorite thing to do, but with a coin of such value missing, her priorities changed. Lighting a lamp and carefully sweeping the house would be a small enough price to pay, even if the job took all day. The rooms had probably never had such a cleaning.

When the job was done, and the coin was in hand, we can imagine her excitement. She had the long-lost coin, and now the collection was once again complete. With great excitement she called in all her neighbors and friends to have a feast. "Let's party!" she said excitedly as she told the story of how she found the coin.

What if she hadn't bothered to look for it? What if she had said, "It's no big deal"? What if she had said, "I hate cleaning"? Then the precious coin would have remained unfound, and this story wouldn't have its greatest lesson. Jesus leaves no corner upswept to find His lost ones, and for that we should be forever grateful.

120 People in Upper Room

Now when the day of Pentecost had fully come, they were all with one accord in one place. And suddenly there came a sound from heaven, as of a rushing mighty wind, and it filled the whole house where they were sitting. And there appeared to them divided tongues, as of fire. Acts 2:1–3

There was great excitement in the air as Jesus' followers gathered for a special prayer meeting in an upper room of Jerusalem. Lots of people were there with them—Mary, the mother of Jesus; and Cleopas, who walked with Jesus on the road to Emmaus. Most likely, Nicodemus and Joseph of Arimathea, blind Bartimaeus, and Lazarus were there also. Jesus had asked them to wait in that room for a special gift, and that is what they did.

While they waited, they prayed for each other and asked God to forgive them of their sins. They prayed for the work of the gospel that was soon to go everywhere like wildfire. And they prayed for the energy to spread the gospel. Jesus had told them, "You will receive power when the Holy Spirit comes on you" (Acts 1:8, NIV). And they believed it. As the days passed, more and more people crowded into the upper room until there were 120 believers gathered there. For more than a week they worshiped God together, and then on the tenth day the sound of a rushing wind could be heard as little flames of fire appeared above the heads of each believer. With the fire came the ability to speak in foreign languages. Many received the power to heal the sick, and they all had love for one another. It was the greatest gift Jesus had ever given His disciples.

What if they hadn't waited patiently in the upper room? What if they had grown tired and gone home? Then the promised gift wouldn't have come. They wouldn't have been able to speak in Arabic, Persian, and Egyptian. They wouldn't have received special powers to heal and preach in Jesus' name. But, praise God, they did, and because they did, they could now stand up for Jesus and even become martyrs like Him, with the peace of heaven in their hearts.

Barabbas

"But you have a custom that I should release someone to you at the Passover. Do you therefore want me to release to you the King of the Jews?" Then they all cried again, saying, "Not this Man, but Barabbas!" Now Barabbas was a robber. John 18:39, 40

Barabbas is one of the most famous people in the entire Bible, but only because Jesus took his place on Calvary. He was a desperate criminal, a robber and murderer, and an enemy of Rome. He was a Jew sentenced to die on a cross with two other thieves. Fortunately for him, there was a custom practiced in Jerusalem: Every year at Passover, a prisoner of the people's choice was pardoned and released from prison. And this happened to be Barabbas' lucky year. Or was it providence?

The scribes and priests stirred up the rabble against Jesus until they became a mob, and then Pilate gave them a choice: Barabbas or Jesus. Calling Barabbas up from the prison in the Antonio fortress, Pilate stood him up against the Man from Galilee. Wow! What a contrast! Thanks to the scribes and priests, the mob chose to free Barabbas. Maybe this was God's way of giving Barabbas a chance at salvation.

What if Barabbas hadn't been given his freedom? What if he had been sent to the cross as Pilate had planned? Then, of course, he would have died in Jesus' place, instead of the other way around. But Jesus did go to the cross, and He did die in place of Barabbas. That must have really touched some cord of gratefulness in the heart of Barabbas, and we'd like to think it made a difference in the life he lived from that day forward. And maybe it did. Christian tradition says Barabbas may have followed the procession of criminals to Golgotha, where he saw Jesus pay the price for his freedom and his sin. If that's so, then it's likely that he later became a Christian. When we get to heaven someday, we'll find out for sure. That's a day to look forward to.

Centurion at the Cross

So when the centurion saw what had happened, he glorified God,
saying, "Certainly this was a righteous Man!" Luke 23:47

If you had been alive two thousand years ago, what would it have taken to convince you that Jesus Christ was the Son of God? His ability to turn water to wine? Seeing Him walk on water? How about healing lepers? Raising the dead? Well, the story of the centurion's reaction when he saw Jesus die on the cross beats them all.

He was a witness to the whole sorry mess of Jesus' trial at the Roman praetorium. He watched his soldiers whip, mock, and shove Jesus up the street toward the place of execution. He watched them nail the Man of Galilee to a cross and then gamble for the clothes they had stripped from His body. He saw Jesus' own people taunt Him, spit at Him, and dare Him to come down off the cross.

The centurion knew little of Jesus. He had heard of the Miracle Man but had never considered Him to be more than a great teacher. However, all that changed when he saw Jesus breathe His last on Calvary. He marveled at Jesus' patience while in pain. He saw the glow of heaven's light surrounding the cross. He heard Jesus' cry of victory, "It is finished!" (John 19:30) And, of course, there was the earthquake that shook Golgotha as Jesus died. It was all more than the centurion could understand. He was impressed and inspired that Jesus was not an ordinary man. His heartfelt confession, "Truly this was the Son of God!" told the whole story (Matthew 27:54).

What if the centurion hadn't opened his heart to Jesus? What if he hadn't been listening to the voice of the Holy Spirit as he watched the crucifixion? Then he would have missed out on one of the greatest epiphanies in history. Jesus was the Son of God, and His crucifixion on Calvary was proof of that. Now that's a discovery of a lifetime!

SEPTEMBER 25

Joseph of Arimathea

This man went to Pilate and asked for the body of Jesus. Then he took it down, wrapped it in linen, and laid it in a tomb that was hewn out of the rock, where no one had ever lain before. Luke 23:52, 53

Joseph of Arimathea was a very wealthy Pharisee in Jesus' day. Christian tradition tells us he gained his wealth as a merchant from business ventures, one of which was a copper mine in the colony of Britain, thousands of miles away. This little snapshot tells us something of the prestige Joseph must have enjoyed in the Jewish megalopolis of Jerusalem.

He is best remembered today for the kindness he showed Jesus after the Savior's death on the cross. However, it's a shame he had to wait until then to show his true colors. Like Nicodemus, Joseph sat on the Sanhedrin, a council of Jewish elders who ruled the nation of Israel. Like Nicodemus, he believed Jesus had been sent from God. He thought the Man from Galilee might actually be the Messiah everyone had been waiting for, and Joseph wanted to be part of the new movement—from a distance. This was his greatest weakness, and others on the Sanhedrin knew it. Like Nicodemus, Joseph was afraid to accept Jesus openly, though he remained a loyal follower in the shadows. This put him somewhere between a rock and a hard place, as the expression goes. When Jesus' ministry approached its fantastic finish during the Passion Week, Joseph was left out on two counts. He was afraid to stand up for Jesus as a disciple, but he wasn't trusted by the Sanhedrin leadership either. That's why they called for a midnight trial, without Joseph or Nicodemus around to gum up the works.

What would have happened if Joseph had been loyal to Jesus from the start? He might have lost his coveted place on the Sanhedrin, although later he lost it anyway when he became a Christian after Pentecost. In the end, tradition says, he donated his wealth to the early church to help spread the gospel. Good move, Joseph—better late than never.

Nicodemus

There was a man of the Pharisees named Nicodemus, a ruler of the Jews.
This man came to Jesus by night and said to Him, "Rabbi, we know that You are a
teacher come from God; for no one can do these signs
that You do unless God is with him." John 3:1, 2

What would you rather be called—a coward or a chicken? What's the difference, you say? A coward is someone who hasn't the courage or character to stand up for the right. A chicken is someone who's a scaredy-cat. Nicodemus was both. He was afraid to stand up for Jesus, and he was just plain chicken because he didn't want anyone to make fun of him.

Here's the story. Nicodemus was a Pharisee and an elite member of the Sanhedrin; he was rich and famous, and he was a godly man. He knew Jesus was no ordinary man, but that was as far as he got. He was not willing to step out in courage and faith to say that Jesus was the Messiah, the long-awaited Savior of the world. Yet he wanted to do the right thing, so he sneaked out under cover of darkness to see Jesus. That way everyone would be happy. His cronies in the Sanhedrin wouldn't see him going to visit the rabbi from Nazareth. Jesus would have a chance to see that Nicodemus was a strong supporter and a potential disciple. Nicodemus would have the best of both worlds. By day he could keep his cushy job in the Sanhedrin, and by night he could sneak around to talk with Jesus in private.

Really? Not a good plan! What if he had accepted Jesus as the Messiah right from the start? After all, what man could calm the angry sea and walk on it? Was there anyone else who could multiply loaves and fishes? Raise the dead? And how many could claim to be the Son of God? Other than Jesus—none! Zero! Zip! Nada! Nicodemus eventually did courageously stand up for Jesus . . . after He was dead. Then he became one of His faithful followers . . . after Jesus rose from the dead. Too bad it took him so long, but that's what you get when you're a coward's chicken.

SEPTEMBER 27

Pilate

When Pilate saw that he could not prevail at all, but rather that a tumult was rising, he took water and washed his hands before the multitude, saying, "I am innocent of the blood of this just Person. You see to it." Matthew 27:24

Pilate is famous for his one-liners: "Are You the King of the Jews?" (Matthew 27:11; Mark 15:2; Luke 23:3; John 18:33) "What is truth?" (John 18:38) "Shall I release to you Jesus or Barabbas?" "Behold the Man!" (John 19:5) "I am innocent of the blood of this just Person." For these clichés—and because he condemned Jesus to a hideous death on a Roman cross, one of the worst forms of torture ever devised by man—Pilate is best remembered. The Jewish priests were determined to kill the Man from Galilee but couldn't execute Him. Only Pilate, a Roman official, could do that.

When he first saw Jesus standing in his court, he was surprised. Jesus had the kindest face—and He looked like a king. He could not be a criminal, and Pilate told the priests and scribes exactly what he thought of their scheme to kill Him. "I find no fault in this Man," he said (Luke 23:4). "I will therefore chastise Him and release Him" (Luke 23:16).

This made the Jewish leaders furious! It seemed that Jesus was going to slip through their grasp once again, and Pilate was the reason. "If you let Him go, you're no friend of Caesar!" they howled. This worried Pilate because he knew the Jews would report him. And so he caved and condemned the spotless Lamb of God. What a wimp!

What if he hadn't given in? What if he had stood firm on his impression that Jesus wasn't guilty? Well, then, we wouldn't be remembering him today as the one who killed Jesus, and Pilate wouldn't have had to live the rest of his life knowing he had sent his Creator to the cross. But wait, there's more! Some five years later, Pilate did lose his job and was sent into exile—the very thing he feared most. As could be expected of a Roman ruler, he considered himself a failure, and in the end, it is said, he committed suicide. It didn't have to end that way!

Pilate's Wife

> While he was sitting on the judgment seat, his wife sent to him, saying,
> "Have nothing to do with that just Man, for I have suffered many things
> today in a dream because of Him." Matthew 27:19

It is difficult to be a politician, and being the wife of one is even more difficult. That's the world Pilate's wife found herself in from A.D. 26 to 36. It couldn't have been much fun for her to live with Pilate in Jerusalem. She had few friends there, and she didn't have much freedom to walk in the streets of the Jewish city, since her husband wasn't a popular man with the Jews. She knew she was living in a man's world, but she also knew Pilate was stubborn and harsh and sometimes clueless. It seemed he was always doing the wrong thing at the wrong time. For example, he spent sacred temple money to build an aqueduct for water and then crucified the Jews who complained about it.

When Jesus was brought to stand judgment in her husband's court early one morning, she knew she must speak up. "He's innocent!" she told Pilate in a message. "Don't have anything to do with the condemnation of this holy Man! Trust me! I've been having nightmares about Him all night!" Pilate must have sweated bullets at this news, because he spent the next few hours trying to get Jesus released. In the end he failed, and that means she failed too. He was her husband, and his future was her future. That's how it goes in politics.

What if she had gotten Pilate to listen to her? What if she had convinced him she was right? What if she had come down to the court herself and told him about her dream? It's possible she might have prevented Pilate from condemning Jesus. Maybe Pilate wouldn't have lost his job and been sent away as a political prisoner himself five years later. Mrs. Pilate wouldn't have had to move away with him to Gaul, in what is now France. She wouldn't have had to suffer after he committed suicide. Wow! Too bad he didn't listen to her.

SEPTEMBER 29

Roman Soldiers at the Cross

And they clothed Him with purple; and they twisted a crown of thorns,
put it on His head, and began to salute Him, "Hail, King of the Jews!"
Then they struck Him on the head with a reed and spat on Him;
and bowing the knee they worshiped Him. Mark 15:17–19

There wasn't a more disgraceful, bloodthirsty bunch of mercenaries than the Roman soldiers who presided over the trial and crucifixion of Jesus. For starters, they scourged him with a cat-o'-nine-tails, a cruel whip made with pieces of metal embedded at the ends of nine leather strands. This, of course, cut Jesus' back to ribbons, making him bleed badly. Then they put a purple cape on Him, a stick in His right hand, and a crown of twisted thorns on His head. Slapping and punching Him, they spit on Him and mocked Him cruelly. "Hail, King of the Jews!" they sneered as they hit the crown of thorns on His head, making the blood run like rivers down His face. When they took Him to Calvary, they drove spikes into His hands and feet and then dropped the cross into a hole in the ground. The pain must have been excruciating, and yet Jesus prayed for the soldiers who were treating Him so badly. If all this wasn't enough, they stripped Him of His clothes to leave Him hanging on the cross naked. What a shameful way to treat another human being—even more so the God of all creation!

What if the Roman soldiers had refused to scourge Jesus and crucify Him? What if they had decided it was wrong to treat anyone that way—especially Jesus, the Son of God. Then history would look a lot different this side of Calvary. Jesus might have died some other way, but the Roman soldiers wouldn't have been the guilty ones. Someday soon the clouds of heaven will split, and Jesus will come again. When that day comes, the Roman soldiers who treated Jesus with such disdain will see Him come in all His majesty. Too late they will realize they helped to crucify the King of kings and Lord of lords.

Simon of Cyrene

Now as they led Him away, they laid hold of a certain man,
Simon a Cyrenian, who was coming from the country,
and on him they laid the cross that he might bear it after Jesus. Luke 23:26

What would you have done if you had been in the Garden the night Jesus was arrested and taken to trial? What would you have done when the temple priests made all those ridiculous accusations against Jesus? Could you have stood by to watch as the Roman soldiers whipped Him and spat in His face, or when they made Him carry His own cross? He was so weak from loss of blood that, the Bible says, He fell beneath its weight. That's when a man named Simon showed up.

We don't know much about him except that he was from the city of Cyrene in Libya, North Africa. He was a Jew with two sons, Alexander and Rufus, and they were visiting Jerusalem for the Passover Feast. He heard the mob shouting obscenities at Jesus as He passed in the streets, and he wondered at the cruel treatment He was given. Simon had heard of Jesus, and though his sons were believers in Jesus, he was not a disciple.

Simon was a good man. He saw that Jesus was about to collapse from the heavy cross he was carrying, and he felt sorry for Him. That was enough for the Roman soldiers, who immediately grabbed Simon. "If you think He's got it so bad, you carry His cross!" they demanded. And that's exactly what Simon did. He lifted the cross to his shoulders and carried it the rest of the way for Jesus. What an honor!

What if Simon hadn't been willing to carry the cross? He didn't really know Jesus, after all. In that case he would have missed an amazing, one-of-a-kind opportunity to do something for Jesus that no one else will ever get to do! But praise God, he did, and it changed his life forever—all because he was in the right place at the right time and willing to help.

Thief on the Cross

But the other, answering, rebuked him, saying, "Do you not even fear God, seeing you are under the same condemnation? And we indeed justly, for we receive the due reward of our deeds; but this Man has done nothing wrong." Then he said to Jesus, "Lord, remember me when You come into Your kingdom." Luke 23:40–42

What was it like to die on a cross? The cross was designed to torture and kill the victim slowly, giving its victim as much pain as possible while there was still life. This was the fate of the thieves who died on either side of Jesus nearly two thousand years ago. In spite of the pain he was suffering, one of the thieves mocked Jesus, showing Him no mercy. "If You are Christ, save Yourself and us!" he said scornfully.

The other thief was outraged. He was suffering incredible anguish on a cross too, but he chewed out the first thief in royal fashion. "Don't you fear God?" he demanded. "You're on a cross just like Him, and you're acting like a moron! We deserve to be crucified! We are being punished because we're criminals, but this Man has done nothing wrong!"

Wow! That was quite a testimony! This hardened criminal was hanging on a cross with nails through his wrists and feet and still had enough courage and common sense to defend Jesus! But it was his final words that really cheered the heart of Jesus. "Lord, remember me when You come into Your kingdom" (Luke 23:42). Jesus was touched by the thief's testimony and said, "You will be with me in paradise. I can promise you that today."

What if the thief hadn't defended Jesus? What if he hadn't asked Jesus to save him a place in the kingdom of heaven? Then he would have died without hope and without the blood of Jesus to cover his sins. Thankfully, we will meet him someday soon.

Ananias of Damascus

And Ananias went his way and entered the house; and laying his hands on him he said, "Brother Saul, the Lord Jesus, who appeared to you on the road as you came, has sent me that you may receive your sight and be filled with the Holy Spirit."
Acts 9:17

How would you like an assignment from God to befriend a man who kills Christians? To go hang out with someone no one trusts? That's what God asked of Ananias. Even more surprising, He asked Ananias to heal the man. Wow! Ananias was scared to death, and though he didn't say no, he didn't say yes right way either. "Lord, I know all about this man!" he sputtered. "He's a hit man, sent to Damascus to knock off as many Christians as possible! If You don't mind, I'd rather not be one of his casualties!"

But God knows His business, and He knows quality when He sees it. That assassin was none other than Saul of Tarsus. God said, "Saul is a chosen vessel of Mine to preach the gospel to Jews and Gentiles alike, and to suffer for My name's sake." So Ananias got his courage up. He went to the street called Straight, entered the house where Saul was staying, and laid his hands on him. "Brother Saul, the Lord Jesus, whom you saw in vision on the road to Damascus, has sent me that you may see again and be filled with the Holy Spirit." And that was it. Saul later said it felt like scales fell from his eyes, and he was healed.

What if Ananias hadn't obeyed God? He could have said no. Many people have done that—Lot's wife, Pharaoh, King Saul, Judas—but we know how things turned out for them. If Ananias had said no, like these notorious characters, he would have missed out on the blessings of bringing sight to the most famous evangelist of all time. To his credit, he helped Saul as he was asked. He healed Saul of his blindness and became famous for it. That's what you get when you listen to the voice of God.

OCTOBER 3

Ananias and Sapphira

But a certain man named Ananias, with Sapphira his wife, sold a possession. And he kept back part of the proceeds, his wife also being aware of it, and brought a certain part and laid it at the apostles' feet. Acts 5:1, 2

This a story about one of the most notorious couples in the Bible—Ananias and Sapphira. Their story teaches us that anyone who thinks they can fool God should think again. And anyone who thinks they can rob God and dishonor His church should watch their back. Stay tuned. The lesson in this story speaks for itself.

We can see it even now. The Christian movement was growing by leaps and bounds, and everyone was excited. With great power the apostles were telling the story of Jesus' death and resurrection. The believers were united and unselfish, and they wanted to share what they had with others. Many who owned land or houses sold them and brought the money to the church. This is how the church helped those in need as they spread the gospel.

This brings us to the story of Ananias and Sapphira. They decided to sell some land and promised they would donate whatever money they received to the church. Nice plan, but after the land was sold they changed their minds and decided to keep back part of the money—and then they lied about it. This didn't go over real well with God because He was looking out for the purity and stability of the early church.

What would have happened to the couple had they been honest with God? What would have happened if they had said, "We shouldn't be greedy"? They would have lived, for one thing. It's hard to tell the story, but Ananias and Sapphira actually died because they lied, and lying is one of the worst sins in God's book. Was that a judgment from God? Absolutely, and we would all do well to pay attention. Lying never pays. Read about it in the Bible.

Barnabas

> And when Saul had come to Jerusalem, he tried to join the disciples;
> but they were all afraid of him, and did not believe that he was a disciple.
> But Barnabas took him and brought him to the apostles. And he declared to them
> how he had seen the Lord on the road, and that He had spoken to him, and how he
> had preached boldly at Damascus in the name of Jesus. Acts 9:26, 27

Barnabas was the coolest leader of the early Christian church. The Bible says he was a good man, full of faith and the Holy Spirit. Early church tradition claims he may have been one of the seventy Jesus sent out on a missionary tour. He loved everyone, and everybody loved him. The stories we read about him describe him as a kind and encouraging man.

For example, when Saul first became a Christian, Barnabas was the only one who would accept him at face value. Even more important, he urged all the believers to welcome Saul into the church and told them about Saul's dramatic conversion story at Damascus.

He and Saul later became missionary partners and traveled the Mediterranean with the gospel story. On one journey, another young man, John Mark, wanted to go with them, and they set off with high hopes. However, partway through the trip John Mark flew the coop and went home, unable to stick it out. Later John Mark wanted to travel with them again, but Saul, now called Paul, would hear none of it. "Not on my watch!" we can imagine him telling Barnabas adamantly. "He'll just run like a chicken as he did before." They argued about it a lot and ended up dissolving the partnership over it.

What if Barnabas hadn't befriended Saul in the first place? And what if he hadn't insisted on giving John Mark a second chance? Maybe both men would have given up their faith, too discouraged to go on. Thankfully, Barnabas didn't abandon them. He encouraged them both and took them under his wing as a mother hen would do for her chicks.

OCTOBER 5

Cornelius

There was a certain man in Caesarea called Cornelius,
a centurion of what was called the Italian Regiment, a devout man
and one who feared God with all his household, who gave alms generously to the
people, and prayed to God always. Acts 10:1, 2

This is one of the most inspiring stories in the New Testament. It's the saga of a man who reached out to God in faith and was rewarded for it beyond his wildest dreams.

Cornelius was a Roman centurion in the coastal city of Caesarea, a family man who was sincere in his worship of God, though he didn't know anything about Christianity. He gave alms regularly to the poor and was a man of great prayer. While he prayed one day, an angel of God came to him in a vision. "Your prayers have been heard by God," said the glorious being standing before him. "Send messengers to Joppa and ask for Peter in the home of a man named Simon, who lives by the sea. This Peter will bring you words of life."

The messengers brought Peter to Caesarea, where he taught Cornelius and his family about the Son of God who died to save mankind. At first Peter was surprised that an angel would ask him to bring the gospel to a Gentile family, but he shouldn't have been. His own vision about a sheet full of unclean animals reminded him that everyone is a child of God. The icing on the cake came when the Holy Spirit descended upon Cornelius and his family—there was nothing left to do but baptize them all in the name of Jesus Christ.

What if Cornelius had not been searching for the truth? What if he had not been a godly man praying for the light of the gospel? Then the angel would not have come, Peter wouldn't have arrived to share the words of life, and the Holy Spirit would not have blessed Cornelius and his family in such a dramatic way. Wow! What a one-eighty Cornelius made in his life!

Elymas

"And now, indeed, the hand of the Lord is upon you, and you shall be blind, not seeing the sun for a time." And immediately a dark mist fell upon him, and he went around seeking someone to lead him by the hand. Acts 13:11

In the Bible you'll find good guys and bad guys. Elymas was one of the bad guys. Paul and Barnabas met him on a missionary tour through Cyprus. He worked with Sergius Paulus, the governor of the island. The governor was very impressed with Paul's preaching and that's where all the trouble started. You see, Elymas was a Jewish sorcerer and enjoyed the influence he had on his boss, Sergius Paulus.

That doesn't even make sense, you might be saying. How could a Jew who believed in God be a sorcerer? Sorcery is the practice of witchcraft in which a man or woman uses the power of demons to do miraculous things. Well, the truth is, Elymas was a false prophet. Paul was suspicious of him, and for good reason. From the start, Elymas gave Sergius Paulus bad advice by turning him away from the message Paul and Barnabas were preaching. When Paul realized this, the Holy Spirit gave him a special message for Elymas. "You son of the devil," he said, "why are you making the path to God complicated for the governor? Because of this you're going to be blind for a while!" Everyone must have been shocked to hear Paul say such a thing, but when Elymas became blind, they realized it was a miracle from God.

What if Elymas hadn't been so jealous of Paul? What if he had said, "I want to be like Paul, who is like Jesus"? Then he would have received the Holy Spirit and gone on to do amazing things for God. He must have been a very smart man, but it's too bad he failed his biggest IQ test of all. Fortunately, this story has a happy ending. Sergius Paulus was amazed when he saw the power of God and became a believer in the gospel message preached by Paul. Perfect.

John Mark

Then after some days Paul said to Barnabas, "Let us now go back and visit our brethren in every city where we have preached the word of the Lord, and see how they are doing." Now Barnabas was determined to take with them John called Mark. But Paul insisted that they should not. Acts 15:36–38

Is there a kid in your school who seems to have everything? Good looks? Money? Lots of stuff nobody else has? That was John Mark, and all his friends may have even resented him for it. He came from an important family in Jerusalem, so it's likely he knew all the big shots in Judea. Pampered and fussed over, he may have been a spoiled brat. And then he was given the opportunity of a lifetime! He was asked to go on a Mediterranean cruise with Barnabas and Paul.

Wow! Very cool! Seeing all those new sites every day and sleeping in a different place every night must have been fun. But eating strange food and getting sick on the high seas probably wasn't much fun for a privileged kid. It was hard to be away from home, where servants did everything. It was hard to be up and out on the road every day before the crack of dawn. Finally, he couldn't take it anymore and jumped on the next ship headed for home. Barnabas felt bad, but Paul was disgusted. "I could have predicted that," he probably said as they headed off to finish the missionary tour. Sometime later, Barnabas suggested taking John Mark with them on their next missionary trip, but Paul said, "No!" and that was a dealbreaker for Barnabas. He felt so strongly about taking John Mark with them that he and Paul split up. Barnabas headed off with John Mark, and Paul paired up with Silas.

Now, we have to ask ourselves, What if John Mark hadn't gone AWOL on that first missionary tour? What if Paul and Barnabas hadn't split up over the whole thing? Well, then, maybe the boy wouldn't have had a chance to mature and later travel with Paul successfully. Maybe he wouldn't have gone on to write the gospel of Mark. Now that's a thought!

Luke

Only Luke is with me. 2 Timothy 4:11

That's a short verse, but it says a lot about Luke. When Paul was in a Roman prison cell awaiting the orders for his execution, everyone abandoned him for one reason or another—everyone but Luke.

Luke was originally from the city of Antioch in Syria and probably one of Paul's Gentile converts. Since he was a doctor, the Roman government officials may have allowed him to stick around and tend to Paul's medical needs. In Roman times physicians treated people with tumors, abscesses, and broken bones, just like today. Even more surprising, many doctors were famous for amputating limbs and doing successful brain surgeries too. That sounds pretty impressive!

Maybe Paul was allowed to have Luke stay with him because the doctor was also a scribe. After all, Paul had many letters to write to all the churches he had started. Rome, Corinth, Galatia, Ephesus, Philippi, and Thessalonica all received letters from Paul, and Luke probably wrote out the later manuscripts because Paul's eyesight wasn't so good. The two of them were the best of friends by now, inseparable during the final days of Paul's life.

Sometime during these years, Luke must have also written his two Bible manuscripts: the Gospel of Luke and the book of Acts. Both books were written no later than A.D. 63. It was his goal in these books to let everyone know that Jesus was the Savior of Jews and Gentiles alike.

What if Luke hadn't become a Christian? Then he wouldn't have traveled with Paul, he wouldn't have met the people in the stories he wrote about, and he wouldn't have gotten two of his books into the Bible. Someday soon we will meet Luke and find out a lot more details about his travels with Paul. God's digital videos in the archives of heaven will be so much fun to watch! I can't wait. How about you?

Paul

But the Lord said to him, "Go, for he is a chosen vessel of Mine to bear My name before Gentiles, kings, and the children of Israel." Acts 9:15

Do you have a nickname? Something like Tam, or DJ, or Shorty? Saul of Tarsus had nicknames. Early on they probably called him the Terminator because of the way he persecuted Christians. But everything changed when God got ahold of him. That's when his name was changed to Paul. Here's how it happened. Saul was on the warpath to kill every Christian in Jerusalem and became their most bitter enemy. He even began hunting them down by going door-to-door, dragging them away to prison.

But persecuting Christians in Jerusalem wasn't enough for Saul. He wanted to go and find them in cities like Damascus too. While on the road to Damascus, he had an experience that changed his life forever. Suddenly a light brighter than the noonday sun shone all around him, and he fell to the ground blinded. As he lay there in confusion and fear, he heard a voice saying to him, "Saul, Saul, why are you persecuting Me?" (Acts 9:4) His companions were blinded by the light and speechless, but they saw no one. Saul recognized who was talking to him, and he was scared—it was Jesus that he was persecuting! They led Saul into the city, but he couldn't see for three days until a disciple named Ananias healed him. The experience humbled Saul, and from that day forward he was a dynamic preacher for Jesus. Everywhere he went, he told people his conversion story, and that's when people began calling him Paul.

We have to wonder, what if the Lord hadn't stopped him on the road to Damascus? What if Saul hadn't humbled himself and given his heart to Jesus? Then he wouldn't have been healed of his blindness. He wouldn't have been stoned or jailed or shipwrecked on dangerous missions for Jesus. Most important, he wouldn't have become the church's greatest missionary evangelist and won thousands of souls for the kingdom of God.

Priscilla and Aquila

And he found a certain Jew named Aquila, born in Pontus, who had recently come from Italy with his wife Priscilla (because Claudius had commanded all the Jews to depart from Rome); and he came to them. Acts 18:2

It must have been a lonely life for Paul, being on the road all the time. He traveled a lot, and when he stopped to preach in the big cities on his trips, he always looked up his friends and went to stay with them. Priscilla and Aquila were some of those friends.

Paul got to know the couple when he went to Corinth to preach the gospel. They were from Italy but had been kicked out of Rome by the emperor Claudius. Paul had something in common with Priscilla and Aquila—they were tentmakers too. Not surprisingly, he stayed with them whenever he came to town and helped them sew tents in their courtyard.

Priscilla and Aquila were strong Christians and very helpful to the young churches in Corinth and Ephesus. Not surprisingly, they were an encouragement to members and travelers alike who came to worship with them each Sabbath. Apollos, a talented young evangelist, got to know them too when he came through Ephesus. He was a new convert to Christianity but didn't know anything about the Holy Spirit. Priscilla and Aquila came to the rescue once again and explained how the power of heaven had been brought to the church through the Holy Spirit.

What if Priscilla and Aquila had said, "Forget it! We're not going to be Christians if we have to lose our home and get booted out of Rome"? Then, of course, they would have never met and worked with Paul, one of the most prolific soul winners of all time. They wouldn't have met Apollos, another amazing missionary for Jesus, and helped train him for even greater service. A neat legacy for Priscilla and Aquila!

Theophilus

It seemed good to me also, having had perfect understanding of all things from the very first, to write to you an orderly account, most excellent Theophilus, that you may know the certainty of those things in which you were instructed. Luke 1:3, 4

W ho was this man Theophilus? His name means "friend of God," and he must have also been a good friend of Dr. Luke, because the doctor addressed both the Gospel of Luke and the book of Acts to him.

We know little else about him, such as where he lived or what connection he had to Luke. Christian tradition tells us he was from the city of Antioch in Syria and possibly a Greek nobleman or high government official. Was he a Christian? We don't know that for sure, but he was probably a Gentile convert since Luke addressed his two books to him. Maybe he was a patient of Luke's at one time. Luke's travels with Paul would have brought him into connection with important people like Theophilus.

Luke called him "most excellent Theophilus," and he wanted to write an accurate account for him about all the stories of Jesus he had heard. He wanted Theophilus to know for sure that Jesus was the Son of God.

What if Theophilus had not been such an upright, godly man? What if he had showed no interest in the amazing things he had heard Luke say about Jesus? What if he hadn't become a Christian? Then, of course, he would have had to give up his claim to eternal life. Without Jesus, there's no such thing as eternal life, and that means Theophilus would have died without hope. Thankfully, through the influence of Luke, it is likely that Theophilus knew and loved God.

Claudius Lysias

Now as they were seeking to kill him, news came to the commander of the garrison that all Jerusalem was in an uproar. He immediately took soldiers and centurions, and ran down to them. And when they saw the commander and the soldiers, they stopped beating Paul. Acts 21:31, 32

What must it have been like to be a Roman officer in the days of Jesus and Paul? Christianity was just getting a foothold in Jerusalem, and the Jewish priests and scribes were not happy about that. More and more Jews were converting to Christianity, and the leaders at the temple were so angry that they wanted to kill every Christian in sight.

While in Jerusalem celebrating Passover one day, Paul got himself into trouble. The priests and scribes sent a mob to the temple to find Paul and beat him to death. Fortunately, Claudius Lysias, the Roman commander in charge of peace and order in Jerusalem, showed up in time to rescue Paul and pull him to safety. He ordered a centurion to put handcuffs and chains on Paul, thinking he must be some kind of desperate criminal. The Roman commander told his soldiers to scourge Paul, but Paul reminded him it was illegal to beat a Roman citizen. When Claudius Lysias learned that Paul was a Roman citizen, it scared him, and he put Paul in protective custody to keep him from being murdered.

What if Claudius Lysias hadn't rescued Paul? To him, Paul seemed like just another Jew. He was weary of all the fighting in Jerusalem caused by the Jewish leadership, so why should he care? If he had not listened to Paul, God would have had to rescue Paul some other way, and the Roman commander might not have heard the gospel story quite the way Paul could tell it. Who knows, maybe Claudius later became a Christian. Someday when Jesus comes, we will find out.

OCTOBER 13

Jailer at Philippi

And he brought them out and said, "Sirs, what must I do to be saved?"
So they said, "Believe on the Lord Jesus Christ, and you will be saved,
you and your household." Acts 16:30, 31

What a job! Imagine that you're the warden of a Roman prison in the city of Philippi. One day you receive two prisoners, along with orders to whip them, throw them in the deepest underground prison cell, and lock their feet in stocks. That's easy enough for a tough Roman officer, but there's a catch. If the prisoners should somehow escape on your watch, the local magistrates will order *your* execution. Ouch! That doesn't sound like a very fun job.

You know the story. The prisoners were Paul and Silas, and they didn't stay locked up for long. They sang praises to God during the first part of their imprisonment. Then, about midnight, a disastrous earthquake hit the city and shook the prison to its foundations. All the doors were knocked off their hinges, the stocks were opened, and the chains fell off the prisoners' hands and feet. The warden was scared nearly to death. Literally. Seeing the prison wide open, he drew his sword to commit suicide but was shocked to hear Paul's voice calling to him. "Don't do it! We're all here, alive and well!" The jailer called for a light and ran into Paul and Silas's cell. "What must I do to be saved?" he asked as he fell to his knees.

"Believe in the Lord Jesus Christ," Paul told him. The warden took the prisoners home to wash their wounds, feed them, and even introduce them to his family. In return, Paul and Silas shared the story of salvation with the jailer and his family and then baptized them all. What a fantastic finish!

What if Paul and Silas hadn't been sent to that warden's prison? In that case he wouldn't have heard them singing hymns of praise to God. He wouldn't have seen their faith in Jesus. He wouldn't have received the message of salvation and been baptized. So, was the warden's risk in having such a dangerous job worth all the trouble in the end? You bet!

Lois and Eunice

I call to remembrance the genuine faith that is in you,
which dwelt first in your grandmother Lois and your mother Eunice,
and I am persuaded is in you also. 2 Timothy 1:5

Timothy had a nice family. His mom and grandma were baptized as Christians when Paul came through the city of Lystra on one of his missionary trips. Their names were Eunice and Lois. Paul praised them for being faithful converts to the early Christian church, which was growing by leaps and bounds. Here are the details.

Timothy's father was a Greek, and his mother and grandmother were followers of Jesus who helped to spread the gospel of Jesus. Paul was grateful for all they were doing to help and for the way they were training Timothy to love Jesus. Maybe they even quoted Solomon: "Train up a child in the way he should go, and when he is old he will not depart from it" (Proverbs 22:6).

On Paul's second journey through Lystra, he invited Timothy to join his ministry team as a disciple. This bond grew to be like that of a father and son. As young Timothy developed as a leader in the Christian church, so did his thankfulness for the faithful witness of his mother Eunice and grandmother Lois.

What if these two women hadn't been faithful as Christians? What if they hadn't done their jobs as mother and grandmother? What if they had said, "Boys will be boys"? Then Timothy would have probably turned out quite different. We would likely not see his name in any of Paul's New Testament letters to the churches. And, of course, we would probably not even know who they were if they hadn't raised Timothy to be a godly young man.

Lydia

And on the Sabbath day we went out of the city to the riverside,
where prayer was customarily made; and we sat down and spoke
to the women who met there. Now a certain woman named Lydia heard us. She
was a seller of purple from the city of Thyatira, who worshiped God. The Lord
opened her heart to heed the things spoken by Paul. Acts 16:13, 14

Lydia ran a prosperous business selling purple garments made from an exotic purple dye. Not just any dye, but a deep purple dye used by kings, princes, and rich merchants. The unique part about the dye is that it came from sea snails and required a complicated process to make the dye. But that's not why we know about her today. Her greatest claim to fame was the fact that she accepted Christianity when Paul came through the city of Philippi on one of his missionary tours. It happened this way.

One Sabbath Paul and Silas went down to the riverside to pray and worship. While there, they visited with several godly women who met at the river regularly. You guessed it. One of them was Lydia, who happened to be a believer in the one true God. As she listened to the things Paul was saying that first Sabbath, the Lord opened her heart to the story of Jesus. She received the truth gladly, and she decided to be baptized. To show her appreciation for their kindness in bringing her the gospel, she invited the missionary team to stay at her house. What a blessing that must have been!

What if Lydia hadn't befriended Paul and Silas? After all, Philippi was her home, and these men were complete strangers. Well, as we can see in Acts 16, these missionaries were beaten and thrown into prison for preaching the gospel in the marketplace. They would need a place to land when they got out, and Lydia's house was the perfect place to go. What a kind woman she must have been to help them out!

Man From Macedonia

And a vision appeared to Paul in the night. A man of Macedonia stood and pleaded with him, saying, "Come over to Macedonia and help us." Acts 16:9

Have you ever had a dream, and when you woke up you couldn't get it out of your head? Paul had one of those, and it was obvious to him that God had sent the dream. He had it one night while he was in the city of Troas on a missionary trip with Silas and Timothy. In the vision, a man from Macedonia was looking at him and begging, "Come over to Macedonia and help us." Macedonia was a region in the area of Europe now located in parts of Bulgaria, Macedonia, Albania, and Greece.

Paul talked it over with his companions, and the next day they left immediately for Macedonia. If God wanted them in Macedonia, to Macedonia they would go. It wasn't an easy trip—they had some life-threatening adventures in Philippi, Thessalonica, and Berea, but they pushed on anyway. They won many souls for Jesus in their travels through the cities of Macedonia. But the biggest question we might ask ourselves is, Did they ever meet the man in the vision? We don't know the answer to that question, but we'd like to think they did. Wouldn't you love to know what they said to each other when Paul told him about the vision?

What if Paul had said, "I'm not going to Macedonia. It was just a dream"? Then he wouldn't have landed in the jail at Philippi and baptized the prison warden. He wouldn't have been attacked by a mob in the city of Thessalonica. He wouldn't have met the believers in Berea who loved the Scriptures and the message of salvation. And he wouldn't have had a chance to meet the man from Macedonia. Good thing he went, don't you think? When the Holy Spirit gives us an impression to speak to someone for Him, we need to obey.

Paul's Nephew

And when it was day, some of the Jews banded together and bound themselves
under an oath, saying that they would neither eat nor drink till they had killed Paul.
. . . So when Paul's sister's son heard of their ambush, he went and entered the
barracks and told Paul. Acts 23:12, 16

Have you ever felt that you don't really matter? That you're just a kid and no one really appreciates you for what you do? If that's the case, you might relate to the kid in this story and the part he played in helping Paul.

Paul was in the hot seat—again. A mob of Jews in Jerusalem had tried to kill him, but the Roman soldiers had saved him, for the moment at least. And that's where the hero of this story enters the picture. We don't even know his name, but here's the story.

A group of forty Jews had banded together to plot the death of Paul. They told the chief priests and elders, "We have bound ourselves under an oath that we will not eat or drink until we have killed Paul." Then they suggested that the Jewish council ask the Roman commander to bring Paul down to the Sanhedrin one more time for questioning. Of course, that was not the real plan. When Paul was on the way to the hearing, they intended to attack and kill him.

Paul's nephew somehow heard about the planned ambush and went to the Roman barracks to tell Paul about it. Paul was grateful and sent his nephew to see Claudius Lysias, the Roman military commander in Jerusalem. Long story short, Claudius Lysias sent Paul that very night on a midnight getaway to the coastal city of Caesarea, with soldiers to protect him.

What if Paul's nephew had been too scared to get involved? He loved his uncle Paul, but what if one of the assassins found out he was the one to break the news to the authorities? He would have been dead for sure. He was just a kid. But that's not the way things worked out. God is good, and He delivered Paul. Thanks much, good nephew.

Possessed Slave Girl in Philippi

A certain slave girl possessed with a spirit of divination met us, who brought her masters much profit by fortune-telling. This girl followed Paul and us, and cried out, saying, "These men are the servants of the Most High God, who proclaim to us the way of salvation." Acts 16:16, 17

How would you like a demon-possessed girl to follow you through city streets and grocery store and even right into your church? How would you feel if she were taunting you about your work for God? Now, let's reverse that. How would you feel if you were that girl saying such things? How would you like being a slave of Satan and used as a fortune-teller or spirit medium to make big bucks for your bosses? That's the way it went sometimes in the old days, and this story proves it.

It happened in Philippi, a city in the country we now call Greece. For several days a slave girl followed Paul and Silas, not giving them a minute of peace. "These men are servants of the Most High God!" she sneered over and over again in a satanic voice. "They've come to tell us all about the way of salvation!"

Finally Paul's patience had reached its limit. Turning to the girl, he said to the spirit within her, "I command you in the name of Jesus Christ to come out of her" (Acts 16:18). The demon obeyed. What choice did it have? When Jesus comes to town, the demons flee.

We don't know what became of the girl in this story, because we never hear from her again. For sure, her slave masters were not happy about losing her services. The income they made from her fortune-telling would zero out, now that she was free from Satan's control. What if she had not followed Paul and Silas through the streets? Then she would not have been marvelously freed from the demons of hell. Wow! What a trade!

Silas

But at midnight Paul and Silas were praying and singing hymns to God, and the prisoners were listening to them. Suddenly there was a great earthquake, so that the foundations of the prison were shaken; and immediately all the doors were opened and everyone's chains were loosed. Acts 16:25, 26

Silas was blessed by God in ways that you and I can only dream of! He got to travel with Paul, one of the most amazing missionary evangelists of all time! Sometimes he had to fight his way through angry mobs, sail through storms, and sit in dark prison cells with rats running over his feet. Wow! That sounds exciting but dangerous! If Silas ever thought travels on the road with Paul might be boring, one night in Philippi changed that.

It all started when angry slave owners stirred up a mob against them. The local magistrates thought Silas and Paul must be serious criminals, and, without giving them a trial, they beat them with rods. After the whipping, they locked them up in prison with chains and ordered their feet to be put in the stocks. Not fun at all! That must have been a night to remember! Silas and Paul refused to be discouraged. To keep up their spirits, they began to sing. We don't know who started singing first, or if either of them could sing well, but it didn't matter, because the angels came to sing with them. How do we know? Around midnight God sent the gift of an earthquake to open wide the prison doors.

What if Silas had not taken the job of traveling with Paul? What if he had said, "Not me! I need those kinds of disasters like I need a hole in the head"? Then today he probably wouldn't be remembered. All those adventures, all those dangerous, heart-stopping episodes with Paul would belong to someone else. All those people won for Jesus might not have been won, like the other prisoners in the jail, and the warden and his family. What a legacy! Thanks for the memories, Silas! You have made our bedtime Bible stories a real treat!

Timothy

And behold, a certain disciple was there, named Timothy, the son of a certain
Jewish woman who believed. . . . He was well spoken of by the brethren who were
at Lystra and Iconium. Acts 16:1, 2

Timothy was just a kid when he started helping spread the gospel in the early
Christian church. OK, he wasn't exactly a child, but he was young. Next to
John Mark and the apostle John, he was one of the youngest Christian workers on
record. Paul met him and his family while on a missionary trip. His mother and
grandmother were Jews, and they became Christians, along with Timothy, after
hearing Paul preach that Jesus was the Son of God.

Before long, Timothy was helping out in the worship services at the church in
Lystra, where he lived. By the time Paul came to town again, Timothy was showing
real talent. How young was he? Probably in his twenties, an age considered young
by church standards. In those days, Jewish men didn't usually become leaders in
their communities until they were at least thirty. Paul was impressed with Timothy's faith and his leadership skills in the young church, and he gave him an offer
he couldn't refuse—the chance to travel with Paul and Silas on a missionary tour
around the Mediterranean. Timothy was a smashing success. Within a few short
years he was a pastor in the church at Ephesus, one of the most wicked cities in the
Roman Empire.

What if Timothy had said he'd rather be out with his friends doing stuff like
surfing on the ocean, or going to watch the gladiators fight, or watching the circus
when it came to town? Then he wouldn't have gotten to travel and see people
give their lives to Jesus. He wouldn't have received letters from Paul like 1 and 2
Timothy. It just goes to show you what a young guy or girl can do for God in the
church. Never be afraid to be like Timothy. Stand up and use your talents for Jesus
even if you think you're too young! Timothy did it, and look how he turned out!

Titus

If anyone inquires about Titus, he is my partner and fellow worker concerning you.
Or if our brethren are inquired about, they are messengers of the churches, the
glory of Christ. 2 Corinthians 8:23

Titus was quite a guy! Evidently, he was young like John Mark and Timothy and also traveled with the apostle Paul on his missionary trips. Titus was not a Jew but a Gentile. He was a convert of Paul and was probably baptized when Paul came through the city of Antioch. The message of salvation brought them together like nothing else ever could. They say the blood of family runs thicker than the water of baptism, but it would be hard to argue it in the relationship we see between Paul and Titus. In fact, there was such a bond between them that the apostle began to think of him as his own son. It appears that Paul never had children, and at the time he was traveling around the Mediterranean he wasn't married either, so it's easy to see why Titus became like family to him. They spent a lot of time together. Paul trusted Titus so much that he began sending him out on missions of his own to help churches in Asia that were struggling. One place was the island of Crete, one of the first places Paul had traveled to early in his ministry. Titus got to hang out with Paul in many scary places, and even in the Roman prison just before Paul was executed by Nero in about A.D. 65.

What if Titus had decided he didn't want to travel with Paul? Going on the road for months and even years at a time can be grueling. And what if he had decided being a preacher in places like Antioch and Dalmatia was not his cup of tea? Then he would have missed out on the blessings of traveling with the greatest missionary evangelist of all time. And he wouldn't have hit the jackpot by having Paul write a letter that was later called the Epistle to Titus, and eventually became part of our Bible. Now that's cool!

Bereans

These were more fair-minded than those in Thessalonica, in that they received the word with all readiness, and searched the Scriptures daily to find out whether these things were so. Acts 17:11

Who were these folks? Today we call them the Bereans, from a passage Luke wrote about them in the book of Acts. They were good friends of Paul and top-notch Christians.

Paul and Silas left Thessalonica for Berea on the overnight express because of all the trouble the Jews were making for him there. However, when they got to Berea, a real surprise awaited them. The willing listeners awaiting them in Berea more than made up for all the headaches they had suffered in Thessalonica. Here's why. When the Sabbath day rolled around again, the two apostles had to make a decision. Should they go to the Jewish synagogue as they usually did? It was the best place to worship, but would they be treated badly as they had been in Thessalonica?

The Jews in the synagogue at Berea turned out to be much more reasonable than the Jews in Thessalonica. They were willing to study the Scriptures for themselves to see if the good news being preached was true. They didn't study it out of curiosity but that they might learn more about the prophecies that pointed to Jesus the Messiah. As they studied, they compared the Scriptures verse by verse. Heavenly angels were beside them to open their hearts and impress their minds that they might understand what they were reading. As a result, many people in the city believed, both Jews and Greeks.

What if the Berean Jews had been ornery like so many others Paul had met? What if they had refused to listen to him even though the things he was teaching were right out of the Bible? Then Paul would have left town, and they would have had no way to hear that Jesus had died and risen again for them. Good thing they listened to the voice of God.

Centurion on Paul's Ship

The soldiers' plan was to kill the prisoners, lest any of them should swim away and escape. But the centurion, wanting to save Paul, kept them from their purpose, and commanded that those who could swim should jump overboard first and get to land. Acts 27:42, 43

Have you ever been advised to do something but didn't do it? That's what happened on a voyage Paul took as a prisoner to Rome. The centurion in charge of delivering Paul to Rome was in a hurry to go, so he urged the captain of the ship to push on. Paul knew how unpredictable the weather could be on the Mediterranean during the fall months of the year, and he warned the centurion and the captain that the voyage would likely end in disaster. Nobody listened, and within a few days their worst nightmare became a reality. The ship was driven out to sea by an October storm, and two weeks later they were still drifting west in the raging tempest. Everyone knew the ship was lost and that they were all doomed to die. However, Paul said he had been told by an angel that they would run aground on an island and not one of them would die. When the ship did indeed hit a shoal and started to break up from the pounding surf, the Roman soldiers wanted to kill all the prisoners on board so they wouldn't escape. However, the centurion wouldn't allow it. He knew Paul was a special prisoner who was due to appear before Emperor Nero himself. And sure enough, just as Paul predicted, no one drowned. All 276 people on board made it to shore.

What if the centurion had listened to Paul when he said the seas weren't safe for travel? Then they wouldn't have gotten lost at sea. And what if the centurion had listened to his solders when they wanted to kill all the prisoners? Then God would have had to rescue Paul some other way. After all, the apostle was scheduled to meet Nero, and nothing was going to stand in the way of that encounter. It would be Nero's last chance at salvation.

Converted Sorcerers in Ephesus

Also, many of those who had practiced magic brought their books together
and burned them in the sight of all. And they counted up the value of them,
and it totaled fifty thousand pieces of silver.
So the word of the Lord grew mightily and prevailed. Acts 19:19, 20

Black magic always has a deep, dark power over its worshipers. In the days of Paul, Ephesus was a center of occult worship for all of Asia Minor. Spirit mediums, palm readers, fortune-tellers, and sorcerers all made a bundle in that city, selling their services to those who would pay for it. And people came from far and wide to do just that. Why? Because in those day many of them were so superstitious that they wouldn't make any basic decisions about life without advice from the spirits.

All that began to change the day Paul came to town. Now, through the Holy Spirit's power, he was preaching to people in the synagogues and teaching them how to study the Scriptures. And they saw him perform miracles of healing for the sick and demon-possessed. It was a life-changing experience, because they now saw the ultimate power that God has over Satan. Hundreds now wanted to start a new life with Jesus and give up their old ways of sin. To prove it, they brought all their books and scrolls about black magic and burned them in a big bonfire in the streets of Ephesus. That was a great victory for God because the value of the books was an astonishing fifty thousand pieces of silver, or the equivalent of 136 years of wages. Amazing!

What if these magicians and sorcerers had decided they didn't want to accept the message Paul preached to them? What if they hadn't burned the books? What if they had loved the money they made from sorcery more than they loved the gospel story? Then they would have gone down the path of ruin and probably ended up demon-possessed themselves. Satan had once been the grand master of their lives, but now Jesus was their all-powerful Redeemer!

Demetrius

"Men, you know that we have our prosperity by this trade. Moreover you see
and hear that not only at Ephesus, but throughout almost all Asia, this Paul has
persuaded and turned away many people, saying that they are not gods which are
made with hands." Acts 19:25, 26

Demetrius was not a happy man, and neither were his fellow idol makers in
Ephesus. They made their living by handcrafting pagan gods out of silver—
especially a goddess named Diana. Their problem? A new preacher had come to
town teaching new ideas that Jesus was the Creator of heaven and earth and that
people should worship Him. The preacher's name was Paul, and wherever he went,
his new message was beginning to stick. Fewer people were buying the small silver
images. And fewer people were paying their offerings of money and flowers and
food at the shrines to Diana; and the number of folks attending the holiday festival
dedicated to Diana had dropped alarmingly.

That was the straw that finally broke the camel's back for Demetrius and all
his buddies in the silversmith trade. "We've got to stop Paul!" he argued angrily
at one of their business meetings, and soon the other smiths were shouting kudos
about Diana and cuss words at Paul.

He and the crowd of angry mobsters went in search of Paul but couldn't find
him. Instead, they found two of his friends, Gaius and Aristarchus, and rushed
with them to the public theater to start a riot citywide. The city clerk showed up
and scolded everyone. "Calm down!" he ordered. "Paul's not breaking any laws of
the land!" and that was that.

What if Demetrius had been wowed by the good news of salvation like everyone else in Ephesus? What if he had accepted the gospel instead of trying to chase
Paul out of town? Of course, he would have had to begin doing something other
than make idols for a living, but God would have blessed him. And, of course, he
would have received eternal life.

Felix

Now as he reasoned about righteousness, self-control, and the judgment to come, Felix was afraid and answered, "Go away for now; when I have a convenient time I will call for you." Acts 24:25

His name was Marcus Antonius Felix, a rather sophisticated title for one who was anything but cool. He was made governor of Judea and Samaria because he was in good standing with Emperor Claudius—and because his wives were from a high social class. His first wife was the granddaughter of Antony and Cleopatra. His second wife was the daughter of Herod Agrippa I. Felix was a cruel, sadistic man, even murdering Jonathan, the Jewish high priest in Jerusalem. Historians tell us he had tried every form of lust in the Roman Empire and "wielded the power of a king with all the instincts of a slave." Today the nicest thing we would call him is uncultured.

Felix shows up in our story when Paul was brought to Caesarea to stand trial. The official reps from the Sanhedrin showed up too, but no charges were ever brought against Paul. Felix was a weak ruler, and to please the Jews he kept Paul under house arrest for two years. Meanwhile, he and his wife Drusilla, who was a Jew, wanted to hear Paul talk about his faith in Christ. As Paul talked about spiritual things like righteousness and the coming judgment, Felix became afraid. "Go away for now," he told Paul, "and when I have a convenient time, I will call for you." From time to time he would send for Paul so they could talk, but secretly he was hoping Paul would give him money for his freedom.

What if he had seriously listened to Paul's message? Here was a man in his court who had met Jesus Himself and knew what was coming for Felix. The governor could have become a Christian and given his life to God, but he didn't. Instead, he said, "Later," and that was the last call he ever received from God.

Herod Agrippa and Bernice

Then Agrippa said to Paul,
"You almost persuade me to become a Christian." Acts 26:28

Herod Agrippa II was a member of a famous family. His great-grandfather was Herod the Great, who tried to kill Jesus as a baby. His father, Herod Agrippa I, persecuted the apostles, even beheading James the brother of John. And like his great-grandfather and father before him, Herod Agrippa II was a monster. He claimed he was a Jew and wanted everyone to think he was a nice man, but he had some nasty habits. For example, it was no secret that he was sleeping with his sister Bernice.

When Governor Felix was replaced by Porcius Festus, there were more trials to see if Paul was guilty of making trouble for the Jews in Jerusalem. The Jewish leaders wanted Paul to come up to Jerusalem for trial, but Paul knew they wanted to ambush him along the way. Porcius Festus wanted to set him free, but Paul asked that his case be taken to the Emperor Nero himself.

Herod Agrippa showed up at the court of Festus with his sister Bernice, all dressed up in the fancy clothes of royalty, and listened to Paul's testimony. Paul gave a short bio about his life and the story of how he had become a Christian on the road to Damascus when he met Jesus in vision. Festus made fun of Paul's story, but Agrippa leaned forward on his throne and said, "You almost persuade me to become a Christian." And then the hearing was over. Paul was sent away, and with him went King Agrippa's opportunity for salvation. He came close to eternal life that day but unwisely let the moment slip away.

What if he had said, "I'm going to give my heart to Jesus; I want to become a Christian"? What a transformation would have come over his life! It would have been difficult, but others like him in ages past had done it. Nebuchadnezzar comes to mind, and he will be in heaven because of it. Too bad you didn't make that choice, Agrippa.

Jason in Thessalonica

But the Jews . . . took some of the evil men from the marketplace, and gathering a mob, set all the city in an uproar and attacked the house of Jason. . . . But when they did not find them, they dragged Jason and some brethren to the rulers of the city, crying out, "These who have turned the world upside down have come here too." Acts 17:5, 6

Have you ever gotten caught in a mob? Let's hope not, but when you serve God it can happen. That's exactly how it turned out for a new Christian named Jason in the city of Thessalonica. When Paul and Silas came to Thessalonica, they stayed at Jason's house. For a while, things went well as Paul preached every week in the Jewish synagogues. However, the leading Jews soon became jealous and stirred up a wild mob against Paul. They rumbled off to Jason's house, but the preacher wasn't there. The screaming crowds were so angry by now that they dragged Jason before the rulers of the city. "This man has two strangers in his home who worship a king called Jesus—not Caesar!" they shouted.

The rulers of the city were troubled when they heard these things, and they knew they had to do something or Jason would be torn to pieces. It was the Jews who were making trouble, not Paul, they said, and soon the cranky crowd melted away into the city. When Paul wrote two letters to the Thessalonians some time later, we can be sure Jason was one of the first to want to read them. After all, he had been through a lot for Paul and Jesus, and seeing those letters must have encouraged him a lot.

What if Jason hadn't been a faithful friend of Paul's? What if he hadn't become a Christian? He wouldn't have gotten roughed up by the mob in Thessalonica, but his story wouldn't be in the Bible either. When Jason became a Christian, his good times outweighed the bad. And the best part? He was now eligible for eternal life.

Nero

"For if I am an offender, or have committed anything deserving of death, I do not object to dying; but if there is nothing in these things of which these men accuse me, no one can deliver me to them. I appeal to Caesar." Acts 25:11

Nero was an evil man! Bad as that sounds, it is the understatement of the century. During the first year of his reign he poisoned his stepbrother, who was the rightful heir to the throne. Then he murdered his mother and his wife, and even those who served in his court were afraid of what he might do next. And yet they gave him their allegiance. He was the emperor of a world civilization, and they worshiped him like a god.

When Paul stood trial before Nero the first time, to everyone's surprise he was set free to visit his churches once again. About this time a terrible fire started in Rome, and nearly half the city was destroyed because of it. Many were suspicious that Nero himself had started the fire and were very angry about it. The emperor realized he was in big trouble, so he turned the blame on the Christians. In the persecution that followed, Paul was brought back to Rome again to stand trial. Everyone was afraid of Nero, but not Paul, and he warned Nero of a coming judgment in heaven. Nero trembled at Paul's words. However, the ruler didn't let him go and finally condemned him to death by beheading.

What if Nero had accepted Paul's invitation to give his heart to Jesus? What if he had given up his crazy life of cruelty and lust? Then maybe God could have helped him save himself and his kingdom. During the last days of his life, Nero's supporters rebelled against him, taking the army with them. Even his bodyguards deserted him, leaving no one to protect him. Finally, afraid that he would be caught and tortured, he killed himself at the young age of thirty.

Onesimus and Philemon

I appeal to you for my son Onesimus, whom I have begotten while in my chains, who once was unprofitable to you, but now is profitable to you and to me.
Philemon 1:10, 11

Can you imagine what it must have been like to be a slave in the days of the Roman Empire? Unfortunately, the laws of Rome allowed slave owners to do whatever they wanted with them. Slaves had no rights and could be bought or sold like cattle in a market. They could be beaten at the whims of the owner or whipped in place of someone else who had broken the law. Owners could force a slave to do anything they wanted. And they could be executed if the slave upset the owner for something as simple as dropping a tray of food or failing to come immediately when they were called.

Let me introduce you to Onesimus. He was a runaway slave from the city of Colossae and a recently baptized Christian. Eventually he found his way to Paul, who was in prison at Rome. Evidently, he knew of Paul because his owner, Philemon, was a Christian. In Paul's day there were many more slaves than Roman citizens in the empire, so runaway slaves were quite a common thing. It is likely that Onesimus may have stolen some of his master's property when he escaped, because Paul later offered to pay any debt Onesimus might have owed Philemon. After much talk, Paul convinced Onesimus to go back to his master. However, before Onesimus left, Paul wrote a letter to Philemon begging for forgiveness and acceptance of Onesimus as a Christian brother.

What if Onesimus had refused? What if he had never gone to see Paul at all? Slaves usually had some sort of mark or tattoo on them, so he was risking his life even showing up in public. He could have easily been caught and thrown into a sports amphitheater to be eaten by wild animals. We don't know the end of this story, but we get the impression it turned out to be a good end for Onesimus. Who knows, maybe he was given his freedom.

OCTOBER 31

Publius

In that region there was an estate of the leading citizen of the island, whose name was Publius, who received us and entertained us courteously for three days. And it happened that the father of Publius lay sick of a fever and dysentery. Paul went in to him and prayed, and he laid his hands on him and healed him. Acts 28:7, 8

Paul met a lot of public officials in his day. Some were from culture centers like Jerusalem, Ephesus, and Corinth. Some were from government cities like Caesarea and Rome. And then there was Publius, a government official on the island of Malta, where Paul was shipwrecked. Two things happened to impress on Publius that Paul was a godly man. First, Paul survived a fatal snakebite, and second, he performed a miracle in Publius's own house.

When Paul's ship crashed on a small island off the coast of Italy, all the passengers on board swam ashore. The islanders welcomed them with food and a warm fire, and that's when Paul was bitten by the viper while putting wood on a campfire. Publius graciously invited Paul to stay at his villa for three days. Paul got to know the family and especially Publius's father, who lay sick with fever and dysentery. The apostle felt sorry for the sick man and prayed with him at his bedside. Then he healed him miraculously. Soon everyone on the island had heard about the miracle and brought those who were sick, and Paul healed them of all their diseases.

Publius was grateful to Paul for his kindness in healing his father, and this prepared his heart to hear the message of salvation. But it might never have happened. When all those prisoners and sailors came swimming ashore that night, he had no way of knowing if some of them might be dangerous men. What if Publius hadn't welcomed Paul? He didn't need to invite Paul to his house, but if he hadn't, his father might have died. And he might never have heard Paul preach the gospel.

Dorcas

At Joppa there was a certain disciple named Tabitha, which is translated Dorcas. This woman was full of good works and charitable deeds which she did. But it happened in those days that she became sick and died. Acts 9:36, 37

What's it like to die and then be given a second chance at life? That would be cool and kind of creepy at the same time, don't you think? The Bible gives us a few examples, and Dorcas's story is one of them.

She was a remarkable Christian who lived on the Mediterranean coast in the city of Joppa. Her name was Tabitha, but she was also known as Dorcas. The Bible doesn't tell us much about her, except that she was a kind, gentle woman and was always doing nice things for others. Sometimes she made meals for those who had nothing to eat or gave a little money to those who were poor. One thing she did especially well was make clothes for orphans and widows.

Then one day she got sick. We don't know what illness she had, but as often happened in those days, she died. Everyone who knew her was stunned! "Why had God let her die?" many asked. She was a wonderful person and had done so much good! Someone sent word to Peter asking if he could come help with Dorcas. We don't know if they wanted him to comfort the family or maybe help with the funeral, but what they got instead was infinitely more. To everyone's surprise, he prayed that God would raise her to life—and He did! Wow! What a surprise that must have been!

What if Dorcas hadn't been such a kind person? What if she hadn't done all those nice things for others? People wouldn't have cried so hard for her at her funeral, and they wouldn't have cheered so much when she was resurrected. However, as nice as it is to be loved by others, we do good deeds because we want to be like Jesus. There's no better reason.

NOVEMBER 2

Emperor Claudius

Then one of them, named Agabus, stood up and showed by the Spirit that there
was going to be a great famine throughout all the world, which also happened in
the days of Claudius Caesar. Acts 11:28

Claudius was the grandson of Caesar Augustus by marriage and a close friend of Herod Agrippa II. Herod had helped him get his throne in Rome, and in gratitude he gave Agrippa more territory in Palestine. Many considered Claudius to be a weak and wavering ruler; others thought he was a nice emperor. It was a matter of opinion.

He ruled from A.D. 41 to 54, a time in the early church when God's people were suffering greatly. The Christians were scattering everywhere because of persecution back home in Jerusalem and Judea. James, the brother of John, was beheaded during the reign of Claudius, and the enemies of the faith tried to kill Peter too, though they were not successful. When a famine hit Palestine in the mid-forties, the Christians in Jerusalem became very poor.

And then Claudius did something rather unusual for a man of his reputation. Early in his reign he was kind to the Jews, but for some unknown reason he now expelled them from Rome. It was during this period that Aquila and Priscilla left Rome and found a home in Corinth.

What if Claudius had decided that he would be kind to the Jews in the empire? What if he hadn't booted them out of Rome? Then the Christians would have been able to stay and continue their work of spreading the gospel, and Claudius' empire would have been blessed by allowing God a place in his kingdom. By doing this, Claudius would have given himself a few more years of grace in which he could have heard the gospel. As it is, we have no record that he ever considered becoming a Christian. Too bad, Claudius. You and Jesus would have looked good together: emperor of Rome and the Master of the universe.

Eutychus

> And in a window sat a certain young man named Eutychus, who was sinking into a deep sleep. He was overcome by sleep; and as Paul continued speaking, he fell down from the third story and was taken up dead. Acts 20:9

Have you ever fallen asleep in church? Maybe you didn't get enough sleep the night before, or maybe the sermon was too boring. Well, it's never a good idea to sleep in church because God might be trying to speak to your heart. And if you happen to be sleeping on the ledge of an open window in the church, it could be a disaster! Here's a story about a guy in the book of Acts who did that very thing. His name was Eutychus, and he was in church one night with all the other believers, listening to Paul preach . . . and preach . . . and preach. This was the last time Paul would be able to speak to the believers in Troas.

The hour grew late, and the air was heavy with sooty smoke from the torches, when suddenly someone gasped. The open spot on the window ledge where Eutychus had been sitting was now empty. One moment he was there, and the next he was gone. Evidently, he had nodded off and fallen out the window. Unfortunately, the room where they were meeting that night was three stories up. In shock and horror, everybody ran downstairs and found that Eutychus was already dead. However, Paul knew that God wanted to raise that boy to life. And that's exactly what happened.

What if Eutychus had stayed awake in church that night? What if he had never fallen out the window? Well, then, he wouldn't have died, and Paul wouldn't have had to raise him to life. Of course, God doesn't want us to do crazy things just so He can perform miracles for us. However, if we stay within His arms of love, nothing bad can ever happen to us—even death, because if God wants us to live like Eutychus, He can raise us to life again.

NOVEMBER 4

Gallio and Sosthenes

Gallio said to the Jews, "If it were a matter of wrongdoing or wicked crimes,
O Jews, there would be reason why I should bear with you." . . . Then all the
Greeks took Sosthenes, the ruler of the synagogue, and beat him before the
judgment seat. But Gallio took no notice of these things. Acts 18:14, 17

Have you ever been called a troublemaker? We all know a troublemaker at
school, on a sports team, or maybe even at church. Sosthenes, the ruler of the
synagogue in Achaia, was a troublemaker. He was always trying to make someone
else look bad—and in this story it was Paul.

Paul's message of salvation was so powerful that Jews and Gentiles alike were
flocking to hear him speak. As the weeks and months passed, many who heard
him preach were impressed and asked to be baptized. Not surprisingly, Sosthenes
didn't like it. Any extra attention Paul was getting would be that much less power
and money for him.

That's when he decided to take things into his own hands. He grabbed up a
gang of thugs in the street and got them to drag Paul before the court of Gallio,
the governor of Achaia. "This guy is a Christian, and that makes him a criminal in
our book!" Sosthenes shouted. However, Gallio was a smart guy and knew exactly
what was going on. "I'm too busy to settle issues for troublemakers like you," he
told Sosthenes and dismissed the case. That was the end of the matter as far as
Gallio was concerned. However, the gang of thugs wasn't happy with Sosthenes
for making fools of them. "You're the troublemaker, not Paul!" they screamed and
began beating him outside the courtroom. Gallio did nothing to rescue him.

Sosthenes was not a nice guy, and some would say he deserved all the trouble
he got. What if he had been kinder to those who listened to Paul? He should've
remembered that what goes around comes around. It's no surprise that Sosthenes
himself got beaten for his shenanigans in the streets that day, but it didn't have to
be that way. Too bad he didn't figure that out sooner.

James of the Jerusalem Council

"Therefore I judge that we should not trouble those from among the Gentiles who
are turning to God, but that we write to them to abstain
from things polluted by idols, from sexual immorality,
from things strangled, and from blood." Acts 15:19, 20

There are several men named James in the New Testament, and one of them became famous at the Jerusalem Council around A.D. 49. This meeting would have turned out to be one big fight if it hadn't been for James. The Jews in the church wanted everyone to keep the law of Moses like they had always done, but the Christians disagreed. Many of those laws didn't make sense to them now that Jesus had died on the cross. All the strict rules about Sabbath observance, circumcision, and feast days kept coming up, and no one knew what to do. Finally, after hours and hours of discussion, James got up and began to speak. "Let's just ask everybody to keep a few of Moses' simple rules that are best for the whole church," he said. "Let's be loyal and pure, avoid eating any food that has been dedicated to pagan idols, and also not eat meat from animals that have been strangled." With these words, James saved the day for the church, and the Jews and Christians began getting along much better.

So, who was this James at the Jerusalem Council? We know he wasn't James, the brother of John, who was executed five years earlier in A.D. 44. He wasn't the other disciple named James either (the son of Alpheus), because after the Christian persecutions in Jerusalem started, we never hear from him again. That leaves another possibility. This James was the half brother of Jesus. Early church historians say he was an important leader in the work at Jerusalem.

Evidently, he was the man of the hour, but what if he hadn't spoken up at the Jerusalem Council? What if nothing was resolved? Then there might have been a split in the church, and it would have been even harder to spread the gospel. Way to go, James!

NOVEMBER 6

Lame Man at Lystra

In Lystra there sat a man who was lame. He had been that way from birth and had never walked. He listened to Paul as he was speaking. Paul looked directly at him, saw that he had faith to be healed and called out, "Stand up on your feet!" At that, the man jumped up and began to walk. Acts 14:8–10, NIV

The ability to walk and climb and run is a blessing we often take for granted. We use this ability when we play sports, when we go from class to class at school, and when we get out of bed in the morning. Only if we lose this wonderful gift do we begin to realize what we have lost.

What if you couldn't walk? What if you never had that ability and were dependent on others or on a wheelchair to get you from place to place? In that case you might understand what it was like for a lame man in the town of Lystra. OK, it's true he didn't have a wheelchair, but that made Paul's gift of healing even more of a blessing.

One day while Paul was preaching, he saw a crippled man sitting nearby. He was impressed that the man had the faith to be healed, so he commanded him to stand up. Immediately the man jumped to his feet and began walking. What a sight that must have been! The crowds listening to Paul got very excited when they saw the miracle, and news of it spread all over town. "The gods have come down to us in the likeness of men!" they shouted. If you've ever seen a miraculous healing like that you would know how these people felt.

What if the lame man hadn't been listening to the voice of God? What if he hadn't taken hold of the faith God had given him? What if he hadn't stood to his feet by faith? Then he wouldn't have been healed. That's the way it is with faith. We don't need much of it; just a smidgen of a tiny grain and God does the rest. Very, very cool. Someday God may even ask you to exercise your faith on someone's behalf, so be sure and listen for His voice.

Paul's Guard in Rome

Now when we came to Rome, the centurion delivered the prisoners
to the captain of the guard; but Paul was permitted to dwell by himself
with the soldier who guarded him. Acts 28:16

How would you like the job of guarding a vicious criminal in prison? Does that sound scary? Well, a job like that has never been easy, but standing guard over Paul in a Roman jail must have been a joke. Paul was no ordinary criminal. He was under house arrest, and his friends could visit him whenever they wanted in the nice apartment where he was staying. Very cool!

By now Paul was not only famous, he was a celebrity. He was a fantastic preacher, a prophet, and a miracle worker using God's power to make bad people go blind, supernatural demons run, and lame folks walk. That's the kind of person Paul was, and the Roman soldiers had been blessed to guard him. It must have been a real treat listening to Luke and Paul talk about all their adventures while sharing the gospel.

Paul was released from his Roman prison only to be brought back again a few years later, this time to die. The soldiers asked to guard him were touched by his faith in God and the peace of heaven on his face. And when it was time for Paul's execution, Nero ordered a squad of only four soldiers to carry out the death sentence because he wanted as few men as possible to be there for Paul's death. It didn't work. Ancient church historians tell us two of the four soldiers who witnessed his execution became Christians.

What if Paul hadn't spent so much time with those guards in prison? What if he hadn't spent so many hours writing and praying? Then his Roman guards wouldn't have had a chance to see his testimony for Jesus. And when he finally was executed for his faith, they probably wouldn't have been inspired to become Christians either.

NOVEMBER 8

People of Lystra

When the crowd saw what Paul had done, they shouted in the Lycaonian language,
"The gods have come down to us in human form!" . . . The priest of Zeus, whose
temple was just outside the city, brought bulls and wreaths to the city gates
because he and the crowd wanted to offer sacrifices to them. Acts 14:11, 13, NIV

What's it like to worship someone one second and the next second be thinking you want to kill them? That's what happens when God is not on the throne in our life and we let Satan take control. Before we know it, we can become more like a demon than a man. Here's an example of how that happened during one of Paul's mission trips.

One day while he was preaching in the city of Lystra, Paul saw a crippled man and healed him. "I'm healed!" the man shouted as he jumped to his feet. The crowds listening to Paul preach got very excited when they saw the miracle, and news of it spread all over town. Soon the Gentiles were all shouting, "The gods have come down to us in the likeness of men!" They called Barnabas Zeus, and Paul they called Hermes, because he was the main talker. Then they called for the priest from the temple of Zeus and brought oxen and garlands of flowers to the city gates. With these they hoped to worship Paul and Barnabas.

When Barnabas and Paul realized what was happening, they tore their clothes to show how upset they were. "Don't do such things!" Paul shouted. "We're just men!" But no one paid them any attention. However, that day there were some Jews who were jealous of Paul in the crowd, and later they stirred everybody up to find Paul and kill him. After stoning Paul, they dragged him out of the town and left him for dead. God kept him from dying, but it just goes to show what can happen when we let Satan control us.

What if the crowd had followed Paul's example to thank God for healing the man? Clearly they would have avoided two extremes that day: worshiping Paul and stoning him. Wow! I think I'd rather they be somewhere in the middle.

Philosophers in Athens

And they took him and brought him to the Areopagus, saying,
"May we know what this new doctrine is of which you speak?. . .
For all the Athenians and the foreigners who were there spent their time
in nothing else but either to tell or to hear some new thing." Acts 17:19, 21

How would you like a job where you just sit around and discuss ideas? Or a job where you get paid to argue? "Hey, that doesn't sound so bad," you might say. "I'm pretty good at arguing, and now someone wants to give me money for it?"

When Paul came to Athens to preach the gospel, people heard him talking in the marketplace and asked him to debate all the smart guys in town. He agreed and went with some of the philosophers to a place called the Areopagus, the most famous meeting place in Athens, where philosophers discussed everything—politics, money, and religion.

The philosophers wanted to know more about the God Paul preached about, but when he told them about Jesus and the resurrection of the dead, some of them started making fun of him. "That's a bunch of baloney!" they sneered. "You're crazy!"

Paul realized that debating people about the Bible doesn't work very well. Either they believe in the power of God and the Bible, or they don't. If they aren't listening for the voice of the Holy Spirit, they won't understand spiritual things anyway. However, when we share the gospel, we have to go where God asks us to go. He'll take care of the rest.

What if Paul hadn't gone to Athens to preach? The smart guys wouldn't have heard Paul share the good news of salvation, even if most of them didn't end up accepting it. However, there were a few converts in Athens who accepted Christianity as their new way of life, and that made Paul happy. After all, it's not important how many we bring to Jesus but that we bring someone to Him.

NOVEMBER 10

Seven Sons of Sceva

And the evil spirit answered and said, "Jesus I know, and Paul I know; but who
are you?" Then the man in whom the evil spirit was leaped on them, overpowered
them, and prevailed against them, so that they fled out of that house
naked and wounded. Acts 19:15, 16

This is one of the craziest stories in the Bible—all because a priest named Sceva
didn't raise his boys to respect the supernatural world. How's that? Sceva was
a Jew, but you wouldn't know it by the way he used sorcery to get what he wanted.
Here was a man who claimed to worship the God of heaven, and yet he used the
forces of darkness to work his magic.

The story took place in Ephesus—where some of the most amazing miracles
in all the Bible happened, like giving handkerchiefs Paul had touched to sick people so they could be healed. But it was Paul's healing of demoniacs that were often
the most dramatic. When he spoke in Jesus' name, the evil spirits had to leave.
Soon, casting out demons was a very popular thing to do. Sceva wanted this power,
but he thought he needed to use sorcery to get the magic.

The seven sons of Sceva got caught up in the frenzy too, and one day they
decided to have some fun by casting a demon out of a local demoniac. "In the
name of the Jesus whom Paul preaches, we command you to come out!" they said,
laughing. Hard to imagine, isn't it? Not surprisingly, the demon in the man was
not amused. "Jesus I know, and Paul I know," he growled, "but who are you?" Then
the man who was possessed by the demon chased the young men down, leaped
on them, tore their clothes off, and beat them mercilessly. The young men were so
scared they ran off naked and wounded.

What if the seven boys had respected the forces of the supernatural world?
What if they had listened to Paul and decided that God wasn't to be taken lightly?
Then they would have left well enough alone. They would have asked God to
cleanse their own hearts and make them like Jesus. That's not how the story ended,
but we can wish it did.

Angels at Eden's Gate

So He drove out the man; and He placed cherubim at the east
of the garden of Eden, and a flaming sword which turned every way,
to guard the way to the tree of life. Genesis 3:24

Guarding the Garden of Eden must have been one of the saddest jobs ever given to heavenly angels. Adam and Eve had fallen for the biggest lie in history. "You shall not surely die," Satan told them, knowing full well that they would die if they chose to listen to him. Jesus showed up just as dusk was falling, and with Him were two cherubim on assignment.

The angels watched sadly as Jesus called Adam and Eve from where they were hiding in the shadows. They turned their eyes away as Jesus made clothes for their naked bodies from animal skins. They bowed their heads as the Creator reminded Adam and Eve how much He loved them and that He would one day die for their sins. They stood amazed as Jesus showed them how to offer a lamb as a sacrifice to represent how that would happen.

Tears fell from their eyes when Jesus told the man and woman they must leave the Garden. Sadly the angels folded their wings as they watched the couple leave through the Garden gate, never to return. Then they drew their swords to guard the entrance to Eden. It was the only thing left to do, by the order of Jesus Himself.

What if they hadn't guarded the Garden gate? If Adam or Eve or any of their children should sneak back into the Garden and eat from the tree of life, the horrors of sin would last forever. That would be a disaster! God knew that the only thing worse than sinners dying would be suffering sinners living forever. And so the angels were left to guard the gate of Eden. For hundreds of years they stood at their posts of duty, until the Flood, when the Garden was whisked away to heaven.

Arioch

> Then Arioch quickly brought Daniel before the king, and said thus to him, "I have found a man of the captives of Judah, who will make known to the king the interpretation." Daniel 2:25

Arioch was a powerful man in Babylon. He was captain of Nebuchadnezzar's military guard, and that pretty much made him top dog when everything was hanging in the balance, like the morning after Nebuchadnezzar had the vivid dream about the image. The king couldn't remember even one little smidgen of it, and he was angry when his wise guys told him they hadn't a clue either. "No one can tell the king about a dream he can't remember himself," they told Nebuchadnezzar, but the king wasn't impressed and decided they all needed to be fed to the lions. Or be fuel for a fiery furnace somewhere.

This brought Arioch into the picture. He was sent to carry out the king's orders and ended up on Daniel's doorstep—not a pleasant task. Everyone liked Daniel, Arioch included. Daniel asked to see the king, requested time, and then prayed to God for help in the matter. That brings us to the end of the story, and again, Arioch shows up. When Daniel told Arioch he had the info the king needed, the captain decided to score a few points with the king. "I've found a man to solve your problem," he bragged. Daniel scored a few points of his own when he told the king all about his dream, and they all lived happily ever after.

What if Arioch hadn't been so accommodating to Daniel? He could have said, "Nah, no one can do such a thing for the king!" In that case God would have had to save Daniel in some other way. After all, He had stuff He wanted Daniel to do for Him. Fortunately for everyone, Arioch had his heart in the right place, and there was great celebration in the palace because of it. Arioch was probably breathing a big sigh of relief too. Executing that many men over a forgotten dream wouldn't be much fun.

Asenath

And to Joseph were born two sons before the years of famine came, whom Asenath, the daughter of Poti-Pherah priest of On, bore to him. Genesis 41:50

Asenath was the wife of Joseph. She was given to him by Pharaoh on the day he was appointed as the prime minister of Egypt. Her father was Poti-Pherah, a pagan priest from the sacred city of On. But what about the rest of the story? Did she know anything about the worship of Jehovah? Did she understand that Joseph's God was the Creator of heaven and earth, that He would one day come to live among men, die for their sins, and then restore them to Paradise lost? Did she know that Joseph's religious values went directly against what she was raised to believe? The Egyptians thought that sacrificing sheep and cattle to the God of heaven was a sacrilege. Did she understand that her reverence for the worship of cobras and cats and crocodile gods was considered by Joseph to be an abomination to the Lord? Did she realize that their marriage would not be a good match, because they would be unequally yoked in every way? Maybe, but it was an arranged marriage, and neither of them had much to say politically about whether or not the knot would be tied.

What if she had never married Joseph? Would we know her name today? Would we even know she existed? Probably not. In those days a woman's identification was linked to a man, even in Egypt where men generally had only one wife. But she did marry him, and in the end she must have become a worshiper of the one true God. She gave birth to sons named Manasseh and Ephraim, both of which were accepted as heirs by Joseph's father on his deathbed. Her name has been recorded for all time on the pages of sacred history, not just because she married the savior of Egypt but because her two boys went on to become famous tribes in the nation of Israel. Today we know more about her than her father or even Pharaoh himself.

Elders of Israel in Egypt

Then Moses and Aaron went and gathered together all the elders of the children of Israel. . . . So the people believed; and when they heard that the Lord had visited the children of Israel and that He had looked on their affliction, then they bowed their heads and worshiped. Exodus 4:29, 31

Everybody wants to be someone important. Everybody wants to be a big shot at some time in their life so they can tell others what to do. Politicians like it, and so do CEOs for big companies. Even church leaders sometimes want to be in charge so they can make all the important decisions. It's always been that way, and the days of ancient Israel were no different. In those times it was the elders who had all the power, but to be an elder you had to be very wise, or very rich, or maybe just very old.

When God asked Moses to come back to Egypt to help set the tribes of Israel free, Moses didn't want to do it. He knew Pharaoh wouldn't like it, but what would the elders of Israel say? Would they believe God had sent him? But Moses didn't need to worry. Angels from heaven had visited the elders and told them the time of their deliverance from slavery was getting close. Of course, nothing is ever easy when Satan's kingdom is threatened, and when Moses told Pharaoh that God wanted His people set free, Pharaoh laughed and doubled their workload by making them gather their own straw for making bricks. This was a real test of faith for the elders, but they trusted in God, and eventually Pharaoh himself drove them out of Egypt.

What if the elders hadn't believed Moses when he said Israel was about to be set free? What if they had chased Moses out of Egypt because they were angry at all the extra work being given to them by Pharaoh? Well, then Israel would have had to wait longer to be delivered from slavery, or God would have had to replace the elders who had so little faith. When God says, "It's time to move forward," we need to get out of the way. Just ask the elders of ancient Israel.

Hagar

The Angel of the Lord said to her, "Return to your mistress,
and submit yourself under her hand." Genesis 16:9

What a life! We often criticize Hagar for making trouble in Abraham's family, but we have to be fair. She didn't ask to be a slave in his household. She didn't ask to become Abraham's mistress or to have his child. She didn't ask that her son be given to Sarah, since Sarah couldn't have children of her own. Hagar had no choice in any of these matters. Considering the circumstances under which she was forced to live, she actually did pretty well for herself.

So, where did she come from, and where did she go after this story ended? We're not sure exactly, but Pharaoh may have given her as a slave to Abraham and Sarah when they visited Egypt. Pharaoh was impressed with Abraham, and giving slaves as gifts was a common thing in those days.

Then Sarah got the big idea that she needed to help God give her husband a son. Having a son was a big deal for women in those days. Without the gift of a son for her husband, Sarah looked bad. So she told Hagar to go sleep with Abraham. Really? Yup, and that, of course, made Hagar a mistress, or a second wife—only slightly lower on the totem pole. However, sparks began to fly, because after having a baby (Ishmael), Hagar began to mock Sarah about not being able to have kids. Bad idea. At that point, things went from bad to worse, and Hagar was eventually booted out of camp, along with her son, to start a new clan.

What if she had stuck it out with Sarah? What if she had stayed with her son in Abraham's village? Then her son, Ishmael, and Sarah's son, Isaac, might have avoided some wars in the years to come. Today the Arab nations are still at odds with the nation of Israel.

Ishmael

So God was with the lad; and he grew and dwelt in the wilderness,
and became an archer. Genesis 21:20

Poor Ishmael. His life didn't start out picture-perfect. To begin with, he was born to a slave woman. Then, he was supposed to inherit everything from his father Abraham; instead, Isaac inherited the bulk of their father's estate. When he was fifteen, the promise of all those riches was taken away because his mom couldn't get along with Sarah, Abraham's first wife.

He was supposed to be the son Abraham and Sarah felt they would never have. Both were too old, well beyond what was considered the age for childbearing. Abraham was at least eighty-five, and Sarah seventy-five. Fifteen years later, Sarah had a son of her own, Isaac. Now, Sarah no longer needed Ishmael to help fulfill God's promise that they would have a son.

Abraham loved Ishmael and hoped he would stick around in spite of how Sarah felt. That's the way it could have gone, but Ishmael's mom got in the way. She was a bad influence on Ishmael and infected him with her attitude toward Sarah and Isaac. It all came to a head at a party held in Isaac's honor, when Sarah caught Ishmael making fun of his baby brother. That was the last straw, and she finally cut the cord that held Ishmael and Hagar to the family. "Send them away!" she told Abraham. In other words, kick them out of the herd.

Sad, isn't it? What if Ishmael had behaved himself? Well, for one thing he would have been able to go on living with his father, Abraham, one of the richest men in Canaan. And he could have been an active big brother in Isaac's life. Instead, he had to leave with his mother and start all over again in the deserts of southern Canaan. Fortunately, God blessed him, and he grew into a great hunter and leader of a powerful nomadic clan.

Job's Ten Kids

> When the days of feasting had run their course, . . . Job would send and sanctify them, and he would rise early in the morning and offer burnt offerings according to the number of them all. For Job said, "It may be that my sons have sinned and cursed God in their hearts." Thus Job did regularly. Job 1:5

Job had seven sons and three daughters, and he loved them to pieces! They got along famously and were always throwing parties at one another's homes. In his heart Job was afraid his kids were doing things they shouldn't have been doing. Perhaps they were drinking alcohol or eating things they shouldn't be eating. Mostly Job was worried that they might be cursing God in their foolish, drunken states of mind. And so it was that every time his kids threw a party, he would offer sacrifices of thanksgiving and repentance. Job prayed that God would save them from their sins.

As it happened, one day Job's worst nightmare came home to roost. His kids were at a party at one of the homes when suddenly a storm hit the house. A great wind destroyed the house and Job's ten children.

What a tragic disaster! Now, Job was thankful that he had been praying for them. He had no way of knowing if all of his kids had died with the peace of heaven in their hearts, but there was hope that God had answered his prayers for them. What if those kids had listened to their father? What if they had lived godly lives instead of going to silly parties? Then they would have honored their father and mother, and left their family with the knowledge that their salvation was assured. Make good choices today, in case tomorrow never comes.

Midianites

Then the children of Israel did evil in the sight of the LORD. So the LORD delivered them into the hand of Midian for seven years. Judges 6:1

The Midianites had a long history of war with the nation of Israel, making them bitter enemies. The sad thing is that Midian and Israel were long-lost relatives. The Midianites were descendants of Midian, who was one of Abraham's sons through his third wife, named Keturah. And the Israelites were descendents of Jacob, Abraham's grandson. So, why all the anger and hostility between the two nations? Blood runs thicker than water, doesn't it? The Israelites and Midianites were family! What we have is a sad tale of bad history that didn't have to happen!

Here's a short history of their run-ins with one another and the string of catastrophes that could have been avoided. For starters, Joseph was sold by his brothers to slave traders from the tribe of Midian, and they in turn sold him to the Egyptians. We criticize his brothers for doing such a thing, but the Midianites were Joseph's cousins. Like his brothers, they were his own flesh and blood. Moses' wife was a Midianite, and his own brother and sister had a little family war going on over that detail. She was darker skinned and an outsider as far as they were concerned.

What about the Midianite women who tempted Israel to worship their gods? Twenty-four thousand people died from that horrendous fiasco. In punishment for this crime, Israel went to war and destroyed five Midianite kings and their tribes in that nation. Finally, Gideon faced the Midianites in battle and destroyed them. With God's help, Gideon's three hundred valiant warriors led the charge that annihilated 135,000 enemy soldiers. All of this happened because of greed and jealousy!

But what if they had decided to get along? That's the million dollar question.

Nero's Household

All the saints greet you, but especially those who are of Caesar's household.
Philippians 4:22

Can you imagine what it would have been like to live in the palace of the most powerful man in the Mediterranean world? Slaves in that household were afraid for their lives—even Nero's children were afraid of their father. Nero's wife and mistresses trembled at the monster of a man who sat on the throne of Rome.

When Paul was on trial before Festus in Caesarea, he asked for a hearing before Nero. It was his hope that if he shared his Christian testimony with the royal family, he might win some souls for the kingdom of God. But was it safe to take the gospel story to the palace where cruel things were done to friends and enemies alike? Clearly, the palace of the Roman emperor was the stronghold of Satan. How could God save people who enjoyed watching gladiators kill each other, or Christians being executed on crosses for their faith?

There were some in Nero's household who were attracted to the message of the gospel. Slaves found the message of eternal life hopeful, and Nero's immediate family members were attracted to this educated preacher, who was sophisticated, witty, and likeable.

More than once Paul was called to appear before Nero and his family to have his case heard. More than once he "entertained" them with the story of his conversion, and each time it brought the royal household closer to Jesus. Thankfully, some in the palace became Christians, which we know because Paul mentioned it in his letter to the Philippians.

What if they had rejected the good news of salvation as Nero did? What if they had feared Nero more than they feared the coming judgment? Then their story would have ended here, and their names would not be written in the book of life. Because they chose Jesus, a crown of life awaits them.

People of Sodom

"For we will destroy this place, because the outcry against them has grown great before the face of the LORD, and the LORD has sent us to destroy it." Genesis 19:13

What must it have been like to live in a city like Sodom? The tropical climate was perfect. Most people living there had lots of leisure time, and trading caravans brought them wealth from nations far and wide. However, with little to do but eat, drink, and be merry, the citizens of Sodom became a nasty bunch. Sodom, Gomorrah, and three other cities on the Jordan plain were among the worst cities in the ancient world. Robberies, murders, and all sorts of sin became part of city life. And crimes of corruption became the trademark of the city.

About this time, Abraham's nephew Lot moved to Sodom with his family. He had great wealth from his years of living with Abraham, and now his business transactions in Sodom made him even richer. As might be expected, the place corrupted his family, and his wife fell in love with the luxuries of Sodom. Unfortunately, the wickedness in Sodom was so great that God decided that it had to be destroyed. When two angels were sent from heaven to destroy the city, they came to warn Lot in person. However, corrupt men came pounding on Lot's door, asking him to send out his guests to be beaten and abused. This was the last straw, and the angels blinded the men. Then they promised to save Lot and those in his family who would leave with him. Lot tried to get all his children and their spouses to flee the city that very night, but they laughed at his warnings and continued their partying.

What would have happened if the people of Sodom had listened to Lot? They would have avoided being destroyed in the fire that fell from the sky early the next morning. Maybe they could have fled with Lot, or maybe God would have spared the city if the people had repented. Today we remember Sodom not as a place that escaped God's judgment but as a city that blatantly ignored it.

Abigail

Then Abigail made haste and took two hundred loaves of bread, two skins of wine,
five sheep already dressed, five seahs of roasted grain,
one hundred clusters of raisins, and two hundred cakes of figs,
and loaded them on donkeys. 1 Samuel 25:18

Wow! That's a lot of food. Was she getting ready for a party? A wedding? A funeral? Actually, she was trying to prevent a funeral. Really, here's how it happened. Abigail was married to Nabal, the meanest, grouchiest man in all of Judah, and everybody knew it, including her. One day her servants came running in to say that her husband had just snubbed David the giant killer, Israel's national hero. Why? Because Nabal was being Nabal—a fool.

Evidently, David had sent some of his men up to Abigail's house to ask for food and had been told to "Get!" The men left, but Nabal's servants knew trouble was coming. Refusing to give food to someone in need was a no-no in those days. Abigail packed several donkeys with food and headed in the direction David's messengers had gone. She hadn't gone far when she was met by a war party led by David himself, coming down from the hills to wreak vengeance on Nabal's household. Unlike her husband, Abigail was the picture of humbleness, proving it when she got down on her knees and begged forgiveness for her husband's rude behavior. David accepted the gift and headed back to the hills. Abigail left for home, no doubt breathing a sigh of relief at their narrow brush with death.

What if Abigail hadn't taken action quickly? What if she hadn't knelt in the dust to beg David's pardon for her husband's insults? Every man in the household would likely have died before David cooled his jets. As it was, Abigail saved her husband's life for the moment, only to have him die from a stroke ten days later. And then she became David's wife, something that wouldn't have happened if David had executed her husband. No kidding!

Demon-Possessed Epileptic

Jesus said to him, "If you can believe, all things are possible to him who believes."
Immediately the father of the child cried out and said with tears, "Lord, I believe;
help my unbelief!" Mark 9:23, 24

Imagine that your son can't speak and has fits of demon possession from time to time. Often he falls to the ground, foams at the mouth, grinds his teeth, and becomes stiff like a dead man. You've heard that Jesus of Nazareth is healing others like your son, but you have your doubts. However, your son's condition only gets worse. When your friends and family urge you to get help from Jesus, you finally agree.

After traveling far and wide, you finally find the Miracle Man one morning, and immediately your son's battle with the supernatural world begins! He falls to the ground in a convulsion, thrashes around, moaning and groaning, his eyes wild like a crazy animal. It's scary to see your son in such pain. "He's been like this since he was very young," you tell Jesus. "Sometimes it throws him into the fire to burn him, and sometimes into the water to drown him." You grab the sleeve of Jesus' robe. "If you can do anything, please take pity on him!"

Jesus shakes his head. "Everything is possible for one who believes," He replies, and you realize that your lack of faith may possibly prevent your son from being healed.

"Please!" you stammer in desperation. "I do believe! Help me overcome my unbelief!"

Hundreds of people like this were brought to Jesus for healing, and when they did, Jesus never turned them away. What if the father in these Bible verses had not believed Jesus could help his son? Or what if he hadn't brought his son to Jesus at all? Well, then, the boy wouldn't have been healed, and he might have even died soon thereafter. The truth is, like the father, often we don't receive because we don't believe. What a shame! What a loss!

Jairus's Daughter Raised

And behold, there came a man named Jairus, and he was a ruler
of the synagogue. And he fell down at Jesus' feet and begged Him to come to his
house, for he had an only daughter about twelve years of age, and she was dying.
Luke 8:41, 42

Have you ever had a near-death experience? Do you know someone who came back from the grave or survived a near-fatal car crash or awoke from a coma? The Bible tells a story about just such a thing happening, and it's a heart-stopping tale that describes how every parent would feel if they lost a child.

Jairus loved his twelve-year-old daughter very much. Unfortunately, she got sick, and Jairus knew he had to find some help fast or she would die. Not surprisingly, when he heard Jesus was in town, he hurried off to find Him. Satan didn't want the little girl to live and arranged for roadblocks along the way. And sure enough, by the time Jesus reached the home of Jairus, the girl had died. What a heartbreaker! Jairus thought Satan had won. He felt lower than low, because he didn't know that Jesus had something special planned. He assured Jairus that the girl was only sleeping and not actually dead. The mourners all laughed, but Satan guessed what was coming and must have been shaking in his boots.

To make a long story short, Jesus had the last word. He raised the little girl to life. That's the way it is when Jesus comes to town. He changes everything, transforming our future like no one else can. But what if Jairus hadn't believed Jesus could help his daughter? What if he hadn't asked Jesus to come to his house? Well, then, no matter how much power Jesus had over the grave, He wouldn't have been able to help Jairus and his little girl. Pretty scary, huh? Like Jairus, we sometimes come very close to missing out on the blessings Jesus wants to give us. Don't let it happen to you.

Paralytic Lowered in a Blanket

Then behold, men brought on a bed a man who was paralyzed, whom they sought to bring in and lay before Him. And when they could not find how they might bring him in, because of the crowd, they went up on the housetop and let him down with his bed through the tiling into the midst before Jesus. Luke 5:18, 19

In today's story, our man made an unforgettable entrance—through the roof. We often hear about people "going through the roof" when they get mad, but this story is nothing like that.

It's quite a tale! This poor man was paralyzed and hadn't walked for years. His friends had made quite a scene to bring him to Jesus, letting him down through the roof in a hammock. They were hoping Jesus would heal him, but the paralyzed man would have been satisfied just to have Jesus forgive him of his sins.

We don't know all the details, but Jesus did. He knew the man had done a lot of bad things. He knew the paralytic, as they called him, had lived a wild and crazy life, doing all kinds of things his mother would not have been proud about. Maybe his friends didn't even know all the bad things he had done, but they brought him to Jesus anyway. It was the man's only chance to find healing. And Jesus healed the man. The first thing he told the man was, "Your sins are forgiven you" (Luke 5:20). This meant all the world to the paralyzed man, and peace came over his face like nothing he had ever experienced before. Then Jesus said, "Stand up! Take your bed and go home!"

What if the paralyzed man hadn't felt remorse for his sinful life? What if his friends hadn't had the faith needed to bring him to Jesus? Then, of course, he would have never walked again. He would have died a broken man without legs, faith, or forgiveness.

Pharaoh III

The LORD plagued Pharaoh and his house with great plagues because of Sarai, Abram's wife. Genesis 12:17

When we serve God, there are certain things we enjoy that are outside what we would call luck or coincidence, such as angelic protection when we drive, or miraculous healings from disease, or unexpected wealth and prosperity. There's no doubt that you and I enjoy some of those perks because we serve the living God, just as Abram did so many years ago. But then there's the other side of the coin. Someone who doesn't worship God or want any part of Him will experience His goodness. In fact, if bad people try to take advantage of God's children, they often pay a heavy price. Pharaoh in Egypt when Abram was a tourist there is one such example. Here's what happened.

As Abram and Sarai were approaching the border checkpoints of Egypt, he told her to lie about their relationship. "Tell them you are my sister," he said, which was true. They had the same father but different moms—this was fairly common in those days. Anyway, everyone knew Sarai was a gorgeous woman, and Abram knew some Egyptian sheik would want her for his own. The truth was that Pharaoh himself had eyes for her, and he sent for her, putting her up for the night in one of his most lavish suites. That's right. He was making plans to add her to his harem of wives. That is, until God intervened, sending a disease epidemic into the palace and a dream to warn Pharaoh. "Keep your paws off Sarai!" God ordered. "She's Abram's wife." "Whoa! Whoa!" we can hear Pharaoh saying. "I had no idea!" Later, he chewed Abram out royally the first chance he got. "Why would you keep such a thing secret?" he demanded.

Good thing Pharaoh was in tune with God's voice, but what if he wasn't? Would God have destroyed him for daring to steal another man's wife? Maybe. He wasn't a worshiper of Jehovah, but he was listening, and that was what saved him. Good move, Pharaoh.

Phinehas (Aaron's Grandson)

Now when Phinehas . . . saw it, he rose from among the congregation and took a javelin in his hand; and he went after the man of Israel into the tent and thrust both of them through, the man of Israel, and the woman through her body. So the plague was stopped among the children of Israel. Numbers 25:7, 8

This is a horribly violent tale, and one we don't often like to share. Phinehas was the star of the show, the hero of the day, and this story is the reason he became famous. His act of bravery was necessary but probably not something any of us would want to have to do. Here's the PG version of the story, minus a few disgusting details. When Balaam failed to curse Israel on the mountaintop for the king of Moab, he came up with another plan. "If you can't beat them, get them to join you," he said, and that's exactly what he managed to do. He arranged to have a gang of prostitutes invade the camp and invite hundreds of Israelite men to join in a heathen festival to worship the gods of Moab. You guessed it. In the end, the party became a wild, drunken party.

The situation got way out of hand when a prince in Israel named Zimri came walking through camp with a prostitute in broad daylight and took her into his tent. Everyone who saw it was speechless, and they knew what Moses would do when he heard about it. Zimri cared little about what Moses thought, or God either, for that matter. But Phineas, son of Eleazar, and grandson of Aaron, cared a lot, and he decided to do something about it. Grabbing up a javelin, he made a beeline for Zimri's tent, walked right in uninvited, and executed the prince and the prostitute together.

Wow! That's quite a story! Unfortunately, twenty-four thousand people died because of a disease epidemic God sent in punishment throughout the camp. What if Phinehas hadn't taken action? It's clear that even more people would have died, and maybe Israel wouldn't have been allowed to go in and conquer the land of Canaan. That would have been a disaster! Good move, Phinehas. You did the right thing.

Purah

The LORD said to him, "Arise, go down against the camp,
for I have delivered it into your hand. But if you are afraid to go down,
go down to the camp with Purah your servant." Judges 7:9, 10

We know almost nothing of Purah except that he was Gideon's servant, probably a bodyguard of sorts. They may have grown up together in Ophrah and
maybe even were the best of friends.

Imagine you are Purah, and Gideon comes to you one day to tell you a heavenly Messenger has visited him. He tells you his God-given assignment is to gather
an army to fight the Midianites who have overrun the land. But first he says there's
a more important job to do. The altar to Baal must be torn down in his father's
courtyard garden, all images must be demolished, an altar to God must be built,
and a holy sacrifice offered on it. It was a big assignment with a scary outcome, and
everyone in town would want vengeance. But you and Gideon must do it anyway,
because you love God and want to see a revolution sweep the country. So you
gather nine others from among the family servants and do the deed in the dead of
night. The next day the city elders come unglued, and when they find out Gideon
is the guilty one, they're furious—you stand by Gideon, and so does his father. By
now your faith in God is strong, but Gideon's isn't yet. He gives God two tests to
see if the command to fight Midian is legit, and God responds with two tests of His
own. In the end it's you who encourages Gideon by going down into the camp of
the Midianites with him. You both hear an enemy soldier talking about a dream in
which Jehovah destroys the Midianite army. Wow! What a rush!

What if Purah hadn't bravely stood by Gideon at every test of faith: the trashed
altar to Baal, the wet and dry fleeces, the dwindling of his army, the midnight visit
to the enemy camp? Purah was a true friend, and it was his courage that pushed
Gideon to do great things for God! Without Purah, the ending of this story would
have been much different.

Slave Taskmasters in Egypt

Therefore they set taskmasters over them to afflict them with their burdens, and they built for Pharaoh supply cities, Pithom and Raamses. Exodus 1:11

How would you like to whip people for a living? Beat them? Make them work out in the hot sun day after day after day? Not much fun, huh? That's a ridiculous question, you might say, but honestly, that's what being a slave taskmaster was all about in ancient Egypt.

The Bible says the Israelite slaves had to make bricks and work on construction projects. How hard did they have to work? The Bible says the taskmasters made their lives bitter with hard bondage. In other words, they worked them like donkeys and beat them as well. It must have been a hard thing to watch, and Moses the son of Pharaoh could not stand it. In fact, one day he caught an Egyptian taskmaster beating a Hebrew slave and decided to get involved. You know the story. He killed the taskmaster and hid the body, then had to flee the country to save his own skin.

It was a sad time for the twelve tribes of Israel. It was hard to be dominated by the Egyptians, but hard as they tried, the taskmasters couldn't break the spirit of the Israelite slaves. God blessed them. He gave them the strength to keep going, and the nation grew in spite of the hard labor. By the time the Israelites were ready to leave Egypt, they were two million strong.

What if the slave masters hadn't been so mean? What if they had been more kind and allowed the slaves to have bathroom breaks and afternoon siestas from time to time? Well, then, it would have gone so much better for them when the ten plagues landed squarely on Egypt. The frogs and grasshoppers and disease hit them all pretty hard, but the death of their firstborns was the hardest price of all to pay. In the end those taskmasters begged the Israelite slaves to leave Egypt and even threw gold and silver jewelry at them to drive them out.

Sons of God

Now there was a day when the sons of God came to present themselves before the LORD, and Satan also came among them. Job 1:6

This is quite a story, and one that has quite a message for us. It's about a meeting somewhere out among the stars of God's great cosmos. It's about a time when the sons of God came together for a rendezvous with God; interestingly enough, Satan was among them. The details of this story draw a contrast between Satan and the other sons of God who came to present themselves before the Ancient of Days. What were these sons of God doing that day as they stood before the Creator on the sea of glass? Likely they were giving reports of what was happening in the galaxies from which they came. Maybe they were asking advice on important decisions that needed to be made in the realms where they ruled.

Satan was there with them, allowed inside heaven's gates to represent earth, which he had stolen from Adam. It must have seemed very wrong that he should stand as their equal before the Almighty God. When it came Satan's turn to report, his line must have seemed so feeble and even pointless. "I've been walking to and fro on the earth, and back and forth on it," he said, as though that was the grandest thing he had ever done.

The rest of the story reveals a mean streak in Satan far different from God's original intention for him. When God first planned the creation of the world, Lucifer had been a son of God too. It was God's plan that he join all the sons of God as they sang in celebration of the coming world. What if he had listened to his friends when they begged him to turn from his rebellion against the Creator? We wouldn't be telling this tale today; he wouldn't have plotted the fall of Adam and Eve; and he wouldn't have schemed to destroy Job years later. What a tragedy for a son of God to fall so low!

Ten Healed Lepers

"Were there not ten cleansed? But where are the nine?" Luke 17:17

Jesus gave many people the gift of healing in His day, but lepers were probably among the most grateful. How could they be anything but thankful? Leprosy was the most dreaded disease of the day, the most despicable, and the most incurable. This story is about one of those miracles, but it's an unusual one because it's about a mass healing.

Evidently, ten lepers in a leper colony decided they were going to go see Jesus. They had heard Jesus could heal them, but would He do it? It was worth a chance. But they were a miserable sight when they finally found Him. Their clothes were rags, and their hair looked mangy. Their bodies were disfigured with missing fingers, toes, and noses. "Go let the priests inspect you," Jesus said, because that was what the Law of Moses required if the men wanted to officially be free from leprosy. The ten lepers must have looked at one another in surprise, but Jesus said nothing more, so they left. Imagine Jesus' surprise to see one of the lepers come running back up the road a few minutes later. Falling at Jesus' feet, he poured out his thanks for healing.

Jesus smiled at the man kneeling before Him and then glanced down the road. "Ten lepers were healed today," He said, "but where are the other nine? Has no one returned to give praise to God except this man who is a Samaritan?"

So the truth came out. Only a Samaritan—a man who was despised by the Jews—returned to praise God. He knew Jesus was his only hope. So we have to ask ourselves, What if the leper had allowed his prejudice to keep him from coming to Jesus? What if he had said, "I won't go to receive healing by a Jew"? Then, of course, he wouldn't have received healing. He would have died a leper, his face unrecognizable, his heart with no hope.

Two Demoniacs of Gadara

When He had come to the other side, to the country of the Gergesenes,
there met Him two demon-possessed men, coming out of the tombs, exceedingly
fierce, so that no one could pass that way. Matthew 8:28

Have you ever seen someone who was demon possessed? It is scary knowing that the person is being controlled by Satan and his demons to say and do all kinds of horrible things. Jesus encountered several demon-possessed people during His ministry. On one occasion, He had just sailed across the Sea of Galilee and reached the shore when he saw a man running toward him on the beach; another man was coming down from a cemetery on the side of the hill—both men were naked. Their bodies were cut and bruised, and their eyes wild with fear. Their hair was full of sticks, dirt, and vermin. Worst of all, they were cursing, swearing, and saying all kinds of terrible things to Jesus.

By now the disciples had all run back to the water and jumped into the boat, but Jesus wasn't afraid. He knew it was Satan who made these men look and act like that, and He felt sorry for them. They had done many bad things to get in this condition, but He loved them and wanted to help them. He knew the men wanted His help, so He told Satan and his evil angels to leave these men and never come back. The demons left in a hurry and entered a giant herd of pigs feeding up on a nearby bluff. Not surprisingly, the pigs went crazy and ran helter-skelter along the steep cliffs until they fell off into the sea.

Wow, what a story! What if Jesus hadn't come to that beach? And what if these demoniacs hadn't wanted His help? Then Jesus would have had to leave them under the control of Satan. Fortunately, they did want help, and the rest of the story is history. They became key witnesses for Jesus. What a story!

DECEMBER 2

Supernatural Secret Service

And He knelt down and prayed, saying, "Father, if it is Your will, take this cup away
from Me; nevertheless, not My will, but Yours, be done." Then an angel appeared
to Him from heaven, strengthening Him. Luke 22:41–43

Did you know that God established the very first secret service detail? When
Satan stole this world from Adam and Eve, God knew it would be a dangerous
place to live—so He set up His supernatural bodyguard. You guessed it. We call
them angels. Those who claim God as their heavenly Father are awarded a personal attendant to watch over and protect them from the day they are born.

Angels also protected Jesus throughout His life and ministry. They warned
Joseph of Herod's plan to kill the newborn Baby Jesus and helped Him escape with
His parents to Egypt. They protected Jesus all those years in the notorious village
of Nazareth. They stood guard over Him for forty days in the wilderness of Judea,
when He was harassed by Satan. They shielded Him from a mob in Nazareth and
kept Him from being pushed off a cliff. For three years they protected Him from
Pharisees, the Herod brothers, and demons who wanted to destroy Him before
He could fulfill His mission as the Savior of the world. During Passion Week they
were His personal bodyguards in the Garden of Gethsemane, at the six rigged
trials by Jews and Romans alike, during the sadistic beatings, and finally when He
was crucified on Golgotha between two thieves.

Angels from heaven were there for Jesus just as they are near us when we need
them most. As we can imagine, they must have often wanted to transport Jesus out
of this world to remove Him from our depraved world. Fortunately, they obeyed
the Father, and Jesus experienced everything we are asked to endure. Aren't you
glad they did?

Caesar Augustus

And it came to pass in those days that a decree went out from Caesar Augustus that all the world should be registered. Luke 2:1

Caesar Augustus is a well-known historical figure in the Roman Empire. Not surprisingly, we've been able to pinpoint the general time when Jesus was born because of the details about Him recorded in the book of Luke. Augustus was born in 63 B.C. under the name Gaius Octavius to a wealthy family in Rome, Italy. His great-uncle Julius Caesar had no children who could take his place on the throne, so he adopted Octavius and named him as heir to his throne. When Julius was assassinated in 44 B.C., Mark Antony and Marcus Lepidus competed with Octavius to rule the Roman Republic. For thirteen years they battled one another as dictators until Octavius finally gained the throne in A.D. 31. At that time he changed his name to Caesar Augustus. Interestingly enough, he renamed the Roman month of August after himself, just as Julius Caesar had done with the month of July.

Caesar Augustus is best remembered as the founder of the Roman Empire and its first emperor from 27 B.C. until his death in A.D. 14. His rule brought the beginning of two hundred years of peace to the empire and enlarged its borders to Africa in the south, Germania in the north, and Spain in the west. The Bible mentions him as the emperor who ordered a world census to tax everyone in the empire, and this brought Mary and Joseph to Bethlehem, where Jesus was born.

Overall, Augustus was a violent man who worshiped many pagan gods. What if he had decided to worship the one true God instead? Then he would have helped prepare the world for the coming of Jesus as the Savior of the world. Too bad he didn't.

DECEMBER 4

Cleopas

Then the one whose name was Cleopas answered and said to Him,
"Are You the only stranger in Jerusalem, and have You not known the things which
happened there in these days?" Luke 24:18

Who was Cleopas? Tradition from the early Christian church tells us he may have been the brother of Joseph, the father of Jesus. We hear of him first in the story when he walked with Jesus from Jerusalem to Emmaus.

On Sunday afternoon, Cleopas and another follower of Jesus made the two-to-three-hour, eight-mile trip. They were very discouraged about Jesus' death on Friday, and although the stories of Jesus' resurrection seemed real enough, they doubted the truth of such tales. While they walked, a stranger joined them on the road. They were surprised that He didn't seem to know anything about the crucifixion of Jesus, but when He quoted Scripture to show what the Messiah had come to do, they began to see things more clearly. Jesus hadn't come to set up an earthly kingdom; He had come to die for the sins of the world. The stranger was Jesus, but they didn't recognize Him.

When they reached Emmaus they invited Him in, and He ate supper with them. As He broke bread, they suddenly recognized Him, but He disappeared. They jumped up from the table and ran all the way back to Jerusalem in the darkness. Bursting into the upper room, they excitedly told everyone what they had seen.

What a day! What a tale they had to tell! What if they had missed out on the walk with Jesus to Emmaus? They had misunderstood the Scriptures but listened patiently, in faith, to the words of Jesus. And they believed. Not surprisingly, Cleopas went on to become a missionary for Jesus, and later he suffered under the persecution of the early church. But it was worth it!

King Darius

And the king, when he heard these words, was greatly displeased with himself, and
set his heart on Daniel to deliver him; and he labored
till the going down of the sun to deliver him. Daniel 6:14

They say kings have no friends, and we find proof for this in the story of Darius. He couldn't trust the advisors in his court, the chamberlains who guarded his bedroom door, or even the cook who put food on his plate. But there was one man he could trust—Daniel. Here was a man who had no hidden agenda, who was loyal, honest, and faithful in service to his king. Not surprisingly, they became the best of friends.

The king admired Daniel so much that he was thinking of promoting him. Daniel's fellow advisors didn't like that idea! Darius should have suspected they were jealous of Daniel, but he fell for the oldest game in the book—flattery. The advisors wrote a decree that put Darius on quite a pedestal. It declared that for thirty days he would be the number one god of Babylon and receive worship during that time. Anyone violating this law would be cast into the den of lions.

Daniel chose to honor the law of his God, but King Darius had to honor the law of the Medes and Persians. Throwing his best friend to the lions was probably the hardest thing Darius ever had to do, and he hated himself for the personal pride that had put Daniel there. With tears in his eyes he committed Daniel to the care of his God and then sealed the lions' den for the night. All night he couldn't sleep. In the morning he discovered that his prayer was answered—Daniel was alive and well! Amazing!

What if Darius hadn't learned to trust Daniel? Or what if he hadn't signed that decree? Daniel no doubt taught him that all things work together for good to those who trust in God, so in a way it was a blessing that Daniel was thrown to the lions. Through this experience Darius was introduced to the God of heaven.

DECEMBER 6

Doctors in the Temple

Now so it was that after three days they found Him in the temple, sitting in the midst of the teachers, both listening to them and asking them questions. Luke 2:46

The temple lawyers and doctors were the big guns, the talking heads, the PhDs. They made the rules, and they always had the last word when it came to God and worship. They held the keys to salvation. At least that's what they taught everyone who came through the doors of the synagogues. And it's what they themselves believed.

Then Jesus came to town for a visit. He was twelve years old when He first showed up at the temple to dialog with the religious leaders, and His presence there changed the way they looked at Scripture—at least for a few hours. They believed the traditions of the Jewish nation were the most important thing for God's people. Jesus said it was Scripture. They believed if a man was rich, his position in heaven was guaranteed. Jesus showed them that those who are poor in spirit are the ones who are truly blessed. They believed that the Messiah would come in with pomp and power to conquer the Romans. Jesus showed them the Messiah must come as a humble Servant to die for the sins of the world.

Jesus did all this with well-phrased questions. After sitting with Jesus for three days, the doctors realized He knew the Scriptures well—even better than they did. But they were proud and stubborn, and because He was from Nazareth and had not been educated by them in their synagogue schools, they rejected Him.

What if they had accepted Him? What if they had said, "No one has ever spoken like this Boy; He speaks with authority and the power of God"? Then the history of the Jewish nation would have been changed forever.

Elizabeth

Now Elizabeth's full time came for her to be delivered, and she brought forth a son. When her neighbors and relatives heard how the Lord had shown great mercy to her, they rejoiced with her. Luke 1:57, 58

Elizabeth was the wife of Zacharias, a Levite priest in Judah. We know that she was a righteous woman who faithfully walked in all the commandments of the Lord, and she was old. We don't know how old, but the Bible says she was well advanced in years, and her husband was sure she couldn't have a baby, even though Gabriel guaranteed it.

She was a kinswoman of Mary, the mother of Jesus. When Elizabeth was six months pregnant, Mary came to see her and shared that she was pregnant too. For three months they celebrated the joys of impending motherhood together, and we can only imagine the good times they had as they worked, prayed, and sang together until Elizabeth's baby was born.

Most important, she was the mother of John the Baptist, one of the most famous prophets in the entire Bible. When he was born, there was some question as to his name. All the relatives wanted to name him after his father, but Elizabeth insisted his name was John, according to the instructions the angel Gabriel had given them.

Most women want to become mothers at some time in their life, and Elizabeth was no different. However, becoming pregnant with a son in old age could bring many problems with it. A baby could be born with birth defects, and his parents might not even live to see him reach manhood. What if Elizabeth had said, "Don't ask me to do this, Lord"? Instead, she cheerfully and courageously took on one of the greatest responsibilities ever asked of a woman. She would raise her son to be the forerunner of the Messiah. Wow! What a privilege!

DECEMBER 8

Esther

And Mordecai had brought up Hadassah, that is, Esther,
his uncle's daughter, for she had neither father nor mother.
The young woman was lovely and beautiful. When her father
and mother died, Mordecai took her as his own daughter. Esther 2:7

This girl had courage! She was called to the palace of Persia at the right time in history to save her people, and she stepped right up to the plate. Challenged to do something many considered to be suicide, she never looked back. That's the story of Esther, and we must admire her for it.

We don't really know how old she was at the time, but she may have been a teenager because she wasn't yet married when the call came to join the king's beauty contest. In those days, girls were usually married as soon as they were able to have children.

First, Esther won the national beauty contest held by the king. After she was crowned queen, she discovered that her people were scheduled to be annihilated by the hate-crazed prime minister. For three days, Esther and her maids fasted before she went to see the king uninvited. God caused King Ahasuerus to honor her bravery, and she invited the king to her palace suite for a banquet—twice. Maybe she couldn't get up the courage to ask for his help the first time. But then again, maybe she was simply trying to build up the suspense. The plan worked! Haman the monster was unmasked and executed on his own gallows, and Esther saved her people.

What if she hadn't mustered the courage for all these adventures? What if she had chickened out and not called on God for help? Then God would have had to find another way to save His people, or they would have all died in the massacre scheduled to follow. Not a good plan at all, but praise God she never lost her nerve!

Ezekiel

"Then I will give them one heart, and I will put a new spirit within them, and take the stony heart out of their flesh, and give them a heart of flesh." Ezekiel 11:19

Have you ever heard the song about Ezekiel's dry bones? "Foot bone connected to the heel bone. Heel bone connected to the ankle bone. Dem bones, dem bones, dem dry bones."

Ezekiel was one of the most famous prophets in the Bible, but did you know he was taken hostage to Babylon along with King Jehoiachin and ten thousand other captives? God allowed him and many of his countrymen to be taken prisoner by Nebuchadnezzar as penalty for their sins. Among other things, they had ignored His warnings about worshiping idols, desecrating His Sabbaths, and murdering innocent people in the land of Judah.

When Ezekiel arrived in Babylon, Shadrach, Meshach, Abednego, and Daniel had already been there for at least eight years. Although these four young men had received high positions of honor in the royal court, many of the Jews were not content to be in Babylon at all. They were upset about having to be captives in a foreign land and angry with God for punishing them.

Ezekiel tried to encourage the people of Judah and reminded them they were supposed to be God's witnesses in Babylon. "Don't be so rebellious," he told them. "Repent and confess your sins. If you do this God will take away your heart of stubborn stone and give you a new heart of flesh." Someday, if they were faithful, God would restore them to their beloved homeland.

Ezekiel received many visions from God in his lifetime about boiling pots, sour grapes, and wheels spinning within wheels. He was called to be a spokesman for God in Babylon. What if he had refused? What if he had said the job was too hard? Then his people in Babylon would have remained in darkness and without hope. Sometimes God asks us to do things we don't want to do, but if we are faithful like Ezekiel, the reward is great.

DECEMBER 10

Ezra

Ezra came up from Babylon; and he was a skilled scribe in the Law of Moses, which the LORD God of Israel had given. The king granted him all his request, according to the hand of the LORD his God upon him. Ezra 7:6

Ezra was a man of many talents—scribe, priest, and administrator. He was well known in Persia, and King Artaxerxes sent him to Jerusalem to help govern the settlement of Jews reestablishing themselves there. The king gave Ezra five thousand gold and silver vessels that King Nebuchadnezzar had stolen from God's temple more than 150 years before. He also sent him with gifts of gold and silver to pay for any building projects. "Go now!" he urged Ezra. "I can't afford to have Jehovah angry with me and my kingdom!"

It took Ezra and his band of exiles several months to get back to Judah, but when they finally arrived, he was shocked by what he found! People were not paying their tithes or keeping the Sabbath properly, and many of them were inter-marrying with local people who worshiped gods like Molech and Chemosh, which required child sacrifice. Ezra was so upset he tore his clothes and pulled hair from his head and beard. This sounds strange to us, but it's what people did in those days to show great sorrow. Then he called all the elders of Judah together, and they had a big powwow. "The jig is up!" he said. "You are being very wicked, and God isn't pleased!" Thankfully, the people repented of their sins. As a result, people stopped worshiping idols, pagan wives were sent away, everyone began paying tithe, and the Sabbath was once again considered sacred.

What if they hadn't listened to Ezra? What if they had tuned him out? Then they might have found themselves in captivity again to relearn the lessons they were supposed to learn in Babylon. Really? Really.

Gamaliel

"And now I say to you, keep away from these men and let them alone; for if this plan or this work is of men, it will come to nothing; but if it is of God, you cannot overthrow it—lest you even be found to fight against God." Acts 5:38, 39

Gamaliel was a member of the Sanhedrin and a teacher and mentor of Saul of Tarsus (later known as Paul). He was well respected in Jerusalem, and when he talked, everybody listened.

The priests and elders of the Sanhedrin were very upset because the disciples continued to preach about the resurrection of Jesus. They commanded them to stop, but the disciples replied, "We must obey God rather than men." The Sanhedrin threw the apostles in prison, but that night an angel of the Lord opened the prison doors and helped them escape. Early the next morning, the Sanhedrin called for the disciples to be brought from the prison for a trial, but they weren't in the prison!

Finally someone found them preaching in the temple again, and they were quietly brought to the Sanhedrin to avoid a riot. The priests and elders were very angry and wanted to kill the disciples, but Gamaliel brought that idea to a screeching halt. He sent the disciples out and warned the council to be careful. "If they are preaching their own ideas, the Christian movement will eventually fizzle. If it is God's idea, you will be fighting against the Lord Himself." And he carried the day. The Sanhedrin listened and set the disciples free.

Wow! What if Gamaliel hadn't stood up for the disciples? What if he had said, "I can't stick my neck out. It would hurt me politically"? Then some of the disciples might have been executed at that time. Good work, Gamaliel. You were God's champion that day, and the disciples had a courtside friend indeed!

Haman

> After these things King Ahasuerus promoted Haman,
> the son of Hammedatha the Agagite, and advanced him
> and set his seat above all the princes who were with him. Esther 3:1

Haman was a nasty man! He was mean, selfish, bad tempered, and he stopped at nothing to get what he wanted. Ancient historians tell us the king of Persia was so impressed with his political skills that he promoted Haman to be prime minister of Persia.

Unfortunately, that was the beginning of the end for him. Scoundrels like Haman are never satisfied. They always want more. He was rich, and now as the prime minister he wanted praise and honor too. He wanted people to bow the knee when he passed in the royal court and on the street. Most people bowed to him, but a Jew named Mordecai would not. Not surprisingly, this made Haman furious, and he set out to destroy Mordecai by building a gallows on which to hang him. Even worse, he plotted to destroy the entire Jewish population in the Persian Empire. Thankfully Esther interfered and petitioned the king to save the Jews. Initially, Haman was ecstatic over the queen's invitation to a private banquet. Little did he know what Esther had planned! When the whole story came out—revealing Queen Esther's Jewish ethnicity—the king was furious and executed Haman on the gallows he had built for Mordecai.

Now that's quite a tale! What if Haman hadn't been so aggressive? What if he had been content to live with the blessings he already possessed? Then he wouldn't have felt the need to be idolized and worshiped by people. He might not have hated Mordecai and written the decree that all Jews would be killed on the thirteenth of March. And most important, he wouldn't have been executed by the king for trying to kill the queen. What a shame!

Hegai

So it was, when the king's command and decree were heard, and when many
young women were gathered at Shushan the citadel, under the custody of Hegai,
that Esther also was taken to the king's palace, into the care of Hegai the custodian
of the women. Esther 2:8

Hegai was the keeper of King Xerxes's, also known as Ahasuerus, harem. Some-
body had to be, because the king had many wives and concubines. In those
days a royal ruler could have hundreds of them (the Bible tells us King Solomon
had at least one thousand).

Then along came Esther, a most unusual young woman. She was beautiful,
classy, sweet, and godly. When Hegai met her, he was very impressed. How'd the
two of them get thrown together? The king had called for a beauty pageant so he
could find himself a new queen. You guessed it. When the royal courtiers found
Esther in their search across the empire, they immediately signed her up for the
beauty contest.

She was scheduled for beauty treatments, but Hegai also gave her a spending
allowance and seven young maidens to attend her. Then he did one better. He
moved her and her maidservants to the best place in the royal harem. As far as he
was concerned, she was the best of all the beauty candidates. When she was chosen
by Xerxes to be queen of Persia above all the others, Hegai wasn't surprised.

What if Esther had not become part of the beauty contest? What if she had
not come to the palace? Then it's likely Hegai wouldn't have been introduced to
her or the God of heaven, who Hegai must have met through observing Esther. She
would have had to be discreet about her faith because she was trying to keep it a
secret that she was a Jewish, but you can't hide faith completely. It comes out in the
smile you wear and the song in your heart.

DECEMBER 14

Herod the Great

> Then Herod, when he had secretly called the wise men, determined from them what time the star appeared. And he sent them to Bethlehem and said, "Go and search carefully for the young Child, and when you have found Him, bring back word to me, that I may come and worship Him also." Matthew 2:7, 8

Herod the Great was the first of the Herods. The name "Great" was not because he did good but because of the lasting impact he had on the Roman Empire in that part of the world and the mark he left on the Jewish nation. He is well known for his building projects: magnificent cities like Caesarea along the Mediterranean coast; thirty-mile-long aqueducts for transporting water; public amphitheaters; sports stadiums; and the rebuilding of the Jewish temple in Jerusalem.

However, he ruled Judea with an iron hand and was one of the cruelest rulers of his day. The Spirit of God was nowhere to be found in this man, but what if he had given his heart to God while still a young man? What if he had decided a life of evil wasn't for him? Then he wouldn't have been such an evil man. He wouldn't have killed forty-five noblemen who opposed him before he came to power in 37 B.C. He wouldn't have executed almost all the members of the Sanhedrin. He wouldn't have killed three of his twelve sons, his favorite wife Mariamne, and her brother, grandfather, and mother. Maybe most important, he wouldn't have ordered the infamous massacre of all the baby boys in Bethlehem. This was done in an attempt to kill the baby Jesus, who escaped to Egypt just in time.

But he was much hated, and he knew there would be great rejoicing in the land when he died. So he called for one final execution to take place on the day of his funeral to force people to mourn properly. Fortunately, that order wasn't carried out, but the fact remains. Without God, Herod was a hopelessly wicked man, lacking hope or happiness.

James

They said to Him, "Grant us that we may sit, one on Your right hand
and the other on Your left, in Your glory." Mark 10:37

James came from the influential family of Zebedee in Galilee. He was the older of two boys in the family, and together they developed quite a reputation as the "sons of thunder." Often James's temper got the best of him. On one occasion when Samaritans wouldn't allow Jesus to enter their city, James and his brother John asked if they could call fire down from heaven on the ungrateful town.

James had aspirations to become a top dog in the new kingdom that he expected Jesus would set up. His mother encouraged these high aspirations in her sons, possibly because she belonged to a well-connected family. Apparently, when his mother wanted something, she usually got it.

Like Peter and his brother John, James was closer to Jesus than the other disciples. He was with Jesus when Jairus' daughter was raised to life. He also was with Jesus on the mount of transfiguration, and again when Jesus agonized in the Garden of Gethsemane.

Unfortunately, he was the first of the disciples to die for the sake of the gospel. In A.D. 44 King Herod had James executed to please the Jewish leadership in Jerusalem. The loss of James was a blow to the early Christian church, but his death helped to spread the gospel when thousands of believers fled Jerusalem to avoid a similar fate.

James was one of Jesus' most faithful disciples, but what if he hadn't accepted Jesus' call by the Sea of Galilee? What if he hadn't decided to be faithful to Jesus and tell the story of Jesus' death and resurrection no matter the cost? He could have avoided becoming a martyr for Jesus, but instead he has a crown of life waiting for him in heaven.

Jonah

Now the word of the LORD came to Jonah the son of Amittai, saying,
"Arise, go to Nineveh, that great city, and cry out against it;
for their wickedness has come up before Me." Jonah 1:1, 2

When people are asked who they most admire in the Bible, Jonah never comes in at first place. However, his roundabout trip to Nineveh is one of the most famous tales in all the Bible. "Pack your suitcase! You're going to Nineveh," God told him. "The people of Nineveh are very wicked and need to hear about it!" But Jonah refused. Can you imagine saying no to God? Jonah could, and did! Instead of going east, he fled west into the waters of the Great Sea, not remembering that God always has the last word.

Jonah's ship hadn't been at sea very long before a violent storm came up. Unfortunately, he knew nothing of this—he was down in the belly of the ship, fast asleep! The ship's captain found him there in the midst of the storm. "Get up!" he shouted. "Pray to your God, or we're all going to die!" But the storm only grew worse, and the men on board finally drew straws to see whose fault it was—Jonah drew the short straw. "Throw me overboard," he said, and when they did, the wind and waters calmed down. Just like that. Meanwhile, Jonah was on his way down into the deep, when a big fish came along and swallowed him up. "Get me out of this fix, and I'll do an about-face," Jonah told God, and that's exactly what happened. He did finally go to Nineveh to preach a doomsday message, and his evangelistic crusade was a smashing success. True story.

What if he hadn't obeyed God in the end? What if he hadn't warned the people of Nineveh about coming destruction? They still wouldn't have known, and God would have had to send someone else with the message. And Jonah wouldn't have gotten the credit for a hundred and twenty thousand baptisms. Good decision, Jonah.

Nathaniel

Jesus answered and said to him, "Before Philip called you, when you were under the fig tree, I saw you." Nathanael answered and said to Him, "Rabbi, You are the Son of God! You are the King of Israel!" John 1:48, 49

Nathanael was a praying man and honest as the day is long. He was one of the original twelve disciples of Jesus and was sometimes called Bartholomew. Nathanael was especially surprised when Philip introduced him to the Man from Nazareth. "Can any good thing come out of that town?" he asked. Then he was impressed when Jesus said, "Before Philip called you, I saw you when you were under the fig tree."

We're not sure what Nathanael did exactly for a living when he met Jesus. He came from the small town of Cana, but he also went fishing with some of the other disciples occasionally. In fact, he was with six of them on the Sea of Galilee following Jesus' resurrection when the Lord helped them miraculously catch a boatload of fish.

Christian tradition tells us Nathanael took the gospel message to Armenia in the first century. Some accounts of his life as a missionary tell us that he traveled with the apostle Philip, others say it was the apostle Thaddeus. According to stories from that part of the world, Nathanael died a martyr's death. Some accounts say he was beheaded, and others say he was crucified upside down.

What if Nathanael had not been a man of integrity? Then he might not have been introduced to Jesus. What if he had not followed Jesus and become one of His disciples? Then he would have missed out on the chance of a lifetime to walk and talk with the Son of God. What if he hadn't been willing to live and die for Jesus? Then he would have lost the glorious privilege of being counted as one of the faithful twelve.

DECEMBER 18

Joseph Barsabas

And they cast their lots, and the lot fell on Matthias.
And he was numbered with the eleven apostles. Acts 1:26

This is the only place we get introduced to Joseph Barsabas in the Bible. His name means "one who is born on the Sabbath" or "son of an aged man," and he even had a Latin surname, Justus. A godly man, he was baptized by John the Baptist, and then he became a follower of Jesus. He was blessed to walk and talk with Jesus from the beginning of His ministry and witnessed His miracles and preaching. When Jesus sent out seventy disciples on a missionary tour in the fall of A.D. 29, Joseph was probably among them. On this trip he was given power to heal the sick, cast out demons, and baptize new followers of Jesus.

After Jesus ascended to heaven, the disciples felt they should choose another disciple to replace Judas, who had committed suicide. Joseph was one of the two selected, along with Matthias, another follower who had spent much time with Jesus. Matthias was the one chosen, and we can be sure Joseph cheered him on, confident that God was in the process. The Bible doesn't mention Joseph again after this story, but most Christian tradition tells us he became a church leader in a town called Betaris. In A.D. 68 he was enslaved and then executed along with other Christians by Emperor Vespasian.

What if he had never followed Jesus to become His disciple? What if he hadn't taken the time to travel with Him throughout the years of His ministry? Then, of course, he would have missed out on the wonderful privilege of hanging out with Jesus. He wouldn't have been one of the two finalists to take Judas' place. He wouldn't have traveled far and wide to spread the gospel. He wouldn't have suffered hardship, persecution, and death. But do you think Joseph ever regretted these choices? Not a chance!

Joshua the High Priest

Then he showed me Joshua the high priest standing before the Angel of the LORD,
and Satan standing at his right hand to oppose him. And the LORD said to Satan,
"The LORD rebuke you, Satan! The LORD who has chosen Jerusalem rebuke
you! Is this not a brand plucked from the fire?" Zechariah 3:1, 2

The story about Joshua the high priest is one of the most symbolic stories in
the entire Bible, demonstrating just how much we need the sacrifice of Jesus.
It didn't take place in the New Testament in the shadow of the cross. Instead, it is
recorded in the Old Testament book of Zechariah. It is a prophecy, showing us that
Jesus' death will pay for our sins.

The Jews had just returned to Judah after the Babylonian captivity, and they
had many challenges to face as they rebuilt the temple and the city wall. Joshua,
the high priest, had quite a job to do in Judah, and the prophet Zechariah stood
shoulder to shoulder with him. At one point Zechariah even had a famous vision
about Joshua himself. In this vision Zechariah saw Joshua the high priest dressed
in filthy clothes standing before Jesus.

Satan accused Joshua before the throne of God. "Joshua is a sinner!" we can
hear him sneering. "He's unworthy to be called a child of God!"

But Jesus wasn't listening. "The Lord rebuke you, Satan!" He said. "Joshua is
like a brand plucked from the fire! He belongs to me!" Then He turned to the angels standing nearby. "Take away his filthy clothes," He commanded. "I am going
to cover him with the rich robes of My righteousness!"

What a vision! What a promise! What if Joshua had said, "No! I don't need
Your help or Your righteousness"? Then he would have died a sinner without hope
in the promise of heaven. Like us, he needed Jesus. We are all sinners and need
Jesus' robe of righteousness to cover our sins. Without it there is no salvation, no
home in heaven, and no eternal life.

Lame Man at the Gate Beautiful

Then Peter said, "Silver and gold I do not have, but what I do have I give you: In the
name of Jesus Christ of Nazareth, rise up and walk." Acts 3:6

When the Holy Spirit was poured out at Pentecost in the days of the early
church, amazing things began to happen. No one had ever seen anything
like it! The power of God was being demonstrated everywhere.

Sometime after Pentecost, John and Peter were on their way up to the temple
when they saw a crippled man sitting at the Gate Beautiful. The man had lived a
life of pain and suffering since the day of his birth. For a long time he had wanted
to be healed by Jesus, but he couldn't travel to the places where Jesus preached.
Finally he convinced some friends to carry him to the temple gate and help him
find Jesus. Sadly, when he got there he discovered that Jesus had been crucified.

He was so discouraged he didn't know what to do, so he began begging beside
the temple gate. "Alms for a poor man!" he called. Peter and John had zero money,
but they wanted to give the lame man something. "We don't have any gold or
silver," Peter said, "but we'll give you what we have. In the name of Jesus Christ of
Nazareth, get up and walk." Peter took him by the hand and helped him up. The
man was so excited he jumped up and down, praising God for his miraculous
healing.

What if he had been angry at the disciples for not giving him money? What
if he had said, "Get lost! I need money, not a confession that you're poor like me"?
Then he wouldn't have been healed. He would have sat there day after day, begging
for money the rest of his life. Whew! Good thing he listened. Good thing he let
Peter give him what he had, even if it wasn't money!

Malachi

"Bring all the tithes into the storehouse, that there may be food in My house, and try Me now in this," says the LORD of hosts, "If I will not open for you the windows of heaven, and pour out for you such blessing that there will not be room enough to receive it." Malachi 3:10

Malachi was the last of the Minor Prophets to preach and prophesy in the Old Testament. His book is also the last of the writings in the Old Testament. His message was written for the Jews who had returned from captivity in Babylon, about four hundred years before the time of Jesus. At this time, Nehemiah had returned to the Persian court in Shushan after rebuilding the walls of Jerusalem.

In the book of Malachi, God reminded His people that He was their heavenly Father and sent them eight separate messages as a call to repentance. They had grown careless in their worship of God, lived like hypocrites, and had backslidden into apostasy. They no longer knew the difference between good and evil—nor did they care. They should have known better. They were the people of Jehovah, and He had brought them back from Babylon to represent Him to the world. Malachi's most famous message scolds the people of Judah for robbing God. The elders of Judah were shocked that Malachi would say such a thing, but he insisted their tithes and offerings belonged to God. They were no longer paying their tithes, and that meant they were robbing God.

What if Malachi had given up when the elders refused to listen to him? Or what if the people had listened to Malachi? Then God would have blessed them and would not have allowed them to suffer through poor crops and famine and pestilence. The message in Malachi's book is especially for us today, and we would do well to listen to it.

DECEMBER 22

Philip the Evangelist

Now as they went down the road, they came to some water. And the eunuch said,
"See, here is water. What hinders me from being baptized?" Acts 8:36

Would you like to be able to fly? How about traveling in a teletransporter, a machine from science fiction that takes people from one place to another in an instant? Sound impossible? Not if you're partnering with the Holy Spirit in evangelism. That's what Philip the deacon did a time or two. We know about one of those episodes when he went on a special trip for God down the dusty road to Gaza. Here's how it happened.

Philip was a great evangelist, and one day an angel sent him on a really bizarre trip. To do what? He wasn't told, but he went anyway. When he saw an important-looking government leader riding in a chariot, he hopped the chariot for a Bible study. For the next few hours they discussed the words of Isaiah—the book that the Ethiopian official was reading and didn't understand. The man was impressed that Jesus was the Savior of the world, and when they came to a flowing stream, he asked to be baptized. Philip was happy to do the honors. But when the official came up out of the water, the evangelist was gone. Where? We don't know the details, but evidently the teletransporter kicked into gear, because the Bible says Philip was caught away to the town of Azotus.

What if Philip hadn't obeyed the angel? For starters, he wouldn't have had a chance to study with the foreign official, who then shared the message of salvation in his home country, Ethiopia. Pretty cool, huh? Absolutely! So, if you have your heart set on traveling in a teletransporter like Philip, make your reservation today. The time when you will be able to travel like that is coming sooner than you think.

Minor Prophets

He has shown you, O man, what is good; and what does the Lord require of you but to do justly, to love mercy, and to walk humbly with your God? Micah 6:8

Who were all these guys, and why were they called "Minor" Prophets? Was it because they were all younger than eighteen? Actually, the term was used because their work was limited in its influence and not as far-reaching as the Major Prophets like Isaiah, Jeremiah, and Daniel.

Some of these Minor Prophets include Hosea, Joel, Amos, Obadiah, Micah, Nahum, Habakkuk, Zephaniah, Haggai, and Zechariah. Among this famous group of prophets were farmers, priests, and princes. They served during times of drought, grasshopper invasion, civil unrest and assassination, Baal worship and child sacrifice, and poverty among God's people.

Zechariah and Haggai worked together to rebuild the temple. Zephaniah came from a royal family. Like Jonah, Nahum was given a message to preach in Nineveh. Amos was a goat herder and raised sycamore fruit. Hosea was married to a prostitute. Each one wrote a book that we now have in our Bibles, and they all loved God and wanted to help His people. The lessons Israel and Judah learned through their writings were hard ones.

What if these guys had decided that God's messages were too hard for them to preach? What if they had all run away like Jonah? Or what if they had griped because they wanted to be Major Prophets instead of minor ones? Then God would have had to humble them and teach them hard lessons of obedience. Or maybe He would have called someone else to do the job—He's had to do that before.

Like the Minor Prophets in the Bible, God calls us to do a job for Him. We might not like the job assignment, but He knows us inside out, and He knows how much we can handle. Are you willing to go on missions for Him even if you are a minor?

DECEMBER 24

Joseph the Father of Jesus

But while he thought about these things, behold, an angel of the Lord appeared to him in a dream, saying, "Joseph, son of David, do not be afraid to take to you Mary your wife, for that which is conceived in her is of the Holy Spirit." Matthew 1:20

Imagine you are Joseph for a few minutes. You have asked Mary to be your wife, and everything is going along fine. You have exchanged vows at the betrothal ceremony, and all the relatives are happy. Your fathers are proud, and your mothers shed tears of joy. Then she drops the bombshell—she's pregnant. "What?" you want to scream. "How could you do this to me? I thought you promised me that you would always and only be mine!"

She is tear-faced, begging your forgiveness. Sobbing, she explains that the Holy Spirit has come upon her. An angel told her it was so. You are, according to the custom of the day, considered her husband already, though you have not yet slept with her, since that is forbidden by the Law of God. But, like Joseph, you are a good man, honorable, and you don't want to make her a public spectacle. To do so would require that she be stoned to death.

So, you quietly arrange for an annulment, a form of divorce that seems very strange, because it's as if you were never actually married. Then God saves the day by sending you a dream in the night. The angel Gabriel comes to you and tells you it is just as Mary told you. She has conceived by the power of the Holy Spirit. "You shall call His name Jesus, for He will save His people from their sins," Gabriel adds (Matthew 1:21). Wow! That's heavy duty!

What if Joseph didn't believe Gaabriel? What if Joseph hadn't accepted Mary's explanation, or Gabriel's? What if he had gone through with that divorce? Then he would have missed out on the greatest honor any man on earth has ever had. To be the earthly father of Jesus was a special privilege beyond all earthly blessings. What an opportunity from out of the blue!

Mary the Mother of Jesus

Then the angel said to her, "Do not be afraid, Mary, for you have found favor with God. And behold, you will conceive in your womb and bring forth a Son, and shall call His name JESUS." Luke 1:30, 31

What a blessed woman she was! Actually, she was only a girl, probably no more than sixteen years of age. Full of life, engaged to the man she loved, and then she found out she was going to have a baby. But not just an ordinary baby. This was going to be the Son of God, the Messiah King who would save the world from sin. Wow! That would be quite a revelation, especially if the angel Gabriel came from heaven to break the news. And that's exactly what happened.

"Don't worry," the angel told her, "God is pleased with you and has chosen you for this very special honor."

At first, Mary didn't know what to think. "How can this be?" she asked Gabriel. "I'm not even married."

"The Holy Spirit has come upon you to give you this Child," Gabriel replied. "Such a thing might seem impossible, but with God, all things are possible."

Mary wanted to believe Gabriel, but what was she going to tell Joseph? Would he understand? Would he believe her? It was an unlikely story, a fantastic tale that could hardly be accepted on anybody's terms, especially hers, since she looked to be the guilty one.

What if she had said, "No, this can't be true! I don't want such a responsibility"? Under those circumstances, would God have forced her to give birth to the Son of God? No, she would have missed out on the incredible privilege of becoming the mother of Jesus, the one who would rock the cradle for the Savior of the world. Now that's an awesome thought!

Philip the Disciple

And Nathanael said to him, "Can anything good come out of Nazareth?"
Philip said to him, "Come and see." John 1:46

Philip was one of the original six disciples Jesus chose to follow Him. Soon after accepting Jesus' call, he brought his friend Nathanael to Jesus too. Though he came from a simple life in the town of Bethsaida, Jesus ordained him with special powers to teach and preach in Galilee. When Jesus offered to feed five thousand people, however, Philip expressed doubt. And then the week before Jesus died, a group of Greek tourists came to Jerusalem in search of Jesus, and it was Philip who found Andrew, and they brought the Greeks to Him. "Show us the Father," he said to Jesus on the night of the Last Supper. Jesus was disappointed at Philip's request and replied, "Have I been with you so long, and yet you have not known Me, Philip? He who has seen Me has seen the Father" (John 14:9).

It was a good learning experience for Philip. He lived through the nightmare of the Crucifixion weekend and met Jesus again in the upper room after the Resurrection. His faith was confirmed that Jesus was indeed the Messiah and the Savior of the world, and he went everywhere preaching that message. Traditional church stories tell us Philip went with Nathanael to Phrygia in what is now the country of Turkey. They preached the gospel there but were persecuted for their faith, and there Philip is said to have died a martyr in the city of Hierapolis.

Philip was impressed with Jesus the first time he saw Him, and he gave his life in service to the Master. What if he hadn't? He would have missed a life of hardship and persecution as he preached the gospel. He wouldn't have died the death of a martyr. But most important, he would have missed out on the privilege of following Jesus.

Rhoda

*And as Peter knocked at the door of the gate, a girl named Rhoda
came to answer. When she recognized Peter's voice,
because of her gladness she did not open the gate,
but ran in and announced that Peter stood before the gate. Acts 12:13, 14*

Rhoda appears just once in the Bible. She was a young Jewish girl turned Christian, and we have to wonder about the rest of her story. Who was she, and how long had she been a Christian? Did she grow up to be a missionary like Peter? Did she die for her faith? We don't know these details, but there were several thousand believers by now, and Rhoda was one of them.

Unfortunately, the Jewish leaders in Jerusalem weren't too happy that belief in Jesus was spreading, and they hoped to stamp out the life of the young church before it could get started. For starters, they killed John's brother James, and then Herod locked up Peter in prison. Rhoda and all the other Christians called a prayer meeting to pray around the clock for Peter's release, and God answered their prayers. The night before Peter's execution, an angel opened the prison doors to let him out. Sneaking up one street and down another, he finally came to John Mark's house, where everyone was praying. Quietly he knocked at the door, but Rhoda was afraid to answer it for fear it might be an enemy. "Who is it?" she called through the door. When Peter answered, she ran back into the house to tell everyone. Not surprisingly, they didn't believe her. "You're crazy," they said. "Peter's in prison." The knocking continued, and they finally opened the door. Sure enough, it was Peter—what an answer to prayer!

What if Rhoda and the other Christians hadn't prayed? Would Peter have been released from prison? Maybe, but perhaps God was rewarding Rhoda and her friends for their faith in His promises. Maybe the angel was sent because Rhoda asked God for it. Maybe it was Rhoda's faith that tipped the scales. Maybe. And when Jesus returns, you can ask her all about it.

Seven Deacons

"Therefore, brethren, seek out from among you seven men of good reputation, full of the Holy Spirit and wisdom, whom we may appoint over this business." Acts 6:3

What's a deacon? Well, in most churches today it's a man who does things like picking up the offering, or mowing the grass, or giving people rides to church. Sounds like they do all the work no one else wants to do, doesn't it?

After Jesus went back to heaven, the Holy Spirit came upon the church in a big way. Miracles were happening everywhere, and thousands joined the church. Many members were widows, orphans, and poor folks, but they had no one to look after them. The apostles knew these people needed clothes and food, but the job of making meals and serving them was beginning to take too much of their time. Because of this, they were spending less and less time preaching the Word of God.

Then someone came up with a bright idea. Why not ask seven godly young men to be deacons in the church so they could help do some of the work? The disciples prayed about it and chose Philip, Prochorus, Nicanor, Timon, Parmenas, Nicolas, and Stephen for service. We don't know much about most of these men, but we do know they were a big help to the young Christian church.

What if they had said, "It's not fair! Why do we have to do all of that work?" If they had, then we would probably not be talking about them today. Fortunately, they followed Jesus' counsel when He said being a servant was the greatest honor of all. Someday when you get to heaven you can ask them all about it. Especially Philip, who went on to become a great miracle-working evangelist, and Stephen, the church's first martyr.

Simon the Sorcerer

But Peter said to him, "Your money perish with you, because you thought that the gift of God could be purchased with money!" Acts 8:20

What is a sorcerer? That's a good question. Peter met one when he was on a trip to Samaria and put a curse on him. Here's how it happened. Philip the evangelist was already in Samaria at the time, preaching the gospel story and healing people with all kinds of sickness and disease. Incredibly, through the power of the Holy Spirit, he cast out demons, made lame people walk again, and gave people back their sight.

Now, there was a man in Samaria named Simon, who had practiced sorcery for many years. He astonished the people with his witchcraft and magic tricks, and people listened to his advice about the future. However, when the Samaritans heard Philip preach about Jesus and the kingdom of God, many accepted his message instead and were baptized as Christians.

Simon also believed, and when he was baptized he spent a lot of time with Philip. He saw all the miracles Philip did, and he wanted that kind of power too. When Peter and John came to town, Simon watched in amazement as they prayed for the Holy Spirit to fill new believers. Simon was very impressed. "How much does it cost to have power like that from God?" he asked.

"Your money perish with you," Peter replied. "Shame on you for thinking the gift of God could be bought with money! You'll live under God's curse with an attitude like that!"

Simon was horrified! He realized his mistake and asked Peter to pray for him. What if he hadn't? Then the power of Satan would have reared its ugly head in his life over and over, and he would have gone on to be demon possessed by the powers of darkness. The lesson for us here? Playing with sorcery is off limits! If we try, we'll always lose.

Three Thousand Converts at Pentecost

Then those who gladly received his word were baptized; and that day about three
thousand souls were added to them. Acts 2:41

The Day of Pentecost had come! One hundred and twenty believers went everywhere in Jerusalem sharing the good news of Jesus' resurrection. When they showed up at the temple, the place was packed. After all, it was the Feast of Pentecost, and thousands of worshipers had come from everywhere to celebrate the religious holiday. The disciples stood up to share the good news of the gospel, and the transformation was amazing! When Jesus died, they had been afraid to speak as witnesses for Him, but not anymore!

They were all excited, and as they began to talk, it became obvious they were speaking in the different languages of the people gathered in the temple courtyard. And it was a good thing! Parthians and Medes were there, and Elamites and Arabs. Travelers from Mesopotamia, Cappadocia, Pontus, Asia, Egypt, Libya, and Rome had come by the hundreds and thousands. The crowds listened in amazement! It was wonderful to hear someone teach the gospel in their own language, whether it was Egyptian or Libyan or Arabic. Some people made fun of the disciples and told everyone they must be crazy—or drunk. "Not so," Peter told them. "The Holy Spirit is speaking through us. You killed the Son of God on a cross, but He has risen from the dead. Today He asks you to repent of your sins and be baptized."

God blessed all the people who were listening to the story of Jesus' death and resurrection that day, and many of them became Christians. But what if they hadn't taken the time to hear the disciples preach? What if they hadn't even come to Jerusalem for Pentecost? Then three thousand of them wouldn't have been baptized and taken the good news back to their own countries. Today the story of Jesus is everywhere because of these people. Praise God!

Stephen

And all who sat in the council, looking steadfastly at him,
saw his face as the face of an angel. . . . Then he knelt down and cried out
with a loud voice, "Lord, do not charge them with this sin."
And when he had said this, he fell asleep. Acts 6:15, 7:60

Stephen was one cool guy! We know little about him before he showed up in the book of Acts, but he climbed the ladder of fame really fast. Not the kind of fame that makes people proud and self-centered, but the kind that gets your name in the Hall of Faith. He was filled with the power of the Holy Spirit, he did many miracles and signs among God's people, and he was an amazing preacher. However, trouble was on the way for him. Satan was not happy about everything Stephen was doing to point people to Jesus, and he stirred up the priests and elders against him. The Jewish leaders knew Stephen spoke the truth about Jesus' death and resurrection, but they hardened their hearts and hated him all the more.

One day, they finally grabbed him and brought him to the Jewish council. Saul of Tarsus, a brilliant young Pharisee, was in charge of the trial, but Stephen was inspired by the Holy Spirit and gave a great testimony. He condemned the leaders of the Jewish council for crucifying Jesus, the Son of God. By now his face was glowing like an angel, and in a vision he saw Jesus in the heavenly sanctuary. The Jewish leaders were filled with hate and rage as Satan took over their minds, and they dragged Stephen outside to stone him. Seeing Stephen pulverized to death by rocks would be scary, but seeing his executioners possessed by Satan would be even worse.

What if Stephen had said, "I'm not going to do it! It's too scary to die for God"? Likely, he wouldn't have died under a big pile of stones. But he wouldn't have had a vision of heaven just before he died, or be remembered today as the greatest champion of Jerusalem's early Christian church.